Activities for Teaching Gender and Sexuality in the University Classroom

Edited by Michael J. Murphy, PhD, and Elizabeth N. Ribarsky, PhD

ROWMAN & LITTLEFIELD EDUCATION

A division of

ROWMAN & LITTLEFIELD PUBLISHERS, INC.

Lanham • New York • Toronto • Plymouth, UK

Praise For *Activities for Teaching Gender
and Sexuality in the University Classroom*

"This book is a series of fascinating exercises, designed to involve students more deeply in their own learning. Overall, I found them instructor-friendly and appropriate for the designated students. This book will be a welcome addition to any instructor's library. After teaching for a while, most of us have a repertoire of activities, but new ones are always welcome. New professors will love this. I would buy this book." —**Rebecca Reviere**, Sociology/Anthropology, Howard University

"This book meets a need as an instructor resource. The types of activities range across many potential course applications. I have not seen another similar book and I am happy this one is forthcoming. Overall, the materials are absolutely appropriate for the college classroom. Many would also be appropriate for an advanced high school student. Additionally, some of the content would lend itself to stand-alone or workshop type training settings. The ideals of active learning are highlighted in many of the sections and the activities in many cases appear to be ones that the student would find memorable and clearly able to make important points. I would both purchase and recommend this book. I was impressed with the content well beyond my expectations. There are numerous activities that read as fantastic experiences for the students and instructors alike. I also enjoyed the abstract content for the activities and the authors' making their cases for why and how they developed and used their activities. I look forward to seeing this work published." —**Rebecca Sanford**, Communication Studies, Monmouth University

"I am so excited about this book! Michael Murphy and Elizabeth Ribarsky's collection of engaging ideas will surely encourage intellectual discovery among college students everywhere. Gender and sexuality studies professors at last have a go-to source for innovative, active-learning exercises that address the politics of diversity and social justice." —**Shira Tarrant**, PhD, associate professor, Women's, Gender, and Sexuality Studies Department, California State University, Long Beach

"*Activities for Teaching Gender and Sexuality in the University Classroom* is a must-have resource for any professor teaching in the field of gender and sexuality studies. Each chapter offers hands-on classroom exercises that offer creative and intellectually rigorous approaches to working with a significant concept, problem or question. This is a wonderful, wide-ranging book whose influence on pedagogy in the field will be felt for a long time." —**John Landreau**, Gender Studies, The College of New Jersey

Published by Rowman & Littlefield Education
A division of Rowman & Littlefield Publishers, Inc.
A wholly owned subsidary of
The Rowman & Littlefield Publishing Group, Inc.
4501 Forbes Boulevard, Suite 200, Lanham, Maryland 20706
www.rowman.com

10 Thornbury Road, Plymouth PL6 7PP, United Kingdom

British Library Cataloguing in Publication Information Available

Library of Congress Cataloging-in-Publication Data

Activities for teaching gender and sexuality in the university classroom / edited by Michael
Murphy and Elizabeth Ribarsky.
     pages cm
  ISBN 978-1-4758-0180-4 (pbk. : alk. paper) — ISBN 978-1-4758-0181-1 (electronic)
1. Gender identity—Study and teaching (Higher) 2. Sex—Study and teaching (Higher) 3.
Curriculum planning. I. Murphy, Michael John, 1965– II. Ribarsky, Elizabeth, 1980–
  HQ1075.A235 2013
  370.81—dc23
                                                                          2013000630

∞™ The paper used in this publication meets the minimum requirements of
American National Standard for Information Sciences—Permanence of
Paper for Printed Library Materials, ANSI/NISO Z39.48-1992.

Printed in the United States of America

Contents

Preface   xi

Acknowledgments   xvii

PART I   EXPLORING ETHICS, VALUES, BELIEFS

1   Where Do You Stand? Assessing Students' Values and Beliefs
—Hazel J. Rozema   3
*Kinesthetic icebreaker exercise for assessing and discussing students'
values and beliefs on a range of "hot button" topics and issues.*

2   Femininity and Masculinity: An Exploration of the Relative Elements
of Gender Identity —Evangeline Weiss & Kerry Poynter   12
*Helps students understand gender as a continuum and the affective
experience of gender nonconformity through a kinesthetic assessment of
their own gender variance.*

3   Is It Theft? Using the Ethics of Crime to Frame a Discussion of
Sexual Consent and Sexual Assault —Mara K. Berkland   17
*Helps students evaluate their moral and ethical stance on rape and sexual
assault through assessing their beliefs about the degree of violation
involved in the crime of theft and then comparing their responses to
similar violations that meet the legal definition of rape.*

4   Bringing the Gender Movements Alive through Role-Play
—Sherianne Shuler   26
*Provides students with an opportunity to learn about the differing
ideologies of the various women's and men's movements through role-play
and other creative activity.*

5   Arguing over Theories of Gender Development—Shelly Schaefer Hinck
       & Edward A. Hinck   35
       *Encourages students to think critically about the assumptions inherent in
       the biological, interpersonal, and cultural theories of gender development.*

6   The Same-Sex Marriage Debate: Gay/Lesbian Rights vs. Queer
       Critiques of Marriage —Elizabeth Currans   47
       *Encourages students to explore the complexity of responses to same-sex
       marriage within lesbian, gay, bisexual, and transgender communities
       while working on public speaking and argumentation skills.*

PART II   SEXUALITY

7   Sexual Secret Cards: Examining Social Norms and Cultural Taboos
       around Sexuality —Shawn Trivette   57
       *Draws on students' anonymously submitted sexual secrets to both engage
       student interest in the course and push past some of the awkwardness that
       often accompanies the charged topic of sexuality.*

8   Beyond Binaries: Seeing Sexual Diversity in the Classroom
       —Robyn Ochs & Michael J. Murphy   62
       *Helps students understand various instruments for measuring sexual
       orientation by anonymously assessing students' sexual identities, histories,
       desires, and fantasies using an anonymous questionnaire, with the results
       acted out by students in class.*

9   Dancing in Class: Choreographing Gendered Sexuality
       —Susan Ekberg Stiritz   71
       *Prepares students to understand script theory and the ways social learning
       shapes our sexual preferences, conduct, and thinking by immersing them in
       contrasting dance scenarios.*

10 Discussing Gender and Human Sexuality "Hot Button" Issues: Considering
       the Role of Religion and Religious Beliefs —Navita Cummings James   78
       *Guides students in dialogue about religion, gender, and sexuality, and the
       role of religion and spirituality in hot button topics such as abortion and
       same-sex marriage.*

PART III   FRIENDSHIPS AND ROMANTIC RELATIONSHIPS

11 Choose Your Own Adventure: Examining Social Exchange Theory and
       Gendered Relational Choices —Elizabeth N. Ribarsky   89
       *Explores the ways in which social exchange theory explains how
       individuals make choices as to whether to enter, continue, or
       terminate a relationship.*

12 Perceptions of Conversations and Gendered Language in Same- and
Cross-Sex Friendships —Allison R. Thorson   95
*Guides students through the process of recognizing their perception of
specific gendered interactional behaviors and, in turn, requires them to
question how, if at all, their perceptions are associated with relationship
attributes and types.*

13 Let's Talk about Sex: Teaching College Students How to Navigate
Sexual Communication Conversations with Relational Partners
—Jessica A. Nodulman   104
*Teaches students how to construct effective sexual communication
conversations with relational partners.*

PART IV   LITERATURE

14 Encouraging Reader Identification with LGBT Literary Characters
through Role-Play —David Hennessee   119
*Helps students relate to and identify with lesbian, gay, bisexual, and/or
transgender (LGBT) characters in literature through role-play.*

15 Designing Utopia: Teaching Gender through the Creation of "Hisland"
—Christin L. Munsch   123
*Utilizes Charlotte Perkins Gilman's novel Herland to help students analyze
the role of gender stereotypes in society and the social construction of gender
through the design of an original version of a utopian society "Hisland."*

16 The Big Bad Wolf Carries a Purse: Restorying Gender Roles in Popular
Children's Stories —Stacy Tye-Williams   133
*Helps students explore alternative ways of thinking about gender and
feminism by constructing alternative storylines to traditional children's
literature and fairy tales.*

PART V   MEDIA AND ARTIFACTS

17 Marlboro Men, Virginia Slims, and Lucky Strikes: The Social
Construction of Reality in Tobacco Advertising —Amie D. Kincaid   141
*Guides students in the analysis of the social construction of gender and
sexual orientation using stereotypical representations found in vintage
cigarette and tobacco advertising.*

18 Writing a Nonsexist Television Advertisement —David Bobbitt   150
*Develops students' creative writing ability by asking them to write
nonsexist scripts for television advertisements for women's personal-care
products and then perform them for the class.*

19   Being a Man: Challenging or Reinforcing Embodied Masculinities in
the University Classroom —Jessica J. Eckstein   155
*Utilizes visual representations of culturally and idiosyncratically
attractive men, to encourage student- and instructor-analysis of diverse,
cultural, and situated masculinities as embodied by individual men.*

20   Communicating Gender Expectations: An Analysis of Boys' and
Girls' Toys and Games —Elizabeth Tolman   162
*Guides students in the description and analysis of gender norms and
expectations in the marketing of toys, based on field research in a toy
store.*

21   Engendering Material Culture: The Gendered Packaging of Bath and
Beauty Products —Michael J. Murphy   170
*Uses personal bath and beauty product packaging to help students see how
longtime cultural beliefs about gender are encoded in mundane consumer
products.*

PART VI   BODY

22   Voicing Gender: Critically Examining Expectations about Gender
and Vocalics —Lisa K. Hanasono   181
*Guides students in analysis of gendered vocalics: the ways that voice is
used to perform gender and how society ascribes gender by interpreting
gendered vocal performances.*

23   Performing and Analyzing Gendered Nonverbal Communication
—Deborah Cunningham Breede   187
*Guides students in description and analysis of gender in nonverbal forms
of communications as performed
by classmates.*

24   Gender-Norm Violation and Analysis —Tamara Berg   194
*Helps students understand the affective experience of and public reaction
to social transgression through the violation of gendered norms in public
space.*

PART VII   WORK

25   Gender at Work: Revealing and Reconciling the Influence of
Gender Norms on Perceived Occupational Roles —Jessica Furgerson   201
*Helps students critically interrogate the function, origin, and implications
of our continued use of problematic normative gender assumptions
through analysis of the sex-segregated labor market.*

26 Analyzing Media Representations of Powerful Women in the
Workplace —Sarah Stone Watt 207
*Reveals important observations concerning representations of
powerful women in the workplace through analysis of language and
representational tropes in the Forbes magazine list "The World's 100
Most Powerful Women."*

27 Let's Go to Work: Discovering the Prevalence and Place of Gender
and Sexuality Expectations in Organizations —Jeanette Valenti 214
*Helps students analyze the presence and expectations of gender roles and
behavior, and also sexuality and relationships, through analysis of the
policies and procedures of different workplaces.*

28 What's the Policy? Exploring Sexual-Harassment Policies in
Organizations —Joy L. Daggs 220
*Guides students in the analysis of workplace sexual-harassment policies,
with a focus on differences in terminology, definition, investigation of
claims, and institutional responses.*

PART VIII   GLOBAL/INTERSECTIONAL ISSUES

29 *Crash:* Seeing the Power of Intersectional Analyses —Sal Renshaw 227
*Provides students with an intellectual toolkit to help them understand the
power of intersectional analyses in thinking about sex, gender, race, and
class through analysis of a scene from the film Crash.*

30 Us and Them: Teaching Students to Critically Analyze Gender in a
Global Context —Amy Eisen Cislo 234
*Guides students in visual and textual analysis of images of non-Western
women used by Western nonprofit organizations to better understand the
way individual, global, and national power imbalances are represented in
popular visual imagery.*

31 Claiming Your Baggage: Gender, Sexuality, and Nation in American
Popular Culture —Christina Holmes 240
*Uses popular women's magazines to introduce students to transnational
feminist analysis of representations of non-Western women.*

About the Contributors 248

Preface

Activities for Teaching Gender and Sexuality in the University Classroom is a collection of innovative, classroom-tested, active-learning exercises for the university and advanced high school classroom. As interest in multiculturalism, diversity, and social justice issues has grown among educators, the number of courses that address gender and sexuality topics has increased significantly. The National Women's Studies Association (NWSA) now estimates that Women's Studies (and similarly named) departments educate nearly one hundred thousand students per year in the United States (Reynolds, Shagle, & Venkataraman, 2007). When the range of courses that address gender and sexuality topics is considered, the number of students receiving instruction in these areas is likely double or triple NWSA's estimate. Beyond the classroom, student-affairs professionals and school administrators now place heavy emphasis on gender and sexuality in diversity and sensitivity trainings, with the goal of creating a more welcoming and inclusive educational environment.

Those who teach about gender and sexuality often place a high premium on active-learning teaching styles. Inspired by feminist and constructivist pedagogical theories, they know active-learning strategies create a more enjoyable experience for learners but also aid retention and application of course content. Active-learning and student-centered activities make knowledge "real" for students in ways that lectures, research papers, and other teaching approaches might not. Regrettably, many instructors lack formal training in active-learning pedagogies, and there are few print or digital resources available for help in teaching about gender and sexuality, topics that are often seen as risqué or difficult to discuss. Until now, word of mouth has been the most effective source of information for sharing active-learning exercises for teaching about gender and sexuality.

Activities for Teaching Gender and Sexuality in the University Classroom is the first interdisciplinary collection of activities devoted entirely to teaching about gender and sexuality. It offers both new and seasoned instructors a range of exciting exercises that can be immediately adapted for their own classes, at various levels, and across a range of disciplines. The activities are designed to generate student interest in gender and sexuality topics while also enabling instructors to broach what are often sensitive issues in the classroom. From over one hundred submissions, activities were selected that are self-contained, classroom-tested, and edited for ease of use and potential to remain current. Each activity is thoroughly described with a comprehensive rationale that allows even those unfamiliar with the material/concepts to quickly understand and access the material, learning objectives, required time and materials, directions for facilitation, debriefing questions, cautionary advice, and other applications. For the reader's benefit, each activity is briefly summarized in the table of contents and thematically organized: Work, Media and Artifacts, Sexuality, Body, and so forth. Many activities include handouts that can be photocopied and used immediately in the classroom. All activities are:

- Designed to be completed in a single class period (or with limited out-of-class preparation).
- Grounded in the relevant disciplinary and pedagogical theory.
- Organized according to a standard outline.
- Accompanied by ideas for alternative uses.
- Supported by references and alternative readings.

Activities for Teaching Gender and Sexuality in the University Classroom will be the standard desk-reference on this topic for years to come, and it will be indispensable to those who regularly teach in the areas of gender and sexuality.

HOW TO USE THIS BOOK

We recommend readers first review the activity titles and descriptive summaries in the table of contents, looking for activities that can be used in their specific classrooms. If an activity on a specific topic is desired, pay attention to the thematic grouping of activities. Activities in each theme are organized by learning skill, from least- to most-challenging. For example, activities simply aimed at soliciting student feedback were placed before application-based activities such as debates or role-playing. Also, many activities under a specific theme are easily modified for different uses (see Alternative Uses within specific activities). For example, many of the debate activities can be modified for a wide range of current issues in gender and sexuality studies, while media and literature activities can be used with almost any visual or textual source. To supplement the thematic table of contents, here is a summary of activities organized by activity type:

- Debate: Shuler; Hinck & Hinck; Currans; James.
- Role-Play: Shuler; Hennessee.
- Assessment: Weiss & Poynter; Rozema; Berkland; Trivette; Ochs & Murphy; Ribarsky.
- Textual Analysis: Munsch; Tye-Williams; Bobbitt; Breede; Furgerson; Watt; Valenti; Daggs; Holmes.

- Visual/Aural/Material Cultural Analysis: Kincaid; Murphy; Eckstein; Tolman; Valenti; Renshaw; Cislo; Holmes; Hanasono.

After identifying likely activities, flip to the activity in the text and read the Rationale and Alternative Uses sections to see if the exercise is for you and how it might be adapted to your classroom needs. Each activity is formatted to include easy-to-follow step-by-step instructions in how to facilitate the activity as well as suggested discussion questions. Feel free to photocopy included handouts or modify them to suit your specific classroom.

SOME CAUTIONARY ADVICE

Activities in this book often ask students to apply course content to their personal lives or employ their bodies in kinesthetic learning experiences. They often take student-supplied information as the basis for class discussion and analysis. Lesbian, gay, bisexual, and transgendered/transsexual, intersexed, queer and questioning (LGBTIQ) students often report that otherwise well-meaning teachers can create an unwelcoming classroom climate when they ask students to reveal private information without thought as to the consequences. As such, it is important for readers and users of this book to avoid exploiting the structural power difference between faculty and students, or taking advantage of student vulnerability by requiring them to divulge personal or private information. This can be especially important at residential colleges or with students in living/learning communities, where classroom experiences often "live on" in the dorms with unintended consequences. No student should be forced to choose between coming out as lesbian in the classroom or prevaricating in order to participate in a classroom activity. Furthermore, in activities grounded in student experience, avoid asking students from racial, ethnic, gender, and sexual minorities to "speak on behalf of their people" (i.e., "Juanita, can you tell the class what's it's like to be Latina?"). Such tokenizing questions overlook individual diversity within communities (no two Latinas share the same experience) while also forcing such students to bear "the double burden of oppression": the consequences of structural inequalities as well as responsibility for educating dominant groups about the workings and experience of oppression. There is a fine line between creating effective learning experiences on the basis of student-supplied information and reducing students to all-knowing representatives of a specific social group.

Accordingly, the editors have included activities that survey student perspectives, backgrounds, beliefs, or values *only* if this information is used to teach a larger concept or theory. Activities that could potentially create a hostile classroom environment, for example by forcing students to choose between deception and potentially damaging self-disclosure, were not accepted for inclusion. All activities that rely on student self-disclosure provide alternative activities for students who opt not to participate, such as a writing, recording, or observing role. Before adopting these activities, it can be helpful to consider a racial, ethnic, gender, or sexual minority student's perspective and ask, "Would I be comfortable having my professor and/or other students know X about me?" Similarly, it is important with the kinesthetic learning activities to remain cognizant of the mobility restrictions of our students and adapt exercises accordingly. Use these activities as a well-thought-out guide, then use your best judgment to create a safe and productive learning environment for all your students.

Some of the activities that focus on visual or textual analysis aim to reveal the heteronormative gender binary that dominates Western culture and society. Although such learning objectives are legitimate, they can unintentionally reproduce the very thing they attempt to describe and analyze. Activities often include alternative questions and extensions for more advanced classrooms or those instructors wishing to highlight the exceptions, paradoxes, and internal contradictions of the dominant gender and sexual paradigm. The focus of the text is on gender and sexuality, and questions of race and ethnicity take a backseat in most of the activities. Although intersectionality is widely considered to be an important concept in the gender/sexuality classroom, many of these activities are designed to teach more introductory material. They usually tackle only one aspect of social experience at a time: usually gender *or* sexuality. However, with the change of a few nouns, many of these activities can be adapted for teaching about a wide variety of kinds of human experience—including examining issues of race and power. We encourage the reader to consider the specific classroom make-up and larger learning objectives, and adapt the activities to suit those needs.

Instructors should use caution in leading discussion about sensitive topics such as rape or sexual orientation and take proactive steps to create a respectful classroom climate. Study after study has confirmed Warshaw's (1994) assertion that 20–25 percent of college women have been the victims of rape or attempted rape. If we add to this number the known incidence of childhood sexual abuse and estimates regarding male rape, we come to realize *many* of our students are survivors of some kind of sexual trauma (Douglas, Collins, Warren, Kann, Gold, Clayton, Ross, & Kolbe, 1997; Tjaden & Thoennes, 1998). Much of the trauma affecting survivors of sexual abuse or violence revolves around a loss of control. Imposing classroom activities having sexually violent content or requirements for self-disclosure without warning or alternatives can have the effect of retraumatizing survivors. We find informing students in advance, both verbally and through the syllabus, often allows survivors to participate in such activities because such participation is a result of *their choice*—a factor which seems to be key. The authors of the individual activities have included helpful advice for guiding effective discussions in the Typical Results and Cautionary Advice sections. Additionally, instructors can prepare for any unintended consequences by identifying a list of campus and community resources for student referral: campus health and counseling centers, LGBTIQ community centers and hotlines, rape and domestic violence crisis centers, etc. We recommend that instructors recognize the limits of their professional training and expertise, and that they refer students to those best trained to help. The majority of the activities should raise no difficulties, but the diverse nature of today's classroom means that student reactions can often be surprising.

It can take several attempts before any instructor becomes comfortable with new learning activities, and we encourage you to try these activities more than once before making final decisions about their permanent inclusion in your curriculum. Instructors often learn about course content and teaching methods through their students' responses and what worked and (regrettably) what did not in the classroom. We encourage you to be in touch with your stories of success and recommendations for modifications to any of these activities. As teachers, we too are always looking for new ideas and suggestions to make our classrooms better learning environments. If you have an exciting active-learning activity about gender and sexuality that you would like to have considered for inclusion in the next edition of *Activities for Teaching about Gender and Sexuality in the University Classroom*, please e-mail the editors at Teach.Gender@gmail.com.

REFERENCES

Douglas, K. A., Collins, J. L., Warren, C., Kann, L., Gold, R., Clayton, S., Ross, J., & Kolbe, L. (1997). Results from the 1995 national college health risk behavior survey. *Journal of American College Health, 46,* 55–66.

Reynolds, M., Shagle, S., & Venkataraman, L. (2007). *A national census of women's and gender studies programs in U.S. institutions of higher education.* Chicago: National Opinion Research Center.

Tjaden, P., & Thoennes, N. (1998). Prevalence, incidence, and consequences of violence against women: Findings from the national violence against women survey. *Research in brief.* Washington, DC: National Institute of Justice and Centers for Disease Control and Prevention.

Warshaw, R. (1994). *I never called it rape: The* MS. *report on recognizing, fighting, and surviving date and acquaintance rape.* New York: Harper Perennial.

Acknowledgments

The editors would like to express their gratitude to the many teacher-scholars who submitted activities for this book and for their patience during the editing process. We are grateful to the anonymous reviewer of the book proposal, whose comments guided our editing process with individual authors, and to Todd Jennings, Rebecca Sanford, Rebecca Reviere, and Barbara Gurr for reviewing the manuscript prior to publication. Their advice and comments have helped improve the book immeasurably. We are also grateful for the many kind words of support and encouragement from friends and colleagues during this lengthy project. A Faculty Scholarship Enhancement Grant from the College of Liberal Arts and Sciences (University of Illinois Springfield) allowed us time away from teaching to work on this project. We are especially grateful to the many publishing professionals at Rowman & Littlefield Education for their tremendous help, guidance, and encouragement during this creative adventure. Special thanks to our long-suffering editor, Nancy Evans, for cheering us on and answering a seemingly endless stream of e-mails, and the inestimable Carlie Wall, for her boundless patience with our innumerable "little" requests.

Michael J. Murphy would like to thank the owners and employees of the Local Harvest Café, Hartford Coffee Shop, and Mokabe's Coffee Shop (all in St. Louis, Missouri) for their kind tolerance of his presence while working on this project. He owes them considerable table rent! He is also grateful for past and ongoing conversations with colleagues interested in active-learning pedagogies in the women's, gender, and sexuality studies classroom, especially Tarah Demant, Amy Cislo, Susan Stiritz, Barbara Baumgartner, Shira Tarrant, and Missy Thibodeaux-Thompson. It has been a pleasure working on this project with Beth Ribarsky, for her shared interest in teaching topics and pedagogies. As always, Michael is grateful for the loving support of his partner, David Ridder.

Beth Ribarsky would like to thank her numerous colleagues and friends across the communication discipline who have been instrumental in their guidance and encouragement in creating an active-learning classroom and composing this book of activities, especially Shelly Hinck, Amie Kincaid, and Cassandra LeClair-Underberg. She is also appreciative of the role Michael Murphy has played in helping guide this tremendous project that was all spurred from a late-night conversation about teaching approaches. And she is undoubtedly thankful for the continued support of her family.

I

EXPLORING ETHICS, VALUES, BELIEFS

Where Do You Stand?
Assessing Students' Values and Beliefs

Hazel J. Rozema, PhD
(University of Illinois Springfield)

Appropriate Course(s) and Level

Any graduate or undergraduate college class that deals with relationships, gender, or sexuality because it provides a content-less form/format instructors can adapt to fit the appropriate theories/concepts they are teaching. Thus, it could be used in communication, women and gender studies, sociology, psychology, and related disciplines. The exercise could also be used in courses on cultural diversity, multiculturalism, history, and other fields by changing the content (e.g., using statements about the causes and effects of poverty or the varying perspectives on the causes and unfolding of the Civil War).

Appropriate Class Size

10–35 students, in classrooms with enough space for students to stand in groups on a 5-point continuum.

Learning Goals

- To see the distribution of where their classmates "stand" on a variety of gender and relational issues.
- To discover how their relational values and beliefs compare to those of their fellow classmates.
- To experience analyzing, explaining, and justifying/debating views by engaging in civil discourse with fellow classmates.
- To practice thinking more critically about views on sexuality and relationships and how those views were formed.

Estimated Time Required

Allow approximately an hour for the exercise. Students will get tired of standing and will get restless after 45–60 minutes.

Required Materials

- Five sheets of paper large enough to be labeled and read from a distance. In bold, large letters, the first sheet should be labeled SA-Strongly Agree. The second sheet: A-Agree. The third sheet: N-Neutral, or Not Sure. The fourth sheet: D-Disagree. The fifth sheet: SD-Strongly Disagree.
- List of statements (see Handout for example statements from a gender communication course).

Rationale

Although we live in a society that bombards us with messages about sexuality, research shows that most people are uncomfortable talking directly about sex (Durham, 2008). Numerous studies have shown that since the majority of parents are uncomfortable talking with their children about sex, the cycle of silence continues. We lack effective role models for how to talk openly and honestly about sex without becoming embarrassed (Galvin, Bylund, & Brommel, 2012; Rozema, 1986). Students also have myths about topics such as the "maternal instinct," the concept of jealousy, and the biological basis for homosexuality (Adresen & Weinhold, 1981; Gamble & Gamble, 2003; Wood, 2009). Because students often have not openly discussed these topics, they may never have critically questioned the basis for or origin of their attitudes/beliefs about sexuality and relationships.

This exercise is educational because it provides a clear example of standpoint theory, which contends that we see the world differently due to our age, gender, race, religion, and sexual orientation (Wood, 2009). The exercise can demonstrate that individuals who are in a one-down position due to race, gender, religion, sexual orientation, or other group affiliation can have a broader understanding of the world (i.e., they understand how to negotiate the world as an African-American but also understand the rules/roles/norms of Caucasian Americans since they have to survive in a white, male-dominated society; Wood, 2009).

In many classrooms, the extroverted students will tend to dominate discussions while the quiet students may rarely voice their opinions. Particularly in a class of 25–30+ students, quiet, less confident, or introverted students may be intimidated and rarely share their opinions. The more controversial the topic, the more likely timid students will be silenced. The majority of the class may be tired of hearing from the "vocal minority" and wonder what the rest of their peers are thinking. Moreover, the silence of the majority may be interpreted as agreement.

The exercise also energizes and involves students. Since all students are now required to get on their feet and literally stand on the continuum, it changes the energy in the room. Students are watching where their peers stand, deciding which position best describes their values/beliefs, and considering why they decided to stand on a particular spot on the continuum. When the instructor asks clusters of students why they chose to stand on that particular spot, discussion and argument flow freely and a wider segment of the class typically voices their opinions.

Preparing for the Activity

1. As the professor, your goal is to create a "safe space" for all students to speak and share their ideas. However, when discussing issues related to sexuality, students may make intolerant statements based on their core beliefs, their religious beliefs, or their aversion to students who engage in nonconforming gender or sexual behavior (according to the standards of society, which privileges white, male, heterosexual behavior). Abusive or demeaning comments about other students based on their beliefs or status are inappropriate in the classroom (Meyers, 2003). At the beginning of the semester, establish ground rules for mutually supportive, respectful, and civil class discussion. You may define your expectations or you may let the class generate rules for positive discussions with your guidance. Suggestions for basic rules are: everyone has the right to be treated with respect, to be treated fairly, to be free from verbal attacks, and to be free from judgment for their attitudes or beliefs. Students are encouraged to engage in critical thinking and to disagree tactfully while maintaining a supportive rather than a defensive or even hostile environment. Listen carefully to what other students are saying, attempt to understand their standpoint/viewpoint, ask questions of clarification, and respectfully share your divergent opinions. If a student makes rude or offensive comments, explain that their comments are inappropriate and are violating the safe space. If they continue to do so, give the student three choices. They can change their inappropriate behavior, remain silent, or be invited to leave the classroom.

2. Prior to the activity, assign students several chapters of a gender-focused textbook that will provide students with an understanding of basic concepts such as the difference between sex (what's between your legs), gender (what's between your ears or in your brain), and sexual orientation (whom you find sexually attractive). The readings should also define and discuss standpoint theory (Gamble & Gamble, 2003; Wood, 2009). If the text does not address standpoint theory, this is an easy topic for an instructor to briefly lecture on.

3. This activity requires sufficient space for 25–30 students to stand across the front of the room. Move desks and other furniture to the back of the room, leaving about one-third of the front of the room empty. Then, place each of the five sheets of paper on the floor equidistant from one another and ranging from SA on one side of the room to SD on the other side of the room.

Facilitating the Activity

1. Explain to students that you are going to read a series of statements, and they will literally decide where to take their "stand" based on their reaction to each statement. Encourage them to take a moment and think about the statement rather than simply looking at where their friends/classmates are standing. Encourage students

to think of the five positions as a continuum rather than discrete points and allow them to stand halfway between positions if they prefer.

2. Begin by reading the first statement. The instructor determines the content and length of the activity by the number and type of statements that are read to the class. It is better to prepare more statements than you expect to use; you can edit, skip, or change them as the exercise unfolds.

3. After each statement, the instructor can elicit feedback from students to explain their particular stances. It is often useful to ask the students who are standing on SD or SA to speak first to establish the affirmative and negative arguments, and then to move to the students who are undecided or who slightly agree or disagree with the statement. Some statements may create a lively, lengthy discussion while others may have most students distributed toward one end of the continuum with only a few outliers who disagree. Typically, the instructor can comment on relevant research during the exercise when summarizing one discussion and before the transition to the next statement (e.g., research shows that women do not have an innate "maternal instinct" and babies will bond with their primary caretaker regardless of their sex). The instructor determines how long the class spends discussing/debating a particular statement or processing the activity.

Discussion Questions

• How did the exercise make you think more deeply about your *standpoint* and how your background/upbringing has affected your sexual/relational attitudes and beliefs?

• What are your reactions to seeing how the class as a whole distributed themselves along the continuum? Why?

• What issue surprised you the most when listening to your classmates explain their stances?

• How many of you hesitated and watched where your friends or the majority of your classmates were headed before deciding where you would stand? What is the role of peer pressure in your daily decision-making?

• What, if any, sex or gender issues are you rethinking after listening to the class discussion? Why?

• What research cited by the professor challenged one of your myths about sexuality and gender?

• How often do you seriously discuss your views on gender and relationships outside of the classroom?

  • When a sensitive sex/gender issue comes up in the future, are you more or less likely to voice your views to family, coworkers, or friends after this exercise? Why or why not?

• Why is it hard to talk about these topics within the family? If it isn't hard for your family to discuss them, why not?

Typical Results

• Students enjoy the continuum exercise and find it thought provoking. Students who are outliers (either very conservative or very liberal) recognize how their views differ from the majority of their classmates. If they were talkative students, they and the class already know this. If they were quiet in the past, the class may feel that they have gotten to know these classmates better. It can serve to create more cohesion and confidence so that formerly quiet students may now participate more in classroom discussions.

- Students reflect on the parents, teachers, religious leaders, and others who have helped shape their standpoints. Students who are convinced that their standpoint on the world is "right" may be surprised at the diversity of viewpoints and values expressed, and they may find their minds expanding. They often hear new arguments since we frequently self-select our friends and our news sources, and we affiliate with people who reinforce our existing attitudes. Students also confront some of their myths about sex and gender.

- Students are not necessarily consistent in the positions they take, so the instructor/observers may be surprised by students' values or how they may be progressive in one area and not in another. Students are surprised at the extent to which they do feel peer pressure to shift a bit toward where their friends are standing.

Limitations and Cautionary Advice

- Before beginning the exercise, you might want to review with students the "rules of engagement" for effective classroom discussions (see Preparing for the Activity). Remind them to treat everyone in the room with respect, and remind them that if anyone engages in stereotyping or negatively labeling a particular gender, religion, sexual orientation, and so forth, you will note that the rules have been broken. If another student recognizes that a hurtful or hostile comment has been made before you notice it, they can say, "Ouch," which is a shorthand way of reminding everyone in the room to be respectful. You can then discuss and dispel the stereotype.

- Note that the exercise is not intended to make any student disclose their sexual orientation or their religious affiliation. Rather, it asks students to nonverbally indicate their attitudes or beliefs by standing on the continuum. Students may choose to disclose that because they are a Catholic or a Baptist, they do not approve of premarital sex. Similarly, students may choose to disclose that because they are gay, they support gay marriage (note that millions of straight allies support gay marriage, so no valid inference can be made that a student who strongly agrees with gay marriage is therefore gay/lesbian). Remind students that demonstrating support for a given belief does not indicate the respondent's religion or sexual orientation; it merely indicates the attitude or belief they hold. If the discussion starts to target a particular student or a group to which they belong, the instructor needs to step in quickly and remind students that the purpose of the exercise is for them to express their individual beliefs, reflect on how they formed those beliefs, and be open to listen and learn from the perspectives of others. Remind students they are not trying to persuade students that they are "right" but rather to understand the diversity of opinions that exist and the basis for those opinions.

- This exercise may make some students uncomfortable if they feel they are being asked to disclose personal attitudes or information. There are three ways to minimize this problem and maintain a safe space for everyone.

- First, as you explain the exercise and the nature of the statements the class will be discussing, you can ask for several volunteers to be observers. That provides an option for students who feel uncomfortable with taking a public, visible stand on sensitive, sexual issues. They can rather watch the exercise, take notes, and see the general distribution of attitudes as class members move about the continuum.
- Second, try to avoid calling on specific students. Rather ask the group of students who are clustered around SA or SD if anyone wants to explain why they are standing there. Usually one to two students will start talking, and others will join the discussion.
  - Third, if you or another student question "Sarah" about why she is standing on a particular spot, she has the option to say, "I pass," or to say, "I agree with what student X said a few minutes before."
- As you adapt the exercise, be careful how you "word" the statements that call for value judgments. Try to avoid inflammatory debates. The instructor needs to model and reinforce how to listen respectfully to all opinions and beliefs. If a discussion starts to get heated, the instructor needs to step in quickly, ask the students to "dial it back," and then ask them to discuss how they can interact calmly when these topics are discussed at home or at family reunions.
- Because religious beliefs often frame students' views on sexuality and marriage, the instructor may not agree with an opinion being expressed but can acknowledge that members of religion X tend to hold this view (i.e., they don't approve of pre-marital sex). Remind students that they are here to listen to a diverse set of voices, to practice supportive listening skills, and not to proselytize their classmates.
- There is a tendency for outspoken students to dominate the discussion. This can be overcome by asking a wider range of students why they are standing on a particular spot on the continuum. If there is an extremely vocal student, calmly say, "Robert, I appreciate your contributions, and I'd like to hear from four or five other students before your next comment. Let's share the air-time so we can practice listening to a diverse set of viewpoints." It is the instructor's role as moderator to ensure that a wider representation of views is heard.

Alternative Uses

- As noted earlier, the format of a human continuum from SA to SD can be adapted to many different topics and disciplines. You could use a series of focused statements around a narrower topic dealing with gender, sexuality, and relationships. You could also use it in a cultural diversity class or sociology class dealing with attitudes toward poverty, welfare, or related issues. It could be used in a history class or in English discussing whether or not students agreed with the thesis of an essay or perspective taken by an author.
- The exercise could be used as an icebreaker during the first weeks of class to get students talking to one another. If so, I recommend the use of low-risk questions since the class hasn't had time to establish a climate of group trust or to trust your responses as the instructor. Low-risk questions can create conversation, reveal the personalities of students, promote laughter, and help develop a relaxed, cohesive classroom climate. A sampling of low-risk questions can be found in the Handout.

REFERENCES

Adresen, G., & Weinhold, B. (1981). *Connective bargaining: Communicating about sex.* Englewood Cliffs, NJ: Prentice Hall.

Durham, M. G. (2008). *The Lolita effect.* Woodstock: Overlook Press.

Galvin, K., Bylund, C., & Brommel, B. (2012). *Family communication: Cohesion and change.* Boston: Allyn and Bacon.

Gamble, T., & Gamble, M. (2003). *The gender communication connection.* Boston: Houghton Mifflin.

Meyers, S. A. (2003). Strategies to prevent and reduce conflict in college classrooms. *College Teaching, 51,* 94–98.

Rozema, H. (1986). Defensive communication climate as a barrier to sex education in the home. *Family Relations, 34,* 531–38.

Wood, J. (2009). *Gendered lives: Communication, gender and culture.* Boston: Wadsworth Cengage Learning.

HANDOUT: SAMPLE STATEMENTS

The range of content for this exercise is varied and can be adapted to many different topics and types of classes. Here are some sample statements used in a gender communication course. The statements range from statements clearly supported by research to ones that may be more reflective of students' personal values and beliefs.

1. Premarital sex is acceptable if the two people are in love.
2. Sex without love (a one-night stand) is acceptable if the two people are consenting adults.
3. When a couple has children, one of the parents should stay at home with the children until the children are in kindergarten.
4. Gay or lesbian couples should be free to adopt children.
5. Females have an innate "maternal instinct," which means young children bond more easily with women.
6. When a heterosexual couple gets married, the wife should take the husband's last name.
7. People who are getting married or entering a civil union should share the same religious beliefs.
8. Living together before marriage is acceptable.
9. Computer dating services provide a good way to meet a mate.
10. Going to a bar is a good way to meet a mate.
11. When men say, "I love you," they usually are sincere rather than using it as a strategy to get their partner to go to bed with them.
12. Gay marriage should be legal throughout the United States.
13. I believe in "love at first sight."
14. Most people can sincerely love several different people in their lifetime vs. having one true love.
15. I value sexual faithfulness and would find it very hard to forgive a partner who cheated on me.
16. Birth control is the primary responsibility of the woman and not the man (in heterosexual couples).
17. Jealousy is a natural part of any relationship.
18. True love means that the relationship is easy; if you have to work at it, it was not meant to be.
19. Psychological/emotional infidelity is more painful/harmful than physical infidelity (having a one-night stand with someone else).
20. Being gay/lesbian or bi-sexual is a lifestyle choice.
21. Males have more invisible privileges in our society than females.
22. Women make better managers than men (or I'd prefer to work for a female manager).
23. A sexually active female is more likely to get a "bad reputation" vs. a sexually active male who is seen as a "player."

Sample Low-Risk/Icebreaker Questions

1. I prefer watching reality TV to watching PBS documentaries.
2. I prefer comedies to dramas.
3. I'd rather read a book than watch TV/movies.
4. I'd rather be visiting a museum than playing a sport.
5. I prefer using public transportation to driving a car.
6. I'd rather be in shorts and sandals (comfortable clothes) than dressed in formal attire.
7. I prefer essay exams to multiple-choice questions.
8. I like to travel to new places more than returning to a favorite beach, cottage, or city for my vacation.
9. I prefer the company of children to that of many adults.
10. I'd rather spend time with someone who is "gorgeous" by cultural standards than with someone who is intellectually stimulating.

Femininity and Masculinity: An Exploration of the Relative Elements of Gender Identity

Evangeline Weiss, MA
(National Gay & Lesbian Task Force),
Kerry Poynter, MA
(University of Illinois Springfield)

Appropriate Course(s) and Level[1]

Introductory courses in sexuality studies, gay and lesbian studies, women's and gender studies, or other courses that address issues of gender expression.

Appropriate Class Size

10–20 students and a classroom large enough for students to line up against one wall.

Learning Goals

- To recognize how gender is both an internal identity as well as an external expression.
- To reflect on how gender is also socially constructed and relative.
- To understand how scrutiny of gender impacts us all, regardless of our gender identity or expression, or sexual orientation.
- To draw parallels between the assumptions we make about gender and the scrutiny that trans and gender queer people face on a regular basis.

Estimated Time Required

45 minutes.

Required Materials

- Two signs: two pieces of at least 8 1/2 x 11 inch paper, one with "Most Masculine" written on it and one with "Most Feminine" written on it.
- Tape, pushpin, or other means of affixing signs to the classroom wall.

Rationale

The history and existence of trans people—those who cross boundaries intended to contain gender—in the United States can be traced to the early days of the women's movement and the beginnings of the modern-day lesbian, gay, bi, trans, queer (LG-BTQ) rights movement (Stryker, 2008). However, trans people can be found throughout history in numerous cultures (Feinberg, 1996; Jacobs, Thomas, & Lang, 1997; Nanda, 1999; Roscoe, 1997). In fact, there is now a growing critical discourse in academia on the existence of multiple genders and sexes (Herdt, 1997). However, gender still exists within a continuum (Beemyn & Rankin, 2011; Bornstein, 1994).

Western culture and college students oftentimes continue to reference a gender binary that relies on individual characteristics and actions to define male or female, masculine and feminine. This binary is enforced in part by gender-based violence against gender nonconforming people. This violence targets victims because of their real or perceived gender, gender identity, or gender expression (Wilchins & Taylor, 2006). Youth are targeted or bullied in primary/elementary education as well as higher education (Rankin, Blumenfeld, Weber, & Frazer, 2010).

> Research shows that hostility toward gender non-conformity starts early and is commonplace. In one recent study, 54% of youth reported that their school was unsafe for guys who aren't as masculine as other guys, while one-quarter (27%) complained of being bullied themselves for not being "masculine or feminine enough." In another, 61% of students reported seeing gender non-conforming classmates verbally attacked, and more than one-fifth (21%) reported seeing them physically assaulted (Wilchins & Taylor, 2006).

These problems oftentimes follow individuals into college and beyond. But for many individuals, college offers students the opportunity to engage in reflective, facilitated conversations about gender and sexuality that can strengthen their identity development, regardless of their sexual orientation. This exercise stresses the need to explore gender identity and expression, apart from discussions of sexual orientation.

This activity helps participants develop self-awareness and compassion. It helps participants think critically about their own assumptions and vulnerabilities as related to gender, body image, and identity, and in doing so, it provides the participants with an intimate and rich discussion that all benefit from, regardless of identity. Students walk away with deeper questions about their own identity as well as how to be better allies to people whose gender identity or expression makes them vulnerable in the larger community. This activity will invariably feel different when facilitated with mostly LG-BTQ students. The ages, economic class, and cultural identities of the participants will also impact the tone of the activity in so far as these factors impact gender expression. Participation requires a minimum of self-disclosure but can elicit some uncomfortable moments (see Limitations and Cautionary Advice).

Preparing for the Activity

1. Facilitators should have specific definitions for gender, gender expression, gender identity, transgender, and gender variant identities, such as those found in Stryker

(2008). This activity would be a good follow-up to a discussion or lecture on the differences between gender identity and sexual orientation, sex role socialization, or another gender-role related topic.

2. Hang the masculinity and femininity signs on opposite sides of the room, making sure there is a clear path for people to stand in line between the two signs.

3. This activity is emotionally risky and should be handled with care, as students are going to be self-conscious of how they might be judged and labeled. Before you get students up to do the activity, it is helpful to frame the exercise as a learning experience and to set some ground rules, for example, participants should not put people where they think they belong; participants should practice curiosity and ask questions; and participants should be nonjudgmental as people share with them. The more vulnerable and authentic students are, the more successful this activity will be. It requires all students to participate. It should be scheduled for midway or later in the semester, once relationships are built and the facilitator knows the students, and their group dynamics more intimately.

Facilitating the Activity

1. Explain that the goal of this activity is for the students to line up from most feminine to most masculine. The ordering will be decided by the students themselves through conversation with each other. This is an opportune time to allow students who may feel uncomfortable engaging in these conversations (perhaps due to fear of disclosure) to serve as observers and take notes on the group's interactions.

2. Instruct students to line up randomly between the two signs.

3. Begin by asking for 2–3 examples of how students might decide where they fall on the continuum, examining how masculine or feminine they are. Sample questions might be "Do you wear perfume or cologne?" "How masculine or feminine do you feel inside?" "What kinds of activities do you like to do in your free time?" and "What kinds of shoes do you have in your closet?" Don't spend too much time generating this list, as you want to get them talking to each other.

4. After generating this initial list, ask students to begin forming one single-file line by arranging themselves from "Most Masculine" to "Most Feminine" through their conversations with and questions of one another. The instructor should engage with students as necessary to make sure they are making good progress or to answer any questions.

5. Allow students about 15 minutes to rearrange themselves along the gender continuum. Larger groups might need more time.

6. Once students are rearranged and the activity is concluding, engage them in a discussion. Asking and answering personal questions about gender performance/gender identity will be uncomfortable for the participants. This is similar to the type of scrutiny that transgender people feel when they interact with us. If you have time, invite people to debrief in small groups or clumps along the continuum. Allow each section to talk among themselves for a few minutes before you bring people to a large-group conversation.

Discussion Questions

- What are examples of some questions that were asked to help movement along the continuum?
- How do appearance, activities, hobbies, and interests influence ideas of what is masculine or feminine?
- What were some questions you wanted (or believe others wanted) to ask but were too afraid to?
- How comfortable are you with where you ended up on the continuum?
- How conscious were you about how you chose to dress today, how you wore your hair, or what shoes you happened to be wearing?
- How, if at all, is gender situational? How, if at all, do people change their gender expression in a church, at a family reunion, in class, etc.?
- How, if at all, are spaces gendered? How, if at all, do we choose certain spaces just because of how they invite us to perform gender?
- How is gender identity different from sexual identity?

Typical Results

- Students often feel very self-conscious when they realize their gender expression is being evaluated. They can react with statements such as "I wish I had worn something different today." They recognize the irony or the silliness of being judged based on a superficial decision such as whether or not to wear high heels or shorts instead of a dress.
- Dialogue shifts at times from appearances (earrings, shoes, clothing choices) to questions about role and behavior (sports, household responsibilities—cooking versus taking out the garbage), and the participants can begin to ask deeper questions, for example, "Do you express your feelings in public?" or "How do you feel about offering comfort?" I have enjoyed the deepening of the questions and the self-reflections about whether these questions represent stereotypical thinking or deeply held beliefs, or at times, both.
- In some cases, people who are gender nonconforming recognize the dissidence between their identity and their gender expression—they may look more masculine on the outside than they feel on the inside. These are wonderful opportunities to help tease out the difference between gender identity and gender expression.

Limitations and Cautionary Advice

- This is an activity about gender expression and identity—not about sexual orientation or sexual identity. Remind students that one's gender expression or identity does not indicate their sexual orientation or identity. Some students may remain reluctant to participate for fear of divulging personal information. As noted, you may offer students the opportunity to serve as observers and to take notes on their observations of the group's interactions.
- Avoid allowing anyone to be placed on the continuum against his or her will.

- Avoid being pulled into a theoretical discussion of masculinity and femininity at the outset of the activity when you are giving instructions.
- This is an activity that has been used mostly with white, middle-class university students who are part of LGBT groups and transgender ally training. Explore how culture, ethnicity, and religion might change decisions and movement in the activity.
- Participants should be reassured that where they end up on the continuum represents only where they are today, at this time, in this group. This is not a static place, and as a matter of fact, we expect that gender expression will change all the time, depending on an individual's whereabouts and the people they are with!

Alternative Uses

- This activity can be adapted to teach about sexuality as a spectrum, particularly as it relates to bisexuality or pansexual identities. An understanding of Kinsey's (1948) view on sexuality would be useful.

NOTE

1. Thanks to our friends at the National Gay and Lesbian Task Force and the University of Illinois, Springfield, who helped us refine this activity and develop our ideas and reflections.

REFERENCES

Beemyn, G., & Rankin, S. (2011). *The lives of transgender people.* New York: Columbia University Press.

Bornstein, K. (1994). *Gender outlaw: On men, women, and the rest of us.* New York: Routledge.

Feinberg, L. (1996). *Transgender warriors: Making history from Joan of Arc to Dennis Rodman.* Boston: Beacon Press.

Herdt, G. (1997). Third genders, third sexes. In M. Duberman (Ed.), *A queer world* (pp. 65–81). New York: New York University Press.

Jacobs, S., Thomas, W., & Lang, S. (1997). *Two-spirit people: Native American gender identity, sexuality, and spirituality.* Chicago: University of Illinois Press.

Kinsey, A. (1948). *Sexual behavior in the human male.* Bloomington: Indiana University Press.

Nanda, S. (1999). *The hijras of India.* Belmont, CA: Wadsworth Cengage Learning.

Rankin, S., Blumenfeld, W., Weber, G., & Frazer, S. (2010). *2010 state of higher education for lesbian, gay, bisexual & transgender people.* Charlotte, NC: Campus Pride.

Roscoe, W. (1997). Gender diversity in native North America: Notes toward a unified analysis. In D. Duberman (Ed.), *A queer world* (pp. 65–81). New York: New York University Press.

Stryker, S. (2008). *Transgender history.* Berkeley, CA: Seal Press.

Wilchins, R., & Taylor, T. (2006). *50 under 30: Masculinity and the war on America's youth.* Gender Public Advocacy Coalition.

3

Is It Theft? Using the Ethics of Crime to Frame a Discussion of Sexual Consent and Sexual Assault

Mara K. Berkland, PhD
(North Central College)

Appropriate Course(s) and Level

Introductory level classes where students might still be resistant to the concept of rape myths or sexual inequity, including gender studies, gender communication, social theory, philosophy, politics and gender, introduction to psychology, interpersonal communication, and human sexuality. Because this activity is meant to facilitate a discussion about rape and sexual consent, any course that introduces students to the struggles that gender bias creates for women and men in our communities could use this activity.

Appropriate Class Size

Up to 40 students, where an instructor can easily facilitate large-group discussion.

Learning Goals

- To help separate students from their bias about sexual assault claims and sexual scripts.
- To introduce a standard of ethics for looking at sexual assault.

Estimated Time Required

60 or 75 minutes, depending on the depth of discussion.

Required Materials

- An article that outlines misconceptions of rape and sexual assault such as "What College Women Do and Do Not Experience as Rape" (Kahn, 2004).
- The survey "Is It Theft?" (see Handout).

- The tabulated results from the survey, preferably in a format such as PowerPoint for presentation to the entire class.

Rationale

It is challenging to get students to understand the complexity of sexual assault and the seriousness of non-stranger rape in terms of the breach of trust, psychological violence, and wholesale disrespect that such an act communicates to the victim. This activity offers a buffer between the preconceived biases about gender roles and sexual norms that take away someone's autonomy and decision-making power. When students decide what counts as theft in the class survey, they are in fact evaluating commonly accepted categories of sexual assault and sexual misconduct (Kahn, 2004; Union College, 2012). When the class discussion juxtaposes student survey results with an examination of what people perceive as rape, it becomes clear what we, as a community, see as problematic behavior, is not being labeled as such once the term "rape" is applied to it. Bringing this dichotomy to students' attention opens the door to asking questions about why many would claim that the taking of money is un-ethical, but would not see sexual encounters that fit the same parameters as equally problematic. The discussions that emerge can help illuminate what potential barriers these socialized expectations create for changing behavior at social and legal levels.

Preparing for the Activity

1. This activity takes a few days to prepare, and it should be started in advance of the class when the discussion will be held. However, it can also be completed in one class period. If the instructor has the time, at least two weeks before the day the instructor plans on discussing sexual assault, s/he will need to prepare the survey "Is It Theft?" (see Handout) and distribute it to the students to either (1) take in class, or (2) take home to fill out and return to the instructor at the following class meeting.
2. The instructor will then collect the surveys and tabulate the results/percentages. These can either be typed into the lecture notes or put into a PowerPoint presenta-tion. The day before the class where sexual assault will be the topic of discussion, the instructor should assign a reading on rape myths or rape scenarios such as Kahn (2004).
3. Administering the survey *well before* students read the coordinated reading helps in two ways. First, by being surveyed about theft before they read the article, students will not recognize the scenarios as being similar to the categories of rape or discussions of rape myths defined in the reading. Second, it increases the likeli-hood that students will have forgotten that they took the survey, allowing for an element of surprise and interest.
4. In addition to the course material preparation, the instructor should also take time to research the most recent statistics on sexual assault, especially the rate and in-cidence among college students. Current data can be obtained from the following organizations:

- The U.S. Department of Justice at www.ovw.usdogj.gov/sexassault.htm.
- The Rape Abuse Incest National Network (RAINN) at www.rainn.org.
- The National Sexual Violence Resource Center at http://nsvrc.org/sites/default/files/Publications_NSVRC_Media-Packet.pdf.
- NOW (National Organization for Women) at www.now.org/issues/violence/stats.html.

Facilitating the Activity

1. A few weeks before the students will have read the assigned article on rape scenarios or rape myths, the instructor should photocopy the survey "Is It Theft?" and take it to class. The survey is two pages long but should not be photocopied double-sided; it should be prepared as a single-sided copy that is stapled together (this will help protect anonymity later). In class, the instructor should tell the students that s/he would like their help with a project s/he is working on about theft by filling out a survey. Students should be told that the survey is anonymous and that they should not put their names on it. Once the students have a copy of the survey, the students should be told, "This survey provides you with eight different scenarios about human interaction that may or may not be considered appropriate. I would like you to read each scenario and then evaluate it for fairness. Because the survey uses a range of responses (Illegal, Unethical, Inappropriate, Fair, Ideal), you are encouraged to circle all of the responses that you feel apply to each scenario you read."

2. When the students have completed their surveys (or on the day that the students are assigned to bring the surveys back), the instructor should ask the students to fold the surveys in half with the blank side up and pass them forward. This step ensures student anonymity, as no one will see their responses.

3. To tabulate the responses, the instructor should first count the number of surveys that were turned in (not all students will have completed the task). Then, focusing on one scenario at a time, the instructor should count how many Illegal, Unethical, Inappropriate, Fair, or Ideal responses there were for each scenario. The instructor should then calculate the percentage based on the number of students who responded. The total percentages for each scenario will not equal 100 percent because some students will choose more than one descriptor. A typical set of statistics for each scenario will likely resemble this: Illegal (76 percent), Unethical (93 percent), Inappropriate (60 percent), Fair (0 percent), Ideal (0 percent).

4. The calculated percentages should be put into a PowerPoint presentation. Each slide should include the exact language of the scenario from the Handout describing the theft and the percentages from the class survey.

5. The day of the activity, the in-class discussion of the reading and survey is best opened with direct questions about what the students think about sexual assault and the issues raised in the reading. It is best to let students share their initial reactions for a few minutes before asking any pointed questions or steering the conversation in any particular direction. The instructor's goal in the class discussion is to guide students through three steps: (1) an assessment of permissible sexual behaviors, (2) an exploration of permissible theft behaviors, and (3) a discussion of the

differences in the two sets of standards. At the point that students have begun to debate interactions in terms of why some students would/would not rate them as sexual assault, the instructor should begin guiding student conversation to the first discussion step by encouraging students to clarify the rules surrounding sexual consent. The instructor should ask students why certain scenarios or experiences, such as alcohol involved sex or coercion, might not be considered rape and let students work out verbally the firmly socially constructed but rarely articulated rules of sexual consent. The instructor should prompt students by asking,

- Who is at fault in this scenario?
- Did anyone behave unethically? Why/why not?
- Did anyone behave illegally? Why/why not?
- What advice would you give to the people in this scenario?
- What went wrong with this situation?

6. Once the instructor is satisfied students have verbalized the social rules of sexual interaction and permissible behaviors, the second step of the class discussion can begin. To start this, the instructor should introduce the theft scenarios that students had previously evaluated in the survey. The instructor will have prepared a visual aid that introduces the theft scenarios and the compiled data from the student survey about the theft of $100. The instructor should again prompt students to explain their thoughts using the same questions concerning what is acceptable behavior. Students will immediately begin to note the overlapping language, and as the class reviews each scenario, it would be appropriate to bring these differing norms to the students' attention.

Discussion Questions

- Why might we define a specific scenario as "theft" but we wouldn't term it "rape"?
- Why might a victim be particularly hesitant to label her/his experience as rape?
- What about the word "rape" makes us afraid to use it to classify a behavior, even if we find that behavior to be a violation of a code of ethics?
- How might the sex of the victim play a role in our desire to believe his/her claims?
- At what point should an unethical behavior be labeled as illegal and appropriately punished?
- If we used the term "sexual theft" instead of "rape," might it change our perception of appropriate norms?

Typical Results

- Because the survey allows the students to select a range of responses (Illegal, Unethical, Inappropriate, Fair, Ideal), the student data highlight how the behaviors might fit on an ethical continuum. The wider degree of responses allows for a discussion of the appropriateness and acceptability of the behavior scenario to be discussed before punishment or labels are assigned. Typically, each scenario presents a range of results that emphasize the inappropriateness, unethical nature, and illegality of the majority of the theft scenarios.

- The only theft scenario that frequently diverges from this pattern is the "Submit to boyfriend" scenario, which, if appropriate for the class, creates an opportunity to talk more in-depth about dating scripts and gendered sexual expectations.

Limitations and Cautionary Advice

- During the discussion, students may struggle with the idea of a punishment linked to legality. Frequently, this is where the discussion becomes most heated. When pressed, students will often concede that they agree an action should be considered illegal, but that they feel potential remedies in the legal system might be too harsh for many scenarios. They will argue that a perpetrator should not be punished heavily because miscommunications between scenario participants might be reasonable. At this point, it is important to prompt them to clarify what types of punishments might be reasonable for different scenarios in both the sex and theft conditions. Walking them through a comparison of acceptable punishments will help to further illuminate their different standards.
- In some instances, the class responses can show ambivalence about theft as well as rape. In such cases, it is important to steer the discussion to one that focuses on the ethics of feminism, and what equal options and opportunities for all humans would/should look like. In that circumstance, it is useful to ask students to devise a standard of ethics in smaller groups, and then apply that ethical standard to the scenarios they had before rated as either Fair or Ideal. It is helpful to emphasize that even if we, as a community, do not label it as rape or theft, that does not inherently eliminate it as an area of concern. It is also imperative to be prepared with statistics to help students understand their concerns that rape victims often make up stories and that good men are often wronged by false accusations.

Alternative Uses

- In the case that the instructor does not want to give out the survey in advance and tabulate it, there are a couple of options to expedite this step. First, the instructor could create the survey on Blackboard (or whichever course software the instructor has access to) and have students take it before they come to class. The software would then tabulate the report.
- Or, if the instructor has access to clickers, the students can take the survey in the classroom at the beginning of class. The instructor can then return to those clicked statistics just as the class discusses the scenarios.

REFERENCES

Department of Justice Office on Violence against Women. (2012). *Sexual assault.* www.ovw.usdoj.gov/sexassault.htm.

Kahn, A. S. (2004). What college women do and do not experience as rape. *Psychology of Women Quarterly, 28*, 9–15.

National Sexual Violence Resource Center. (2012). *Media packet: Info & stats for journalists.* http://nsvrc.org/sites/default/files/Publications_NSVRC_Media-Packet.pdf.

Rape, Abuse & Incest National Network (RAINN). (2009). *Statistics.* www.rainn.org/statistics.

Union College. (2012). *Sexual assault examples.* www.union.edu/offices/dean/sart/assault/examples/index.php.

ADDITIONAL READINGS

Burt, M. R. (1980). Cultural myths and supports for rape. *Journal of Personality and Social Psychology, 38*(2), 217–30. doi:10.1037/0022-3514.38.2.217.

Fisher, B., Cullen, F., & Turner, M. (2000). *Sexual victimization of college women. Bureau of Justice Statistics.* Washington, DC: U.S. Department of Justice. www.ncjrs.gov/pdffiles1/nij/182369.pdf.

Hickman, S. E., & Muehlenhard, C. L. (1999). "By the semi-mystical appearance of a condom": How young women and men communicate sexual consent in heterosexual situations. *Journal of Sex Research, 36*(3), 258–72.

Katz, J., & Tirone, V. (2009). Women's sexual compliance with male dating partners: Associations with investment in ideal womanhood and romantic well-being. *Sex Roles, 60*(5/6), 347–56. doi:10.1007/s11199-008-9566-4.

McGregor. J. (2005). *Is it rape? On acquaintance rape and taking women's consent seriously.* Surrey, UK: Ashgate Publishing.

Peterson, Z. D., & Muehlenhard, C. L. (2004). Was it rape? The function of women's rape myth acceptance and definitions of sex in labeling their own experiences. *Sex Roles, 51*(3/4), 129–44.

Warshaw, R. (1994). *I never called it rape: The* Ms. *report on recognizing, fighting, and surviving date and acquaintance rape.* New York: Harper Perennial.

HANDOUT: "IS IT THEFT?"

In the following survey, please evaluate each circumstance and select the appropriate rating concerning the legal and/or ethical evaluation of each. In some cases, you may choose to select more than one. (All scenarios adapted from Kahn [2004].) All of the circumstances begin with the following scenario.

It is Pat's birthday, and as a gift, Pat's grandmother has enclosed in the birthday card a crisp $100 bill as a gift. Pat immediately plucks the bill from the card and tucks it in a pants pocket for safekeeping. (The demographic characteristics of Pat will change in each scenario so as not to reflect bias about what is right for a male or female.)

Circumstance 1

Pat's best friend, Terri, has found out about the $100 and has spent the entire day begging Pat to give it to her so she can buy a new dress. The pestering began in the morning when Terri was complaining about an upcoming evening out and having nothing to wear. At lunch she pointedly asks Pat to give her the money, and by the end of the day she is insulting Pat and saying that Pat is a terrible friend and she won't be friends with her anymore if Pat doesn't give her the $100. Eventually, Pat, afraid of losing a trusted friend, gives in.

Terri's actions are

A. Illegal
B. Unethical
C. Inappropriate
D. Fair
E. Ideal

Circumstance 2

Pat's best friend, John, has found out about the $100 and begins teasing him about taking it. As they are rough-housing, the punches become less playful, and John, who is larger than Pat, tackles him, forces him to the ground and with Pat's arm locked in a half-nelson, John takes the bill from Pat's pocket. After John safely stashes the bill in his own pocket, he offers his hand to help Pat up and smilingly slaps him on the back while saying, "No hard feelings!"

John's actions are

A. Illegal
B. Unethical
C. Inappropriate
D. Fair
E. Ideal

Circumstance 3

Pat is an eight-year-old girl, whose fourteen-year-old cousin, Mindy, babysits her regularly. Mindy sees the $100 bill sticking out of Pat's pocket and takes it. When Pat protests, Mindy tells Pat that if she tattles on her, then she will tell Pat's parents that Pat was naughty and needs to be grounded. Mindy then tells Pat that she will buy her ice cream if she doesn't tell.

Mindy's actions are

A. Illegal
B. Unethical
C. Inappropriate
D. Fair
E. Ideal

Circumstance 4

Pat is asleep and he has left his jeans on the floor. While he is sleeping, his roommate comes home from work and sees the pants lying there. He plucks the $100 bill from the pocket.

The roommate's actions are

A. Illegal
B. Unethical
C. Inappropriate
D. Fair
E. Ideal

Circumstance 5

Pat is at a bar with a group of friends from work and he is happily telling them that he is planning to buy a new golf club with the money his grandmother has given him. After some trash talk about who is going to dominate on the course this summer, Pat heads to the restroom. While Pat is washing his hands in the bathroom, Terry, an acquaintance of Pat's and a friend of one of the people he works with, walks in the door. Terry says, "I heard that you have your eye on a fancy new wedge." Pat laughs and admits that that is the club he needs to round out his bag. Terry then, who is a bit drunk, mumbles about how he is going to screw with his game, swings at Pat. A scuffle ensues and Terry successfully pulls the bill out of Pat's pocket and leaves.

Terry's actions are

A. Illegal
B. Unethical
C. Inappropriate
D. Fair
E. Ideal

Circumstance 6

Pat is walking home from the library after it has closed for the night. As she rounds a corner, a masked person jumps out of the bushes waving a knife. The stranger tells her to give him her purse and empty her pockets. He makes off with everything she has, including her $100 bill.

The stranger's actions are

A. Illegal
B. Unethical
C. Inappropriate
D. Fair
E. Ideal

Circumstance 7

It's Pat's twenty-first birthday and she has been celebrating with friends. One friend finally has the presence of mind to walk her home. As Pat stumbles toward her apartment, her friend holds her hair as she vomits into the bushes. When they finally get to Pat's home, her friend helps her brush her teeth and drink some water. They both laugh about the crazy evening and the list of shots that Pat had to drink. As she covers Pat up, Pat's friend grabs the $100 bill out of Pat's back pocket.

The friend's actions are

A. Illegal
B. Unethical
C. Inappropriate
D. Fair
E. Ideal

Circumstance 8

Pat's best friend, Sarah, has just died tragically in a car accident. Pat's good friend, Matt, has been encouraging her to use her $100 to buy them tickets to hear U2, a band Pat and Sarah had seen perform together a number of times. Matt loves the group as well and thinks that going to the concert will help Pat celebrate Sarah's life and give her a chance to enjoy herself again. Pat has been really depressed since Sarah's death and doesn't feel ready to confront the emotion that this concert could bring. Matt, however, will not let the issue drop and continues to bring it up until eventually Pat relents and buys the tickets.

Matt's actions are

A. Illegal
B. Unethical
C. Inappropriate
D. Fair
E. Ideal

Bringing the Gender Movements Alive through Role-Play

Sherianne Shuler, PhD
(Creighton University)

Appropriate Course(s) and Level

Introductory to advanced students in courses related to women and gender studies or other courses that examine women's and/or men's movements.

Appropriate Class Size

10–30 students.

Learning Goals

- To increase knowledge of the diverse ideologies of historical and contemporary women's movements.
- To increase knowledge of the diverse ideologies of historical and contemporary men's movements.
- To encourage perspective-taking through role-playing of diverse ideologies.
- To engage in critical argument analysis.
- To practice oral argumentation skills.

Estimated Time Required

The two activities can be combined and adjusted to fit into as little as one 50-minute class period, but they work best in one or two longer sessions.

Required Materials

- Handout of the various strands of the women's and men's movements as covered in your text. Create your own that parallels the readings on the women's and men's movements you assign. See Handout for an example.

- Paper or poster board and markers for the men's movement.
- A gavel, a podium, and any other "props" you would like to use to make your classroom seem more like a conference setting (sometimes I bring refreshments) for the women's movement.

Rationale

In gender-related courses, some topics almost automatically generate controversy (and thus vigorous discussion), and others are less likely to pique the students' interest. The historical information about gender movements tends to fall in the latter category. It is important in introductory gender-studies courses to provide historical context by covering gender-related movements, or students will assume how we currently "do gender" (West & Zimmerman, 1987) is how it has always been done. Part of the foundation of most gender-studies courses is the notion that gender is a social construct that varies historically and cross-culturally. But just how do notions of gender change? In my experience, contemporary college students have a vague notion that things have progressed since their parents were their age but are unable to fill in any details about how and why changes have occurred. Many students seem to forget that progress toward gender equality has not simply happened automatically over the years but through the hard work of committed people who often sacrificed a great deal to make their beliefs known. Further, today's college students tend not to identify "feminism" as a positive term or to consider themselves to be feminists (Rowe-Finkbeiner, 2004). According to Baumgardner and Richards (2000), however, the vast majority of women and men actually do support the goals, values, and achievements of feminism, if not the label. If students are uninformed about the diverse beliefs and goals of the various women's movements, they are often even less informed about men's movements.

Here I demonstrate two engaged role-playing activities that attempt to make up for these deficits by deepening students' understanding of the similarities and differences between the ideologies of the various branches of the women's and men's movements. Engaged role-playing promotes learning about ideological differences between groups, and it offers an opportunity to do some perspective-taking. Students enjoy the activity but also report "getting it" more deeply than reading or lecture/discussion allows. As Nyquist and Wulff (1990) noted, "The experience can be particularly useful when students encounter situations or play roles that force them to view a situation from a variety of perspectives" (p. 352). The act of having to articulate the opinions of another promotes empathy, especially when the opinions are those with which we disagree. This is a major benefit of the activity.

Preparing for the Activity

1. For the day(s) you will conduct this activity, assign students the corresponding chapter(s) in your text or from outside readings covering the women's and men's movements (see Additional Readings for suggestions). Remind students that it is particularly important they complete their reading for this day, as they will need

to use the material in class, and it will be hard to "hide" that they did not complete their readings.

2. Review the women's and men's movements as presented in your assigned reading, and also explore online resources of current movement organizations to get a more in-depth feel for their ideologies (see Additional Websites for Instructor Preparation for suggested organizations' websites).

3. Create a handout that outlines the women's and men's movements in a way that parallels your assigned readings. Since which movements are included and how they are labeled and covered varies between readings, it is not practical to provide a universally applicable handout with a list of movements. However, an example that fits with one popular textbook (Wood, 2013) is provided (see Handout). The text that I use covers men's and women's movements in separate chapters, so my example is formulated as two discrete activities for use in two successive class periods. Others may wish to combine men's and women's movements into one activity if the assigned reading covers the movements together.

4. On the women's movement day, the instructor will embody the voice of liberal feminism at a conference convened by NOW and presided over by its president. To prepare, visit NOW's website (NOW, 2012) to learn the name of the current president of NOW, and also take a look at some of their current issues so you can fully embrace your role.

5. For the men's movement day, the instructor will be the organizer of a "men's rally" that is about to take place on the quad. The activity is written with the instructor being a generic men's group leader. However, for the fullest embodiment of this role, find out if your campus or community has a men's group, and prepare for the role as leader of that group by familiarizing yourself with their mission and activities, and presume they are sponsoring the rally.

Facilitating the Activity

Women's Movements

1. Open class by handing out your previously prepared list of women's movements that corresponds with the way they are covered in the reading, and let students know that they should use it to take notes.

2. Then, assign each student one movement for which they will be responsible. If you have more students than movements, you can put students into groups and have each group explore one movement. Do not assign "liberal feminism" to any group because that is the role that you will take as the instructor.

3. Allow students 10–20 minutes (or no more than one-third of the class time) to review what they learned in the reading about their particular movement, either individually or in groups. Encourage them to think about/discuss their movement's main values and goals and what makes their group similar or different from the others in the chapter.

4. When 10–20 minutes have passed and/or students seem to be finished reviewing the material on their assigned groups, bang a gavel on the podium and say, "Let's

get started." To best explain how to facilitate this activity, I have provided the narrative below that you may use or adapt to your classroom.

> Okay, let's get started. Please feel free to grab some coffee or doughnuts as we talk today. I want to welcome you to this historic and miraculous gathering. My name is Terry O'Neill and I'm the president of NOW and the convener of this conference on "Gender: Past, Present, and Future." I thank all of the participants from various women's movements for being willing to travel great distances, in some cases even across time, to be with us today. Some of you have worked together in the past, but others are meeting for the first time today. For that reason, please state the name of the group you represent when you rise to speak.
>
> As many of you know, ever since 1963 when Sister Betty Friedan wrote about "the problem that has no name" in *The Feminine Mystique*, NOW has been a leader in helping women escape their boring and meaningless lives as housewives and live up to their potential. While women can now do anything men can do, there are still not enough women in the military, government, the pulpit, or at high levels of many organizations. We certainly still have work to do. Who here is with us in our quest for true equal rights for women? Anyone?

At first, students will likely be pretty confused. As the instructor continues the opening spiel, it will slowly dawn on them what is going on. The ones who are less prepared will get a little worried, but most students will be quick to catch on to the game. After posing the above question, the instructor should look at the students expectantly and wait. Perhaps it is the first-wave women's rights suffragettes who finally speak up to describe how they actually came up with the idea of equal rights in the first place. Or, perhaps it is a radical feminist who says, "Well, we're certainly not in favor of just having women join such a broken system," etc.

5. At this point, when it is clear that the students understand what is expected of them, the instructor's role becomes that of facilitator. Keep the list of all the groups handy, and check them off as you go. Use prompts like "Is there anyone else here who agrees with that?" "I wonder if there's anyone here who does *not* share this goal," or "Thank you for your honesty, although it hurts. Anyone else think the real problem is feminism itself?" If something unclear or incorrect is said about a group, say something like "Oh, perhaps I was misinformed. I thought you were from the revalorist group. Would you like to explain and clarify your stance a bit more?" If you get to the end and a group has not jumped in, say something like "The power feminists have been awfully quiet so far and that's not like them. Is there someone here from that group who can speak about women living up to their full potential?" Continue in this manner until all groups have spoken at least once and you are satisfied that the important distinctions between groups have been surfaced.

6. After all the groups have spoken, say, "Thank you so much for your fine participation. I think we are well on our way to making some progress on the topic for today. Now let's open up the floor for further dialog and discussion." At this point, end the role-playing and ask for questions and move to further discussion about the various groups (see Discussion Questions).

Men's Movements

1. The next class period, open in a similar way as above by assigning a men's movement to each group of students.
2. As with the women's movements, provide your prepared list of groups covered in
   your reading to the students for the purposes of note taking and keeping track of
   what has been covered.
3. Bring large pieces of paper (like from a flip chart) and markers to class. Then,
   open with some version of the following:

   > Gentlemen. I think we know why we are here. There is a sickness sweeping our
   > land and that sickness is contemporary manhood. Let's be men and speak up and do
   > something about it! As you know, the rally on the quad starts soon. Between now
   > and then your goal is to get your message across—capture the spirit and the beliefs of
   > your group in protest signs, chants, and brief speeches. Paper and markers are spread
   > throughout the room. Be both clear and creative.

4. Then offer students 20–30 minutes (or one-third to one-half of the remaining class
   period) to prepare their signs. Circulate among the students to make sure they
   understand that their goal is to get across the fundamentals of their group through
   chants or brief protest speeches as they hold up their protest signs. Remind them
   the "rally" is about the problems with contemporary masculinity, but each group
   should frame the "problems" differently, so they should make sure their protest
   artifacts show what makes them unique.
5. After the preparation time has expired and/or the students seem to be ready to
   share, call them back to order and start the role-play as follows:

   > Okay, brothers. Before we head out to the quad for the rally, let's psych ourselves
   > up. I see that the profeminist men think that women and men should "unite and take
   > back the night!" Would you explain that please?

At this point, have the students hold up and explain their signs and do their
chants and/or rally speeches. To facilitate interaction between the groups, say
things like "Who will stand with these fine brothers in this quest?" or "Oh, I
think you've stepped on some toes. Who is offended?" Continue in this fashion until all the groups have shared their rally preparation and then move to
a discussion of the similarities and differences between the men's movement
groups. After all the women's and men's movements have been covered, it
is valuable to take some time to tie the movements together and examine the
similarities and differences among the groups (see Discussion Questions).

Discussion Questions

- How similarly or differently did your group fundamentally see men and women?
- How much did class and race matter to your group?
- How welcoming of an environment do you believe your group would create for
  gay/lesbian individuals?

- What points, if any, do all the groups agree upon regarding the women's movement or men's movement?
- What do you believe were the key points of disagreement among your men's movement and women's movement groups?
- What projects could some groups work together on? (equal pay, violence against women, getting dads more involved in fatherhood, etc.)
- How relevant do you believe your group's movement is to today's modern issues?
- Is there a new movement needed now? What would its goals be?

Typical Results

- This exercise helps students grasp that the historical and contemporary gender movements involve(d) real people with strong beliefs, which can be difficult to fully realize by just reading a chapter. Some expectations we have today (e.g., women voting, women being allowed to major in whatever they choose, fathers being allowed to miss work for the birth of their children, sexual harassment being a crime) are taken for granted, but they were gained because committed people worked in groups to make change. By having to take the perspective of a group whose beliefs they may not really share, students also gain empathy for others. The varying techniques of role-playing and the creation of signs, chants, and speeches help students to understand the varying ideologies on a deeper level than is otherwise possible.

Limitations and Cautionary Advice

- If the class does not seem to be getting into the activity enough, or especially if the students don't do a great job on the first try of drawing distinctions between the various groups' beliefs, try to provoke arguments between groups by asking questions that will bring out their points of disagreement ("We all think traditional feminine activities like cooking and housekeeping are demeaning, right?"). The more students embody the group ideologies and interact with the members of the other groups, the more they learn.
- Consider trying to "rig" the groups somewhat so students get a group they would ordinarily not be comfortable with. Having to articulate an opposing group's position promotes perspective-taking and empathy, so I often will assign conservative groups to the more progressive students and vice versa.
- Allow students to poke a little fun at groups by representing their extremes, but be prepared to rein them in and emphasize that the goal is to understand each group on its own terms and not to belittle people. For example, I might allow the separatists to say, "Okay sisters, society is so far gone there's no fixing it, so let's all move to a ranch in Montana to set up our own perfect society and live communally. No more makeup or shaving!" Students may need to be cautioned to speak as if they are members of the group. Promise Keepers, themselves, would not say, "We're extreme bigots who don't like women or gays," and you may have to challenge

students to do a little more perspective-taking and represent a group like this more fairly.

Alternative Uses

- I spend a week on the gender movements, which might be a limitation for some instructors. To save time, it is possible to combine the men's and women's movements into one big conference and/or rally, especially if the course text includes them all in one chapter.
- Alternatively, you could assign movements ahead of time so preparation can be done outside of class instead of taking class time to work in groups. I have preferred not to do this, as the element of surprise has made the activities lively in my classes.
- Consider using a take-home essay question on the exam that asks students to create a movement that addresses a current gender-related problem. What would be the name of their movement? What strategies would they use to get their message across? Which existing groups would they build on? Why is a new group needed? What are existing groups not doing that the student thinks needs to be emphasized? One could also imagine turning this into a project rather than an exam question.

REFERENCES

Baumgardner, J., & Richards, A. (2000). *Manifesta: Young women, feminism, and the future.* New York: Farrar, Straus, and Giroux.

Friedan, B. (1963). *The feminine mystique.* New York: Norton.

NOW. (2012). www.now.org.

Nyquist, J. D., & Wulff, D. H. (1990). Selected active learing strategies. In J. A. Daly, G. W. Friedrich, & A. L. Vangelisti (Eds.), *Teaching communication: Theory, research, and methods* (pp. 337–62). Hillsdale, NJ: Lawrence Erlbaum Associates.

Rowe-Finkbeiner, K. (2004). *The F-word: Feminism in jeopardy.* Emeryville, CA: Seal Press.

West, C., & Zimmerman, D. H. (1987). Doing gender. *Gender and Society, 1,* 125–55.

Wood, J. (2013). *Gendered lives: Communication, gender, and culture.* Belmont, CA: Thomson Wadsworth.

ADDITIONAL READINGS

Baumgardner, J., & Richards, A. (2000). Ch. 2: What is feminism? In J. Baumgardner & A. Richards (Eds.), *Manifesta: Young women, feminism, and the future* (pp. 50–86). New York: Farrar, Straus, and Giroux.

Flood, M. (2007). Men's movements. In M. Flood, J. Kegan Gardiner, B. Pease, & K. Pringle (Eds.), *International encyclopedia of men and masculinities* (pp. 418–22). New York: Routledge.

ADDITIONAL WEBSITES FOR INSTRUCTOR PREPARATION

- Eve Online: Ecofeminist visions emerging (http://eve.enviroweb.org/index.html)
- Fathers' Rights (www.fathersrightsinc.com/)
- MenWeb (www.menweb.org/)
- NOMAS (www.nomas.org/)
- Promise Keepers (www.promisekeepers.org/)
- Third Wave Foundation (www.thirdwavefoundation.org/)

HANDOUT: GENDER MOVEMENTS (SEE WOOD, 2013)

1. Women's Movements
   (a) First wave
       1. liberal branch "women's rights"
       2. cultural branch "cult of domesticity"
   (b) Second wave
       1. liberal feminism
       2. radical feminism
       3. lesbian feminism
       4. separatist feminism
       5. revalorists
       6. ecofeminism
       7. womanists
       8. multiracial feminism
       9. power feminism
   (c) Third wave
2. Men's Movements
   (a) Profeminist
       1. NOMAS
       2. men's antiviolence groups
   (b) Masculinist
       1. men's rights
       2. fathers' rights
       3. mythopoetic men
       4. Promise Keepers
       5. Million Man March

Arguing over Theories of Gender Development

Shelly Schaefer Hinck, PhD (Central Michigan University),
Edward A. Hinck, PhD (Central Michigan University)

Appropriate Course(s) and Level

Introductory gender communication course, communication theory, or possibly a political communication course. Additionally, the exercise could be used in an interdisciplinary course on leadership in a unit on differences between masculine and feminine communication styles or in an introductory-level course in sociology to examine theories and styles regarding gender.

Appropriate Class Size

15–45 students.

Learning Goals

- To develop knowledge of the main tenets of each major theoretical perspective explaining gender development.
- To compare strengths and weaknesses of theoretical perspectives of gender development.
- To identify and apply criteria to compare and evaluate theoretical perspectives.
- To examine gender differences in conflict and argumentation.

Estimated Time Required

The debate requires at least a 75-minute class period, but the exercise should be assigned a week prior to the actual debate in order to give students time to think about the strengths and weaknesses of each theoretical perspective.

Required Materials

• Optional handouts (see Handouts).

Rationale

This activity challenges students to debate theoretical points of view regarding gender development. In addition to comprehending multiple theoretical perspectives, students must also apply basic principles of argumentation—the ability to make a claim and present support for the position. This skill entails a deep understanding of the material since students must anticipate opposing points of view and prepare answers to those arguments. Perkins (2009) argued performance is the key to engaged, deep learning. In particular, debate calls for performance to demonstrate engaged learning.

The theories that will be addressed range from biological approaches to gender to interpersonal and cultural theories of gender development. Biological theories of gender development focus on how sex chromosomes, hormones, and the brain impact individuals (Wood, 2011) while interpersonal theories (Psychodynamic, Social Learning, Cognitive Development) address how relational factors influence gendered behavior. Cultural theories (Anthropology, Symbolic Interactionism) privilege the cultural context and its assumptions as to what it means to be masculine or feminine in that particular environment.

This exercise provides students with the opportunity to learn what each theory represents and to think carefully as to what each theory can explain and what each theory cannot explain. Students are required to present and defend the assumptions of their assigned theory while noting the limitations of the other theories and the evidence presented. Although some may argue that one theory cannot adequately explain gender development, requiring students to argue for a particular theory forces students to compare and contrast the theories' abilities to explain and/or predict gendered behaviors. The exercise encourages students to put aside personal assumptions about the construction of gender and to rely on the evidence they have gathered as a way to support their theories, hence developing important critical-thinking skills.

The activity also provides students with the opportunity to experience gender differences manifested in advocacy. Research on masculine and feminine communicator styles and patterns point to differences between the way men and women argue. These differences are brought to the surface as students directly experience and observe those communication behaviors when working together on teams to build cases. Not everyone on each team will agree about how to best support their theoretical perspective. The arguments about how to solve those problems are worth discussing in relation to the problem of how men and women disagree while trying to resolve differences. Instructors can invite students to consider how gender differences enable or problematize complex problem-solving. Additionally, the debate offers an opportunity to observe men and women negotiate the role of advocacy. These performances and observations open up the possibility of discussing how gender expectations affect the perception of men and women as leaders in social, organizational, and political situations.

Preparing for the Activity

1. Instructor should provide information concerning a general look at theories of gender development.

2. Instructor should explain what constitutes a unit of argumentation. A basic explanation of the three primary components of Toulmin's (1958) model of argument should suffice: claim, data, warrant. Instructor should be prepared to offer one or more examples of the kind of discourse that counts as a basic argument in support of the theory assigned. For example, for the biological theory, the claim might be that biological differences determine communication behavior; the evidence might be that the hormonal differences between males and females are objective, measurable differences that affect behavior. Since these differences are accepted by professionals from many disciplines and are grounded in science, the biological theory would be, therefore, a strong explanation for gendered behavior.

3. Instructor should introduce the stock issues for a proposition of value. Basically, the students need to understand that they must argue for one or more criteria of what counts as the best theory and apply the criterion or criteria to the theories under discussion. Additionally, students should be given information that helps them think about how to critique arguments, including type of evidence provided, assumptions of the sources of the evidence, and generalizability of the claims presented (see Handout A). This information will enable students to think critically when examining the assumptions of the theories for gender development.

4. Instructor should explain criteria for evaluating theories. Frey, Botan, and Kreps (2000) offered a summary of six basic criteria that can be used for this exercise (see Handout B). After providing the Handout and explaining the six basic criteria, the instructor will need to make sure that the teams know they need to select one or more criteria, apply them to the theory they are assigned to defend, be prepared to compare and analyze the competing theoretical perspectives, and be prepared to defend the criteria they selected as appropriate or most appropriate for the debate. In the example provided above, the team defending the biological basis for gender development might want to select a criterion for evaluation related to a theory's capacity to explain a phenomenon on the basis of observed facts. In the case of biology, the observed facts that explain gender differences would be the scientific measure of hormonal differences.

5. The day of the debate, to help facilitate the activity the instructor will want to prepare the room for the debate, and remind the class of the debate expectations. The instructor will want to have a podium and/or desk at the front of the room where each speaker will present their case. Additionally, team members will want to sit together so that they will be able to discuss the debate as it proceeds.

Facilitating the Activity

1. A week before the debate day, to allow ample time for research, students should be randomly assigned to 4 teams: 3 advocacy teams and 1 team of judges. Each advocacy team can be composed of up to 10 students. Each team should select 3

advocates and the remaining students will serve as support staff to generate arguments, explanations, and examples. The instructor could allow more than three people to speak for a given team depending on interest levels of each team. Each advocacy team is responsible for developing a case to support the theoretical perspective they have been assigned. The team of judges is charged with identifying criteria for evaluating theoretical perspectives on gender development and developing a ballot that can be used to critique the debate and render a decision (see Handout C for an example). It is important that students are randomly assigned to groups. An integral part of the learning experience occurs when students are asked to defend a theory that they don't initially support.

2. After placing students in teams, the instructor will need to explain the structure and the format of the debate activity (see Handout D).

3. Once the teams have been created and students understand the format of the debate activity, teams are assigned readings from their textbook that address various gender development theories (biological/social learning/cognitive learning/cultural/symbolic interactionism). Students are also required to find at least four additional pieces of evidence that they can use to either support their theory or that will address the limitations of the other theories.

4. Once teams understand the assignment, each group will need to identify who they would like to deliver each of the speeches mentioned in Handout D. To get as many students actively engaged in the activity as possible, the instructor may encourage different students within each group to present the various speeches; this includes presenting in "two-person" teams if students are apprehensive about speaking in public.

5. In an effort to make the activity an enjoyable experience, the instructor should ask that each team behave like a "team." Students should be encouraged to clap for and support their teammates after they have finished speaking; they may choose to dress in a similar manner (team uniform) or they may "name" their team if they desire.

6. The day of the debate, it is important that the instructor reminds the class of the speaking expectations (time requirements for each speaker as well as the purpose of each presentation). If time permits, the instructor may want to offer 10 minutes at the beginning of the class period so that the teams can go over any last-minute speaking assignments or address changes in speaking assignments. The initial 10 minutes at the beginning of the class period also allows the judging team to pass out critique sheets to the judging team members.

7. The instructor facilitates the debate, serving as a moderator and providing time signals for the speakers following the format provided in Handout D.

8. After the debate concludes, the judges will confer and then announce their decision concerning who won the debate. The judges will explain, using the criteria they selected, how they arrived at their decision. Although it may initially seem as if the judges are not as actively engaged in the debating process, the students soon find that being a judge is difficult. To effectively evaluate the arguments made by the three teams, it is important that the judges be knowledgeable about all the theories presented in the textbook. The judges are also required to construct the

critique sheet that they will use to evaluate the debate performance. Constructing the critique sheet encourages the judges to think about which criteria are important when evaluating arguments. Finally, the judges must be able to present their decision as to which team argued the most persuasively, offering support for their decision and answering questions if needed.

9. Process the debate using the provided Discussion Questions.

Discussion Questions

Describe

- What types of arguments were used?
- What types of arguments did you find the most persuasive?
- What types of arguments were not persuasive?
- What were the most persuasive pieces of evidence?
- What did you see as a limitation/strength of each of the theories presented?

Infer

- Did you have to argue a position you didn't agree with? What was that like?
- What did you find surprising from the debates?
- Is there one perspective that resonates with you more than the others? Why or why not?
- What could one theory explain that the other theories couldn't?
- Can we say as scholars that one of the perspectives offers definitive proof? Why or why not?
- How does this influence your understanding of how gender develops?

Transfer/Connect

- Are there gender differences in arguing, and if so, how do gender differences become manifested in theoretical arguments about gender?
- What theory best explains the gendered differences in arguing?
- When it comes to working through disagreements about important issues, are gender differences valuable? If so, describe how.
- What do the differences contribute in terms of resolving disagreements that would be missing if only one gendered style of arguing was used?

Typical Results

- As a result of having spent considerable time learning about an assigned theory, students often indicate that they now see the strengths of their assigned theory, more than before the activity. In fact, students often indicate that they have changed their mind concerning the theory they initially believed to explain gender development, often in favor of the theory they were asked to support and defend.

- Because students are more comfortable with the theories, they often reference the examples used in the debate to support the theories as well as the assumptions of the theories throughout the semester.
- Students are initially wary of critiquing other theories and need to be encouraged to think critically about the strengths and weaknesses of each of the theories. If an instructor doesn't take the time to discuss how to argue and/or critique positions, the debate may not engage the class and may simply be a presentation of information void of critical analysis.

Limitations and Cautionary Advice

- Not all students will feel comfortable arguing; students may have limited experience in formulating and evaluating arguments. The instructor will need to "coach" students in terms of developing arguments that address the limitations of the theories. Many students feel more comfortable stating the assumptions of the theory assigned rather than addressing the limitations of the other theories. Graff (2003) argued that students have argumentation skills, however they often don't know how to utilize them in an academic setting.
- It is important that students have sufficient time to prepare for the debates. The exercise can be assigned a week prior to the actual debate, therefore giving students time to research their positions. Additionally, the instructor may want to give the students time in class to prepare their speeches and to work within their groups/advocacy teams.
- The instructor may need to clarify any information presented that is not accurate after the debate is complete. Students may misunderstand the assumptions of a theory or propose an example that illustrates a theory that isn't accurate.
- The debate topic does not offer much of an opportunity to discuss issues regarding transgendered identities. Although not intentional, the exercise tends to view gender through a construct with binary masculine and feminine categories. The issue of transgendered identities might come up in the debate as a way to compare the theories of gender development. Transgendered identities might also be considered a variation of the debate topic (see Alternative Uses).

Alternative Uses

- The instructor could encourage students to interact through the use of online instructional programs, for example, through an online course educational suite. Many online educational tools have a feature that allows instructors to create groups to work on projects. The group feature allows students to interact online. Students could use the group pages to exchange ideas outside of class in preparation for the debate. Combining the use of online instructional programs with face-to-face interaction in the classroom could ensure that students are well prepared for the debate.
- An alternative proposition for debate might be what criteria should be used to determine the gender of an individual entered for Olympic competition. A recent

article in the *New York Times* framed the controversy over what criteria should be used to determine gender-defining characteristics. The controversy would draw forth a close study of the biological theory of gender development but also pose issues that indicate the degree to which gender is a socially developed construct.

- Additionally, the instructor could propose a debate topic related to the problem of constructing gender categories. For many students, gender is understood in a binary construct of masculine and feminine qualities. A binary construct of gender categories limited to two alternatives makes it difficult to discuss gender along a continuum or to consider issues posed by transgendered individuals.

REFERENCES

Frey, L. R., Botan, C. H., & Kreps, G. L. (2000). *Investigating communication: An introduction to research methods.* Needham Heights, MA: Allyn and Bacon.

Graff, G. (2003). *Clueless in academe: How schooling obscures the life of the mind.* New Haven, CT: Yale University Press.

Jordan-Young, R., & Karkazis, K. (18 June 2012). You say you're a woman? That should be enough. *New York Times.* www.nytimes.com/2012/06/18/sports/olympics/olympic-sex -verification-you-say-youre-a-woman-that-should-be-enough.html?_r=1&ref=sports.

Perkins, D. (2009). *Making learning whole.* San Francisco, CA: Jossey-Bass.

Toulmin, S. E. (1958). *The uses of argument.* New York: Cambridge University Press.

Vilain, E. (18 June 2012). Gender testing for athletes remain a tough call. *New York Times.* Retrieved from www.nytimes.com/2012/06/18/sports/olympics/the-line-between-male-and -female-athletes-how-to-decide.html?ref=sports.

Wood, J. (2011). *Gendered lives: Communication, gender, and culture.* Boston: Wadsworth-Cengage.

ADDITIONAL READINGS

Anderson, K. V. (1999). "Rhymes with rich": "Bitch" as a tool of containment in contemporary American politics. *Rhetoric and Public Affairs, 2,* 599–623.

Benhabib, S. (1992). *Situating the self: Gender, community and post modernism in contemporary ethics.* New York: Routledge.

Brockriede, W. (1972). Arguers as lovers. *Philosophy & Rhetoric, 5,* 1–11.

Brockriede, W. (1990). Where is argument? In R. Trapp & J. Schuetz (Eds.), *Perspectives on argumentation: Essays in honor of Wayne Brockriede* (pp. 4–8). Prospect Heights, IL: Waveland.

Brown, L. M., & Gilligan, C. (1992). *Meeting at the crossroads: Women's psychology and girls' development.* New York: Ballantine.

Bruner, M. L. (1996). Producing identities: Gender problematization and feminist argumentation. *Argumentation and Advocacy, 32,* 185–98.

Campbell, K. K. (1998). The discursive performance of femininity: Hating Hillary. *Rhetoric and Public Affairs, 1,* 1–19.

Canary, D. J. (1990). Marital arguments. In R. Trapp & J. Schuetz (Eds.), *Perspectives on argumentation: Essays in honor of Wayne Brockriede* (pp. 73–85). Prospect Heights, IL: Waveland.

Crenshaw, C. (1996). The normality of man and female otherness: (Re)producing patriarchal lines of argument in the law and the news. *Argumentation and Advocacy, 32*, 170–84.

Dow, B. J., & Tonn, M. B. (1993). "Feminine style" and political judgment in the rhetoric of Ann Richards. *Quarterly Journal of Speech, 79*, 286–302.

Ehninger, D., & Brockriede, W. (1971). *Decision by debate*. New York: Dodd, Mead, & Co.

Foss, S .K., & Griffin, C. L. (1995). Beyond persuasion: A proposal for an invitational rhetoric. *Communication Monographs, 62*, 2–18.

Fulkerson, R. (1998). Transcending our conception of argument in light of feminist critique. *Argumentation and Advocacy, 32*, 211–12.

Gilligan, C., Rogers, A. G., & Tolman, D. L. (Eds.). (1991). *Women, girls, and psychotherapy: Reframing resistance*. New York: Harrington Park Press.

Makau, J. M., & Marty, D. L. (2011). *Cooperative argumentation: A model for deliberative community*. Long Grove, IL: Waveland.

Palczewski, C. H. (1990). Argumentation and feminisms: An introduction. *Argumentation and Advocacy, 32*, 161–69.

Tannen, D. (1998). *The argument culture: Moving from debate to dialogue*. New York: Random House.

Trapp, R. (1990). Arguments in interpersonal relationships. In R. Trapp & J. Schuetz (Eds.), *Perspectives on argumentation: Essays in honor of Wayne Brockriede* (pp. 43–54). Prospect Heights, IL: Waveland.

HANDOUT A: CRITIQUING ARGUMENTS

The level of critical analysis can be developed along two lines: examining the individual lines of argument used to support the stock issues and examining the integrity of each line of argumentation. The questions under Stock Issue Analysis for a Proposition of Value will assist you in examining how well the case for each theory is constructed. The questions under Claims, Evidence, and Reasoning will help you identify limitations of each line of argumentation. As you become more familiar with how these questions can help identify strengths and weaknesses in the argumentation, your understanding of the competing theories will develop.

Stock Issue Analysis for a Proposition of Value

- Did the team identify the criteria to use in evaluating the theories?
- Did the team explain the criteria to be used in evaluating the theories?
- Did the team provide reasons for selecting those criteria?
- Did the team select criteria that were logically consistent?
- Did the team apply the criteria to the theory that they were assigned?
- Did the team compare the other theories in relation to the criteria?
- Were the criteria applied to the theories in a logically consistent way?
- Did the application of the criteria reflect an accurate understanding of the theories?

Claims

- Were the claims clearly and concisely stated?
- Did the debaters avoid shifting their claims in the course of the debate?
- Were the claims of individual arguments related to the stock issues?

Evidence

- What evidence was used?
- Was the type of evidence used appropriate for the claim?
- Did the use of evidence pass the tests for use of evidence?

Reasoning

- Did the team explain why the evidence supported the claim in their arguments?
- Did the team identify the type of reasoning used?
- Did the reasoning pass tests for that type of reasoning?

HANDOUT B: CRITERIA FOR EVALUATING THEORIES

Explanation

- What is the scope of the theory's explanatory power?
- What is the basis for the validity of the theory?
  - Is the theory internally consistent, free from contradiction?
  - Is the theory externally valid in that it is consistent with observed facts?
- How parsimonious is the theory? Can it explain the phenomenon in a more simple, powerful way than competing theories?

Prediction

- Does the theory offer predictions that can be tested scientifically?
- Has the theory been tested in scientific research?
- Does the research provide support for the theory?

Control

- Can the theory explain and predict phenomena to the extent that it helps human beings gain knowledge that can be used in some way?

Heuristic Value

- Does the theory generate new insights that lead to new questions and new insights, discoveries, or understanding about the phenomena?

Communicative

- Does the theory generate interest sufficient for scholars to discuss and debate its implications?

Inspiration

- Does the theory generate excitement, stimulate human imagination, and generate understanding about the phenomena? Does it help solve important puzzles about human concerns?

NOTE

1. Adapted from Frey, L. R., Botan, C. H., & Kreps, G. L. (2000). *Investigating Communication: An introduction to research methods.* Needham Heights, MA: Allyn and Bacon.

HANDOUT C: JUDGES' GUIDE
FOR EVALUATING ARGUMENTATION

The evaluation rubric is designed to measure basic public-speaking skills, basic argumentation skills, basic understanding of gender theories, and an ability to respond fairly to competing ideas in a debate framework. The team assigned to listen and evaluate the arguments has a formidable task. To fairly listen and evaluate the arguments, the team assigned to judge the discourse must fulfill the following expectations:

- Understand all of the theories.
- Be able to analyze the issues for a proposition of value.
- Understand criteria for evaluating social-scientific theory.
- Be able to apply standpoint theory in evaluating responsiveness.
- Listen carefully to all of the arguments in order to provide a compelling critique.
- Develop and present reasons in support of their critique.

HANDOUT D: ARGUING OVER THEORIES OF
GENDER DEVELOPMENT, THEORETICAL PERSPECTIVES
FOR EXPLAINING GENDER DEVELOPMENT TO BE COVERED

- Biological Theory
- Interpersonal Theory: Psychodynamic Theory or Psychological Theory
- Cultural Theory: Anthropological Theory, Symbolic Interactionism

Objectives

- To develop knowledge of the main points of each major theoretical perspective.
- To identify strengths and weaknesses of each theoretical perspective.
- To initiate discussion of theoretical perspectives for explaining gender development.
- To identify and apply criteria for evaluating theoretical perspectives.

Team Formation

Students will be randomly assigned to 4 teams: 3 advocacy teams and 1 team of judges. Each advocacy team will be composed of typically 10 students: 3 advocates and 7 support staff to generate arguments, explanations, and examples. Each advocacy team is responsible for developing a case to support the theoretical perspective they have been assigned. Each team must use four new pieces of scholarly information (in addition to the information from the textbook) to support their case. The team of judges is responsible for developing a ballot that can be used to critique the debate and render a decision.

Proposition

- Resolved: _____ theory best explains gender development.

Format

- Constructive Speech—Team #1—5 minutes
- Constructive Speech—Team #2—5 minutes
- Constructive Speech—Team #3—5 minutes
- Rebuttal Speech—Team #1—6 minutes
- Rebuttal Speech—Team #2—6 minutes
- Rebuttal Speech—Team #3—6 minutes
- Summary Speech—Team #1—2 minutes
- Summary Speech—Team #2—2 minutes
- Summary Speech—Team #3—2 minutes

Speaker Duties

- Constructive Speech

1. Identify the assumptions of the theoretical perspective your team is defending.
2. Outline the main points of the theoretical perspective your team is defending.
3. Offer two pieces of additional evidence (this can be in the form of examples, statistics, authority evidence) not found in your textbook.
4. Describe the criteria your team believes is most appropriate for evaluating the theories.
5. Explain how your theory satisfies those criteria.

- Rebuttal Speech

1. Refute the arguments presented against your theory.
2. Compare your theory to its competitors to show how your theory is a more adequate explanation of gender development.
3. Share two additional pieces of evidence not found in the textbook.

- Summary Speech

1. Summarize the case against your theory's competitors.
2. Summarize the case for your theory.

Throughout the debate each team will have 5 minutes of preparation time (total) to use to prepare for the next speech. Explain where this time can be used. Enjoy the experience! Clearly explain your positions, provide examples, and engage your audience. Good luck.

The Same-Sex Marriage Debate: Gay/Lesbian Rights vs. Queer Critiques of Marriage

Elizabeth Currans, PhD
(Eastern Michigan University)

Appropriate Course(s) and Level

Introductory or mid-level courses in LGBTQ studies, women's/gender/feminist studies, sociology, communication, or American studies.

Appropriate Class Size

Works best with 30 students or less but is possible with up to 40 students.

Learning Goals

- To expose students to the range of perspectives about same-sex marriage within LGBTQ communities, including critiques informed by feminist and critical race perspectives.
- To provide a concrete example of intersectional analysis.
- To help students understand perspectives different from their own well enough to argue for or against them.
- To provide an opportunity to practice making arguments.
- To have students practice public speaking.
- To build teamwork skills.

Estimated Time Required

75–90 minutes.

Required Materials

- Readings about same-sex marriage and the queer critique of marriage (see References and Additional Readings).

Rationale

This exercise serves four primary goals: practicing making concise arguments, practicing critical-thinking skills, getting students to understand the diversity within LGBTQ communities, and teaching about intersectional analysis. Active, performance-based teaching techniques such as debates encourage students to interact with ideas and concepts in embodied as well as intellectual ways. They also keep students more engaged (Pedelty, 2001) and enable more effective learning. According to Kennedy (2009), "students learn more effectively by actively analyzing, discussing, and applying content in meaningful ways, rather than by passively absorbing information" (p. 225). Debates provide this active engagement while also encouraging students to better understand points of view they don't agree with, teaching them how to better defend their own points of view and helping them evaluate arguments.

In-class debates also help students create arguments. In contrast to lecturing, which encourages memorization, Omelicheva and Avdeyeva (2008) found "educational debate . . . can help students learn how to formulate clear, precise, and logical arguments" (p. 604). In debates, most students will be arguing positions they don't entirely support or positions they even actively disagree with, which can enhance their understanding of how arguments are crafted.

Debates provide an opportunity to practice critical-thinking skills. Kennedy (2009) explained debate not only requires understanding content, but

> it also demands the mastery of critical thinking skills such as defining the problem, assessing the credibility of sources, identifying and challenging assumptions, recognizing inconsistencies, and prioritizing the relevance and salience of various points within the overall argument, which can be applied to new information and changing situations. (p. 226)

Thus, students are able to practice skills they can use in a variety of situations both inside and outside of classrooms. Although this debate model can be applied to numerous topics, I find it helpful to facilitate a discussion of same-sex marriage.

Discussions of same-sex marriage are generally presented as disputes between, on the one hand, a liberal inclusion model, and, on the other hand, a conservative and often religious perspective, leaving the range of points of view about marriage within LGBTQ communities obscured. This exercise provides a window into the diverse views within LGBTQ communities and, ideally, allows students to articulate nuanced positions that take arguments against marriage as a social institution *and* arguments for same-sex marriage rights into consideration.

Because different perspectives about gay marriage are often influenced by individuals' social position, gender identity, and engagement with feminist and queer theory, this exercise requires students to address how one topic (same-sex marriage) can have distinct meanings for different people. In defining intersectionality, Crenshaw (1991) explained women of color's experiences can only be understood by taking race, class, and gender into account. Recent discussions of LGBTQ lives have reinforced her point while emphasizing the need to address sexual orientation and the effects of societal homophobia, heterosexism, and transphobia, thus expanding our understanding of intersectionality to include sexual orientation and gender expression (Ferguson, 2003;

Manalansan, 2005; Muñoz, 1999). In short, every person experiences the combination of their oppressions and privileges based on race, gender, sexuality, class, and other factors. Exploring an abstract concept such as intersectionality through a concrete example such as same-sex marriage enables deeper understanding. Because people's responses to national and local campaigns for same-sex marriage reflect their gendered, raced, classed, and sexualized experiences and their engagement with feminist and queer activism and theories, this topic can be useful in helping students better understand how intersectionality works in practice.

The homophobia of many arguments against same-sex marriage is easy for students to recognize. However, many prominent supporters of same-sex marriage utilize misogynist, classist, and racist language and arguments, which can go unnoticed in the emotionally charged debates between proponents of same-sex marriage and homophobic opponents (Duggan, 2004; Kandaswamy, 2008). Few arguments for marriage rights address long-standing feminist critiques of the institution of marriage even when they can be used to support same-sex marriage (Bevacqua, 2004; Jeffreys, 2004). Additionally, although same-sex marriage is billed as a top concern for LGBTQ communities nationwide, concerns unique to transgender people are seldom addressed (Lorenz, 2005; Robson, 2007). Impoverished people are also rarely considered in these conversations despite the fact that marriage rights will ideally help couples save money on taxes and health insurance (Kandaswamy, 2008). Since women of color have often been targeted by campaigns that encourage wedlock as a response to poverty and supposed moral inadequacies, addressing the simultaneous demonization of some people for not being married and others for wanting to get married can demonstrate how privilege and oppression function in complex and divergent ways (Ferguson, 2003; Kandaswamy, 2008). Questions about access to marriage rights and privileges are much more complex than simply considering the moral standing of same-sex relationships.

PREPARING FOR THE ACTIVITY

1. Assign and make available a variety of readings—at least one article that provides either a feminist critique of marriage (e.g., Jeffreys, 2004) or a popular-culture discussion of women and marriage (e.g., McGinn, 2006); at least one articulation of a queer critique of marriage (e.g., Duggan & Kim, 2005); at least one argument in support of same-sex marriage (e.g., Bonauto, 2003); at least one text that provides an anti-racist critique of same-sex marriage (e.g., Kandaswamy, 2008); and at least one exploration of transgender people's responses to same-sex marriage (e.g., Robson, 2007). Students are unlikely to do all of these readings; therefore, designating one or two readings as required for all and then assigning one additional reading to each student will ensure all areas are covered.

2. Explain that students will turn in an evaluation of other team members the class period following the debate, and they will be evaluated on their preparation for the debate as well as their contribution to crafting the argument and/or presenting the argument before the judges. Each student will turn in a one-page description of who did what and what they learned during the exercise.

3. The class period before the debate, assemble students into three groups: a group of 2–3 judges (2 if you have an even number of students, 3 if you have an odd number of students); a group that will argue in support of same-sex marriage; and a group that will provide a critique of marriage based on queer and feminist arguments. I generally ask for students who don't have strong opinions about the topic to raise their hands and choose the judges from this group and then have the rest of the students number off to create the other groups. This way each group includes students with a variety of views about same-sex marriage.

4. Explain to students that each team will designate a primary speaker and a secondary speaker. The primary speaker will make the initial argument and rebuttal. After the initial argument and rebuttal are presented, the team will decide whether the primary or secondary speaker will make the closing argument.

5. Ask students to think about who they think would be good speakers. Remind them that a good speaker is able to present an argument, listens to his or her teammates, and can respond to the arguments made by the other team. Scheduling the debate at least halfway through the term will allow students to better assess who among them is comfortable speaking in public, who presents good arguments, and who is good at responding to others' comments.

6. It's also helpful to explain that all team members help make a good argument. Although only one or two students from each team will actually debate, all team members will help craft the argument. The strategy sessions provide time for the entire group to come up with talking points and the individual parts of the argument that the speakers will make. One way to ensure all students are prepared is to ask that each student bring three points, drawn from assigned readings that will help the speakers make their arguments.

7. After assigning groups, put students into their groups for 10 minutes so they can begin planning their strategy for the next class period when the debate will happen. Ask that they not make the final designation of the speakers until the day of the debate in order for students to have time to evaluate who will do the best job and whether or not they will be comfortable being a speaker.

Facilitating the Activity

1. On the day of the debate, students are likely to be nervous. Remind them that grades are based on whether or not they participate rather than whether or not they are on the winning team. It's also helpful to describe this activity as helping them build public-speaking and argument-making skills that they will be able to apply to specific class assignments and in their future careers. Reinforce that it doesn't matter whether they are arguing for a position they support, but rather, that they understand the reasons people make these particular arguments.

2. On the day of the debate explain the timeline for the activity.
   - Strategy meeting: 10 min
   - Opening argument
     ○ Team 1: 3 min
     ○ Team 2: 3 min

- Rebuttals
  - Team 1: 2 min
  - Team 2: 2 min
- Strategy meeting: 5 min
- Closing arguments:
  - Team 2: 2 min
  - Team 1: 2 min
- Judges deliberate: 5 min
- Decision: 3 min
- Debrief: 10–25 min

3. While the two groups who will debate are crafting their arguments, meet with the judges. Encourage them to come up with a system of some kind for making a decision. I usually leave this up to the students, but a particularly innovative strategy one set of students devised was a 1–5 scale that each judge used each time a speaker presented an argument or rebuttal. The scores were then averaged to come up with a numerical score for each team.
4. Flip a coin to see which team will present their opening argument first.
5. During the exercise you will keep time. It's best to be pretty firm so there is enough time at the end for debriefing.
6. After the groups finish, send the judges out of the room to make the decision. When they return, ask that they explain their decision. If there are only two judges, you will serve as the tiebreaker if one is needed.
7. After the judgment is delivered, lead the debriefing session by focusing on two themes: the experience of the debate, and how people's views have changed or not changed by doing the exercise.

Discussion Questions

- Why do people want legalized same-sex marriage? What are the rights and privileges they are seeking to access?
- Why do people critique the institution of marriage? What are their concerns?
- How is marriage different from domestic partnership?
- What are the current laws in your state? Have there been any recent statewide campaigns? What were the results of these campaigns?
- If same-sex marriage were legalized today, would it provide the same amount of rights and privileges to all people under the LGBTQ umbrella? Why or why not?
- Should same-sex marriage occupy a prominent position on the agenda of LGBTQ organizations? Why or why not?
- What does this debate show us about the diversity of perspectives within LGBTQ communities?

Typical Results

- For many students, this exercise allows them to gain a deeper understanding about why people support or critique efforts to secure same-sex marriage rights. The debriefing session allows students to articulate positions between the poles of the debate, and it allows, potentially, for a conversation about how debates limit the terms we use to discuss difficult issues by keeping the options limited to two oppositional positions.

- Students are able to practice critical-thinking skills while developing a deeper understanding of a contemporary issue.
- This exercise also helps students understand how arguments are constructed using evidence, and this exercise can serve as an example when explaining how to write an argumentative paper or exam question. Because many students will be arguing for positions different from their own personal views, in-class debates allow them to understand better how to craft an effective argument supported by textual evidence.

Limitations and Cautionary Advice

- Although some students will express anxiety about in-class debates, research has shown that most students not only see debates as valuable, they also identify them as a good teaching technique (Kennedy, 2009). Because only one or two students will speak during the debate, shyer students are able to contribute through helping craft and judging the effectiveness of arguments.
- Occasionally, some students have such strong opinions that they are unable to effectively argue for the other side. In these cases, I generally let the groups monitor (and usually replace) a speaker or allow the judges to explain that a speaker wasn't convincing. Students nearly always rise to the occasion.
- There is a risk that people will not use the debriefing time to explore complex positions. In these cases, you may need to initiate a conversation about the limits of polarized discussions of an issue. Being prepared with some examples of more complex approaches is helpful.
- Be prepared for the possibility that the debriefing session will be emotionally charged. There is a risk that some students may be hurt by the critiques of same-sex marriage, or they may experience those that support gay marriage as classist, racist, or transphobic. Hopefully, you'll have already established a norm of respectful dialogue so such responses can be effectively addressed.

Alternative Uses

- Debates can be used to explore a variety of issues. I find it the most useful to use this framework to highlight perspectives not usually addressed in mainstream media and politics. So for example, rather than having students debate whether or not abortion should be legal, it might be useful to have students advocate for a reproductive justice framework versus a pro-choice framework (Silliman et al., 2004). Like a debate that explores perspectives supporting same-sex marriage versus queer critiques of marriage, such a debate encourages students to learn more about an issue and exposes them to perspectives not generally addressed outside of activist communities.

REFERENCES

Bevacqua, M. (2004). Feminist theory and the question of lesbian and gay marriage. *Feminism & Psychology, 14*(1), 36–40.

Bonauto, M. L. (2003). Civil marriage as a locus of civil rights struggles. *Human Rights, 30*(3), 3–7.

Crenshaw, K. (1991). Mapping the margins: Intersectionality, identity politics, and violence against women of color. *Stanford Law Review, 43*(6), 1241–99.

Duggan, L. (2004). *The twilight of equality: Neoliberalism, cultural politics, and the attack on democracy.* Boston: Beacon Press.

Duggan, L., & Kim, R. (18 July 2005). Beyond gay marriage. *The Nation.* www.thenation.com/doc/20050718/kim.

Ferguson, R. (2003). *Aberrations in black: Toward a queer of color critique.* Minneapolis: University of Minnesota Press.

Jeffreys, S. (2004). The need to abolish marriage. *Feminism & Psychology, 14*(2), 327–31.

Kandaswamy, P. (2008). State austerity and the racial politics of same-sex marriage in the United States. *Sexualities, 11*(6), 707–26.

Kennedy, R. (2009). The power of in-class debates. *Active Learning in Higher Education, 10*(3), 225–36.

Lorenz, R. D. (2005). Transgender immigration: Legal same-sex marriages and their implications for the Defense of Marriage Act. *UCLA Law Review, 53*(2), 523–60.

Manalansan, M. (2005). Race, violence and neoliberal spatial politics in the global city. *Social Text, 84–85,* 141–56.

McGinn, D. (5 June 2006). Marriage by the numbers. *Newsweek,* pp. 40–49.

Muñoz, J. E. (1999). *Disidentifications: Queers of color and the performance of politics.* Minneapolis: University of Minnesota Press.

Omelicheva, M., & Avdeyeva, O. (2008). Teaching with lecture or debate? Testing the effectiveness of traditional versus active learning methods of instruction. *PS: Political Science and Politics, 41*(3), 603–7.

Pedelty, M. (2001). Teaching anthropology through performance. *Anthropology & Education Quarterly, 32*(2), 244–53.

Robson, R. (2007). A mere switch or a fundamental change? Theorizing transgender marriage. *Hypatia, 22*(1), 58–70.

Silliman, J., Gerber Fried, M., Ross, L., & Gutierrez, E. (2004). *Undivided rights: Women of color organize for reproductive justice.* Cambridge, MA: South End Press.

ADDITIONAL READINGS

Bailey, M. B., Kandaswamy, P., & Richardson, M. U. (2004). Is gay marriage racist? In M. B. Sycamore (Ed.), *That's revolting: Queer strategies for resisting assimilation* (pp. 87–93). Brooklyn: Soft Skull Press.

Braun, V. (2003). Thanks to my mother . . . A personal commentary on heterosexual marriage. *Feminism & Psychology, 13*(4), 421–25.

Chauncey, G. (2004). *Why marriage? The history shaping today's debate over gay equality.* New York: Basic Books.

McCreery, P. (2008). Save our children/let us marry: Gay activists appropriate the rhetoric of child protectionism. *Radical History Review, 100,* 186–207.

Sherman, S. (1992). *Lesbian and gay marriage: Private commitments, public ceremonies.* Phila-
    delphia: Temple University Press.
Sullivan, A., & Landau, J. (1997). *Same-sex marriage: Pro and con.* New York: Vintage.
Warner, M. (1999). *The trouble with normal: Sex, politics, and the ethics of queer life.* Cam-
    bridge, MA: Harvard University Press.
Weeks, J. (2008). Regulation, resistance, recognition. *Sexualities, 11*(6), 787–92.

II

SEXUALITY

Sexual Secret Cards: Examining Social Norms and Cultural Taboos around Sexuality

Shawn Trivette, PhD
(Louisiana Tech University)

Appropriate Course(s) and Level

Upper-level social-science courses (sociology, anthropology, communication, women's/gender studies, etc.) dealing with sexuality.

Appropriate Class Size

20–60 students. Very small class sizes would make maintaining anonymity difficult. The activity could be adapted for classes larger than 60 (see Alternative Uses).

Learning Goals

- To help students explore the social norms around different sexual behaviors and desires and consider the ways in which certain sexual activities are considered taboo.
- To help students see the great diversity of sexual experiences, fears, and interests among their classmates.
- To help students become more comfortable with openly discussing sexuality related issues.

Estimated Time Required

5–10 minutes in one class session for activity explanation; 20–30 minutes (or up to an entire class period) in a later class session, ideally two classes later.

Required Materials

- Blank index cards.
- Poster board.

Rationale

Social norms theory contends we behave according to our perceptions of a social norm, perceptions that are often inaccurate (Berkowitz, 2005). Though originally developed to counter college binge drinking, the theory can be applied to expanding one's understanding of sexual behaviors and desires. Perceiving that certain sexual interests (whether the student shares this interest or not) are not socially acceptable, students may be reluctant to discuss them openly and frankly in a classroom environment. Our culture generally teaches us not to discuss sexuality in an open forum, and students often enter a class on sexual behaviors, identities, and politics with many strongly held beliefs about what is acceptable and unacceptable when it comes to sexuality.

This activity serves a dual purpose of helping to quell anxiety and showing students that many sexual "secrets" are actually quite common and relatively mundane (in the words of one of my former students, "Most of these secrets aren't that weird") by providing an accurate (and anonymous) picture of students' sexual behaviors and desires. It shows them that sexual interests are diverse, and many interests that they believe to be rare or fringe are actually quite common. When students are able to see this reality held up against their preconceived notions, the result is a more open, honest, and accepting classroom environment. Further, in facing down some of the more challenging topics to be discussed during the term, students develop a greater comfort level with both the instructor and other students.

Preparing for the Activity

1. Given the sensitive nature of the topic of this activity, lay the groundwork for a civil and respectful discussion with these five simple classroom agreements on the syllabus:
   - In class, be positive, willing, and prepared.
   - Be on time.
   - Do not use cues (packing up early, snapping binders shut, etc.).
   - Be authentic (honest, real, true).
   - Be respectful. I spend a little time on the first day of the term discussing what these mean. For example, being respectful does not mean we have to agree with everything someone else says. Instead, it means that we recognize that some topics we cover in class may be controversial, and we agree to both listen to other points of view with respect as well as share our own views in a way that encourages others to listen. I remind students of these agreements throughout the semester, particularly when they seem to have been forgotten or when it may help diffuse what may be a particularly tense or sensitive discussion (such as this particular activity).
2. Other than this, little to no preparation is needed for the activity itself other than bringing the blank index cards and later taking the time to put them on the poster board.

Facilitating the Activity

1. At the end of class (ideally at the end of the first week of the term), give each student a blank index card. Their weekend homework is to write one of their sexual secrets on one side of the card by the next class. The only requirements are that it be something related to sexuality (broadly) and that it be something no one else knows (except any partners who may have engaged in the act with them, if the secret is some sexual activity). Students should be told not to put any identifying mark on their cards (such as names) so as to preserve anonymity. *This is extremely important*; sexuality can be a very charged topic, and some students may be nervous about revealing such personal information. Assure them that no one (not even the instructor) will know who submitted what card. Students are welcome and encouraged to be as creative as they like in designing the card. They can use markers and crayons, make a collage, or even design something on the computer and print it onto the card. If they have a distinctive handwriting, they should consider collage, printers, or markers as a way to help make their cards more anonymous. The community art project PostSecret (www.postsecret.com) can serve as a source of inspiration for this activity.

2. In the next class session, collect the secret cards by passing a lidded box or large envelope around the room; this will allow students to anonymously submit their card. It also gives a discrete "out" for students too nervous or embarrassed to turn one in. *Remind students that they should not have their name on the card.*

3. Between that class session and the next, tape all the cards up to pieces of poster board. Do not pack them in too tightly or there will be crowding as students try to look at them later. Plan to arrive to class a few minutes early on the day the cards are to be presented; this will allow students a bit more time to examine the cards. Allow students the first few minutes of class to peruse the cards.

4. At the start of the discussion (see Discussion Questions), remind students about any class rules or agreements regarding respect and civility. The secrets they are about to discuss come from some person in the room. A little circumspection in how the secrets are discussed can go a long way toward helping everyone in the class feel comfortable and safe even while discussing such a charged topic.

5. I like to allow a little time at the end of class for students to take another look at the secrets before leaving. This is especially useful for students who did not arrive early and didn't get much time to examine the cards before class.

Discussion Questions

- What was it like to write or create your card? (*Do not tell us which card is yours!*)
  - Some students may confess that they didn't turn a card in for some reason (most often because they were too uncomfortable writing down their secret). Encourage students to address this during discussion.
- If you spoke with someone outside of class about your card, what was the reaction?
- How do you feel now that the assignment is done? Liberated? Ashamed? Scared? Relieved? Something else?

- In looking at the cards displayed, what do you notice? Are there any trends? What topics have people covered?
- What surprised you?
- Raise your hand if you saw any displayed (besides your own) that could have been *your* secret.
  - Each time I have asked this nearly every student raises a hand. This is the point at which students begin to lower barriers, open up, and empathize with each other. As they acknowledge their ability to relate to other secrets besides their own, remind them that those other secrets were submitted by someone else in the class. They are not just acknowledging another secret; they are acknowledging their connection to their fellow students.
- What do these secrets tell us about our society's treatment of sexuality? That is, what makes the things described in these secrets taboo? Do some seem more "serious" than others? Why do you think so?

Typical Results

- When the assignment is first announced, students are often simultaneously nervous and excited. In the end, though, most students really get into it. They will draw pictures, color, tape together words and pictures from magazines or printed from the Internet, and in general show a truly creative flair. Also, expect a diversity of secrets, but also expect a few to be very similar, and expect some secrets to be highly gendered in both subtle and not-so-subtle ways.
- This exercise helps many students grasp an interesting paradox about sexuality in contemporary U.S. culture. Although many sexual desires and behaviors are considered taboo, they are in truth relatively common. Students are able to see, then, that the perceived norms around sexual topics do not always line up with the sexual reality.
- Discussing their secrets (anonymously) early in the term also increases both students' interest in the subsequent course material and their comfort in discussing such hot topics. Students often reference the activity throughout the term and are able to use it to make links to some of the more complex topics in sexuality theory. For example, I draw students' attention back to this activity when teaching Michel Foucault's (1978) "repressive hypothesis" (using the cards to show how sexuality is both hidden/repressed and widely known and understood) and Gayle Rubin's (1984) idea of the "charmed circle" (to discuss what we consider "good" and "bad" sex).

Limitations and Cautionary Advice

- Be prepared for students to opt-out of the assignment or to be very nervous prior to turning it in.
- Emphasize the anonymity of the project: no one will know who turned what in, including the instructor.

- During the discussion, be mindful of the tone people use and remind them of the need for civility and respect—after all, *someone* in the room turned in the secret they are discussing.
- Also remind students that they should at no point feel any pressure to share something that may reveal which secret is theirs.
- Since there is no way to return cards to students confidentially, I have kept all secret cards from past terms in a secure space in my office. If you have no secure place to store them, they should be destroyed at the end of the course. *Do not simply put them in the trash or recycling bin (they should be either shredded or burned)!* I recommend against disposing of them prematurely, as you may find a use for them in a later class-related activity or lecture (and students will likely refer back to the activity throughout the term).

Alternative Uses

- In larger classes, it may not be possible for students to have time to view all cards. As long as students have had the opportunity to view some of the cards, the discussion should still be fruitful. In this situation it may be helpful to have students begin discussion in small groups around a certain subset of cards (perhaps the poster-board display nearest to them), and then have each group share their discussion with the larger class. If you have teaching assistants, they could be tasked with monitoring discussion in groups to ensure confidentiality and civility.
- Alternatively, instructors could display cards using a projector.
- For online or distance-learning classrooms, cards could be scanned and uploaded to a course management program (Blackboard, Moodle, etc.) prior to student discussion.

REFERENCES

Berkowitz, A. D. (2005). An overview of the social norms approach. In L. Lederman & L. Stewart (Eds.), *Changing the culture of college drinking: A socially situated health communication campaign* (pp. 193–214). Cresskill, NJ: Hampton Press.

Foucault, M. (1978). *The history of sexuality: Volume 1, An introduction.* New York: Vintage Books.

Rubin, G. (1984). Thinking sex: Notes for a radical theory of the politics of sexuality. In C. Vance (Ed.), *Pleasure and danger: Exploring female sexuality* (pp. 267–319). Boston: Routledge & Keegan Paul.

Beyond Binaries: Seeing Sexual Diversity in the Classroom

Robyn Ochs, EdM,
Michael J. Murphy, PhD (University of Illinois Springfield)

Appropriate Course(s) and Level

Courses across a variety of disciplines that discuss issues of sexual orientation and expression, including sociology, women's and gender-studies courses, human sexuality, etc. Appropriate for upper and lower division—depth of analysis and conversation can be altered through use of the Discussion Questions.

Appropriate Class Size

Works best in a class of 20 or more to protect students' privacy.

Learning Goals

- To understand the complexity and diversity of sexual experiences, desires, and identities.
- To examine the benefits and limitations of the major methods and survey instruments used to measure sexual orientation.
- To realize that sexual experiences, desires, and identities do not always correspond and can change over the life course.
- To produce a more respectful and inclusive classroom environment through greater knowledge of students' peers while protecting privacy and confidentiality around sensitive subjects.
- To increase student awareness and understanding of identities and experiences that differ from their own.

Estimated Time Required

Activity can be completed in a 50-minute class period, though for upper-level courses, it is best conducted over two class periods: one for the lecture, one for the activity.

Required Materials

- Handout with models for measuring sexual orientation (Klein, Storms, Kinsey, etc.) and questionnaire related to sexual experiences, desires, identities, etc. (see Handout).
- Box of black or blue pens (to ensure untraceable comments on questionnaire).
- 7 sheets of paper numbered 0 through 6 (a Kinsey scale) in very large print (one number per piece of paper), or the same numbers written on a chalkboard across the front of the classroom.
- Tape or other means of adhering sheets of paper to front of classroom (if needed).

Rationale

The diversity of human sexual experiences, desires, and identities is often obscured by taboos surrounding discussion of sexuality and dominant cultural discourses that privilege monogamous, heterosexual behavior in the context of romantic relationships. Moreover, inequality for lesbians, gay men, and bisexuals often inhibits the disclosure of these identities or related experiences, especially by young students in the classroom context. Objective or abstract approaches to human sexuality can lead to a failure to recognize the diversity of sexual experiences and identities in the classroom. As a result, students can make unintentionally harmful or exclusionary comments about marginalized or non-normative sexual identities or experiences that might be represented, albeit silently or covertly, in their own classrooms. Finally, the apparent straightforwardness of descriptors like "straight" and "gay" can prevent students from seeing that even these sexual identities are complicated and multifaceted constructs that social scientists have struggled to accurately describe and measure (Evans & Wall, 1991; Sedgwick, 1990; Sell, 1997).

Preparing for the Activity

1. We recommend assigning the overview of methods for measuring sexual orientation (Sell, 1997) for the day you will conduct this activity.
2. Make enough copies of the handouts for distribution in class. Because students will be returning the questionnaire, double-sided copying is not recommended.
3. Depending on the level and background of your students, prepare a short lecture on the history of the most popular scientific models of sexual orientation. This can be as brief or in-depth as you like, depending on the length of your class time and level of the course.

Facilitating the Activity

1. Distribute the Handout (with sexual orientation models) in class and deliver your short lecture.
2. Segue to the activity by describing the activity and explaining its purpose: to help students understand who's in the room as well as the larger issues about human sexual diversity and incongruence between sexual behavior, identities, and desires and shifts over the life course.

3. Distribute questionnaire and blue or black pens if students need one. It is very important that students use a common (black or blue) ink color so no one can trace answers back to a specific student. Read the instructions aloud. Give students about 10 minutes to answer the questions. Note: Inform students that they are not to put their names on the questionnaire and that all answers will be kept confidential.

4. While the students work, tape numbered sheets (0 on the left and 6 on the right) across the front wall of the classroom allowing enough space between them for students to stand in groups during the second part of the activity. Spacing of 4–5 feet between numbers works well in classes up to 30 students. The more space between numbers, the easier it will be to see on which number people are standing. Adjust according to the size of your class and configuration of your classroom. In classrooms with large chalk/whiteboards at the front, it is sufficient to write the numbers (0–6) on the board with sufficient lateral spacing between the numbers.

5. Again, remind students that their names should not appear anywhere on the questionnaire. Ask students to fold their questionnaire in half with the blank side facing out when finished.

6. After collecting all the sheets, shuffle them by "dealing" the pile into three separate piles, then stacking the piles and repeating until you are confident that they have been randomized. Make it clear that you are not looking at any individual sheet's answers while shuffling. *It is important that you make an effort to not show an interest in a specific student's responses!*

7. Announce you will be redistributing the sheets. *Explain it is highly unlikely anyone will receive their own sheet back, but on the unlikely chance someone did, no one else would know unless the student exclaimed, "I got mine back!"* Ask students to respect the person whose sheet they draw the same as they would wish the person who has their own questionnaire/information to respect them.

8. Redistribute the sheets to the class. When all the sheets have been distributed, ask students to stand and move to the front of the classroom while you move to the back so you can "orchestrate" their movements. Read the first question and ask students to line up under the number for question 1 on their sheets. Remind them they are "performing" the answers on the questionnaire in their hand, not the answers they provided earlier. In this way, everyone's responses can be made known while individual student responses remain confidential.

9. When everyone has settled under a number, direct the class to make some observations about the distribution. Then, move on to each question in succession, having students move to their indicated position.

10. Before reading question 9 (on the questionnaire), ask everyone to return to their answer to question 1. Tell participants that you will be calling out identity words, such as "gay," "straight," "bisexual," "asexual," "pansexual," "queer," "questioning," "choose not to label," etc. Ask them to raise their hand each time a word that is on their sheet is said, and say that you want to honor every identity in the room and thus will ask students at the end to call out any identity word that has not yet been said.

11. Ask students to return to their seats and proceed with the Discussion Questions.

Discussion Questions

- When discussing sexual orientation, we usually group ourselves into two (or three categories): gay or straight (or bisexual). This classification system describes our own gender identity (or sex) in relation to that of those to whom we are attracted. Why do we sort ourselves this way?
  - What are some other ways we could sort ourselves?
  - In some cultures, if two men have sex, only the man who takes a passive or receptive role is considered gay. What if we defined our sexual orientation by other factors: active/passive/switch; "top"/"bottom"/"switch"; or by specific desired sexual practices?
- Most of us, if someone told us they were "straight," would instantly imagine them to be a Kinsey 0. Yet the data from this exercise (and from sexuality research in general) tell us that "straight" covers a wider range: usually—in our experience—from 0 to 2. All of our sexuality labels, as we see, cover ranges. And someone who identifies as bisexual might be just as heterosexual as (or more heterosexual than) someone who identifies as straight, or just as homosexual as (or more homosexual than) someone who identifies as gay or lesbian. What then is the usefulness of these categories? What do we need to keep in mind when someone tells us how they identify?
- How, if at all, do you think people's Kinsey scores may vary over their lifetimes?
- Are we attracted to someone because of their sex (male/intersex/female) or because of their gender identity (man-ness/gender-queerness/woman-ness) or because of their gender expression (masculinities/androgynies/femininities)? Why or why not?
- Introducing the Kinsey Scale, Alfred Kinsey wrote, "Males do not represent two discrete populations, heterosexual and homosexual. The world is not to be divided into sheep and goats. It is a fundamental of taxonomy that nature rarely deals with discrete categories . . . The living world is a continuum in each and every one of its aspects" (Kinsey et al., 1948, p. 639). How, if at all, do the data from this exercise support Kinsey's assertion?
- Where does bisexuality begin and end?
  - If we view sexuality as a spectrum, how much territory does the word "bisexual" cover?
  - How much bisexual attraction and/or behavior does it take to make a person bisexual?
  - Is the concept of bisexuality meaningful across cultures? Why or why not?
  - Do you believe bisexuality encompasses people whose attractions change over time? If you are once bisexual, are you always bisexual? Is there a statute of limitations? And for each of these questions, who gets to decide?
- A more typical way of gathering data about sexual orientation identities is to ask, "What is your sexual orientation (check one): ___ straight ___ lesbian/gay ___ bisexual?" Discuss the value and limitations of this method of collecting sexual orientation data.
- How, if at all, has doing this activity changed your understanding of sexuality? What are assumptions that you had previously made that you wish to no longer make?

- What are limitations of doing research on sexuality?
  - How comfortable do you think some people—even some people in this class—are answering honestly questions about their fantasies and sexual behavior?
  - How do you think results to this questionnaire might vary if everyone filled out the questionnaire knowing that they would be required to represent themselves on the scale or if they were filling out this questionnaire anonymously online?

Typical Results

- Responses vary dramatically, depending upon the class. Sometimes, not all numbers are covered. However, there is always a continuum.
- There are some students (most often on 0) who stay in one place during the entire exercise. Some students move but within a small segment of the scale. Others move moderately. Yet others move dramatically.
- In our experience, "straight" or "heterosexual" usually spans 0, 1, and 2 of the scale in a triangular shape (with most respondents on 0, a smaller number on 1, and a smaller number on 2). "Lesbian" or "gay" usually spans 4, 5, and 6, but the shape is different. (Most fall on 5 or 6, but distribution is unpredictable, and 4 is usually the smallest. Ochs described this shape as that of a bottle facing inward.) "Bisexual" and "pansexual" usually span 2, 3, and 4, and sometimes extend further to 1 and/or 5. "Queer" normally spans 2 to 6. It is not uncommon for 1 to 3 participants to step off the scale with an NA answer to one or more questions.
- Geography and campus culture have a dramatic effect on results. On some campuses, "queer" is the most common identity label (other than "straight"/"heterosexual"). And there are other campuses where not a single participant will identify as such.
- Expect students to express amazement about the range and diversity of responses as well as the (sometimes significant) movement of individuals as you work through the questions. These "Ah ha!" moments are when the real learning occurs!
- Depending on your class, an emerging awareness of the sexual diversity and identity of fellow students can be disconcerting, especially if you conduct this exercise early in the semester. It is important to allow sufficient time for debriefing and processing the knowledge produced during this activity.

Limitations and Cautionary Advice

- Remember to read the guidelines aloud and ask students to be frank and honest in their answers.
- Clarify the difference between the terms "sex" and "gender."
- Take steps to ensure that this exercise is as anonymous as possible and also to ensure that it is perceived as such. This exercise should not be done with a group of less than 20. It can provide extra "cover" (or confidentiality) to bring together two classes to do this exercise together; to invite students to bring guests; to bring in a few extra people yourself; or to invite students from your campus LGBT group to participate.

- Before students fill out the questionnaires, make sure they know that this is an anonymous exercise, and that they will not be identified with the answers on their own questionnaire.
- Have extra copies of the survey available just in case someone accidentally doodles or writes their name on theirs.
- If the area available for enacting the exercise is limited and the 0 group is crowded, you may wish to ask all students holding sheets in which all answers to questions 1–8 are 0 to raise their hands. You can then invite these students to be seated, reminding students to imagine, throughout the exercise, that these people arc all standing at 0. Doing this will make it easier for all students to observe movement between 0 and 1, and to see that not all for whom 0 is their first answer remain on that number for every question.
- Before leaving the room, collect all questionnaires from the students and let students know they will be recycled or trashed.

Alternative Uses

- The questionnaire includes space for bonus questions, for example:
  - With 0 being "very uncomfortable discussing sex with my closest friends" and 6 being "very comfortable discussing sex with my closest friends," assign yourself a number between 0 and 6.
  - Write in how old you were when you first met someone you knew was lesbian, gay, bisexual, or transgender.
- Were you taught sex education in secondary school?
  - If so, were lesbian, gay, bisexual, or transgender people mentioned in this curriculum?

REFERENCES

Evans, N. J., & Wall, V. A. (1991). *Beyond tolerance: Gays, lesbians, and bisexuals on campus.* Alexandria, VA: American College Personnel Association.

Ochs, R. (2009). What is bisexuality. In R. Ochs & S. E. Rowley (Eds.), *Getting bi: Voices of bisexuals around the world* (pp. 7–9). Boston, MA: Bisexual Resource Center.

Sedgwick, E. K. (1990). *Epistemology of the closet.* Durham, NC: Duke University Press.

Sell, R. L. (1997). Defining and measuring sexual orientation: A review. *Archives of Sexual Behavior, 26,* 643–58.

ADDITIONAL READINGS

Bem, S. L. (1981). *Bem sex-role inventory professional manual.* Palo Alto, CA: Consulting Psychologists Press.

Berkey, B. R., Perelman-Ifall, T., & Kurdek, L. A. (1990). The multidimensional scale of sexuality. *Journal of Homosexuality, 19*(4), 67–87.

Friedman, M. S., Silvestre, A. J., Gold, M. A., Markovic, N., Savin-Williams, R. C., Huggins, J., & Sell, R. L. (2004). Adolescents define sexual orientation and suggest ways to measure it. *Journal of Adolescence, 27,* 303–17.

Gonsiorek, J. C., Sell, R. L., & Weinrich, J. D. (1995). Definition and measurement of sexual orientation. *Suicide and Life-Threatening Behavior, 25,* 40–51.

Kinsey, A. C., Pomeroy, W. B., & Martin, C. E. (1948; 1998). *Sexual behavior in the human male.* Philadelphia: W.B. Saunders; Bloomington: Indiana University Press.

Kinsey, A. C., Pomeroy, W. B., Martin, C. E., & Gebhard, P. (1953; 1998). *Sexual behavior in the human female.* Philadelphia: W.B. Saunders; Bloomington: Indiana University Press.

Klein, F., Sepekoff, B., & Wolf, T. J. (1985). Sexual orientation: A multi-variable dynamic process. *Journal of Homosexuality, 11,* 35–49.

The Klein Sexual Orientation Grid. (1978). American Institute of Bisexuality. www.bisexual.org/kleingrid.html.

Ochs, R., & Rowley, S. E. (Eds.). (2009). *Getting bi: Voices of bisexuals around the world.* Boston, MA: Bisexual Resource Center.

Sell, R. L. (1996). The Sell assessment of sexual orientation: Background and scoring. *Journal of Lesbian, Gay and Bisexual Identity, 1*(4), 295–310.

Storms, M. D. (1980). Theories of sexual orientation. *Journal of Personality and Social Psychology, 38,* 783–92.

Weinrich, J. D., Snyder, P. J., Pillard, R. C., Grant, I., Jacobson, D. L., Robinson, S. R., & McCutchan, I. A. (1993). A factor analysis of the Klein Sexual Orientation Grid in two disparate samples. *Archives of Sexual Behavior, 22,* 157–68.

THE KINSEY SCALE

0   1   2   3   4   5   6

Exclusively heterosexual

Predominantly heterosexual, only incidentally homosexual

Predominantly heterosexual, but more than incidentally homosexual

Equally heterosexual & homosexual

Predominantly homosexual, but more than incidentally heterosexual

Predominantly homosexual, only incidentally heterosexual

Exclusively homosexual

HANDOUT
Models of Sexual Orientation

Robyn Ochs
www.robynochs.com
robyn@robynochs.com

Males do not represent two discrete populations, heterosexual and homosexual. The world is not to be divided into sheep and goats. It is a fundamental of taxonomy that nature rarely deals with discrete categories... The living world is a continuum in each and every one of its aspects. (Kinsey, p. 639).

THE STORMS SCALE

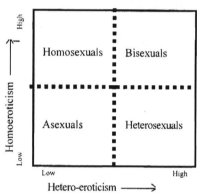

Klein Sexual Orientation Grid

Variable	Past	Present	Ideal
Sexual Attraction			
Sexual Behavior			
Sexual fantasies			
Emotional preference			
Social preference			
Het/Homo lifestyle			
Self-identification			

People rate themselves on a 7-point scale as follows:
1. Other sex only
2. Other sex mostly
3. Other sex somewhat more
4. Both sexes equally
5. Same sex somewhat more
6. Same sex (G/L) mostly
7. Same sex (G/L) only

Other-sex attracted				Same-sex attracted		
0	1	2	3	4	5	6

PLEASE READ: Many of the questions refer to the spectrum at the top of this page. All questions that refer to sexual experience refer only to consensual experience. If a question doesn't apply to your experience, it's fine to put "n/a" (not applicable) or to write in a comment.

WHERE WOULD YOU PUT YOURSELF ON THIS SCALE, TAKING INTO ACCOUNT ....

1) ... your sexual orientation overall? _____

2) ... your sexual attractions   overall _____ ;   before age 16 _____ ;   in 2008 _____ ;   in the past month _____

3) ... your sexual experience, including making out,   overall _____ ;   before age 16 _____ ;   in 2008 _____ ;   in the past month _____

4) ... your fantasies   overall _____ ;   before age 16 _____ ;   in 2008 _____ ;   in the past month _____

5) ...your romantic/emotional attractions   overall _____ ;   before age 16 _____ ;   in 2008 _____ ;   in the past month _____

6)   Where do your closest family members think you are on this scale? _____

7)   Where do most of your friends think you are on this scale? _____

8)   If you could be anywhere on this scale, where would you choose to be? _____

9)   Why? _____
_____
_____

10) What word(s) (i.e., gay, straight, etc.) do you use privately to describe your sexual orientation? _____

11) What word(s) (i.e., gay, straight, etc.) do you use to describe your sexual orientation to others? _____

Note: This exercise was designed by Robyn Ochs (www.robynochs.com) drawing from the work of Kinsey, Klein, Storms, *et al.* You may use and adapt this exercise providing you give credit to the author and inform her when you do so. Suggestions/feedback welcome.Adult/short version/ revised September 2009.

Dancing in Class: Choreographing Gendered Sexuality

*Susan Ekberg Stiritz, MBA, PhD, MSW
(Washington University in Saint Louis)*

Appropriate Course(s) and Levels

Introductory to graduate courses in women's/gender/sexualities studies, sociology, culture studies, dance, anthropology, law, history, ethnic studies, American studies, social work.

Appropriate Class Size

Up to 40 students.

Learning Goals

- To give examples of Gagnon's three levels of a society's sexual scripts: intrapsychic, interpersonal, and cultural.
- To list at least three ways three different dances express the social values of a particular culture.
- To understand that cultural practices, such as dance, can be "read" and interpreted just as a written or verbal text might be.
- To transfer what students learn about dancing to sexuality and sexual practices and to explain how sexual practices express cultural values.

Estimated Time Required

60–90 minutes, depending upon how many dances students perform and analyze and whether the instructor addresses relevant readings in the same class period as the exercise.

Required Materials

- Classroom with movable desks and enough floor space for students to dance (required space will vary with class enrollment).
- Traditional musical instruments: drums, rattles, sticks.
- Index cards and small pencils to use as "dance cards" for ballroom dancing.
- Examples of dance music, such as Native American powwow, big band, rock and roll, samba, hip hop, rap. For contemporary music, ask students in advance for examples.
- Classroom technology to play music loudly enough for dancing.
- First two chapters of Gagnon (1977; see References) or a similar article(s) which addresses development of sex roles and scripts.

Rationale

The social construction of sexuality and gender seems difficult for undergraduates to embrace. Students often resist the notions that culture shapes something as foundational as gender and as personal as sex and that gender and sexual constructions further political agendas. Belief in social construction must vie with the certainty of students' faith in their autonomy. "How could sexuality and gender be determined from the outside? They are the most personal, basic parts of my identity. I am me because of the sex and the orientation with which I was born. How I act sexually results from my choices, certainly not from pressure from society," students often protest. Thinking that the foundations of our identity are plastic can be threatening. Gaining insight experientially creates a deeper, more certain knowing than learning vicariously through reading and listening to lectures (Gardner, 2011; H'Doubler, 1940).

Performing a small multicultural dance repertoire with a partner in an academic classroom teaches students to see how scripts shape universal activities, like dancing and sexuality, in an array of ways. Students rarely will forget drumming, waltzing, or grinding in the classroom, and analyzing their experiences encourages them to analyze other social rituals for their pretexts and subtexts. Further, identifying the meanings different dances embody and express pushes students to acknowledge that social interactions and rituals teach people's bodies their culture's values, while eluding their conscious consideration. The importance of this learning is that insight into the social construction of a conventional embodied practice exposes its availability to being deconstructed and reconstructed.

Both a site of oppression and a source of empowerment (Vance, 1984), sexuality can mystify students with its paradoxes. Learning how to read sexuality sociologically can provide students with that "click" moment feminists celebrate as "scales falling from eyes" when they realize "the personal is political" (Hanisch, 1969). Besides augmenting critical thinking, academic success requires sociological and critical insight that can increase young people's life-course agency (Carpenter, 2010) by helping them to identify and resist forces of oppression. It can also help them strategize for social justice by teaching them that change is possible and that theory can force description into critique.

The purpose of this exercise is to convince students that human (hetero)sexuality is neither entirely hardwired by a reproductive imperative nor entirely voluntary, the result of autonomous choice. The goal is to help students apply to sexuality what Novack (1990) explained about dance: "This is not to say that dancers consciously plan these changes; like all participants in a culture (to paraphrase Marx), they make their own dances, but within a set of rules they do not always personally create" (p. 141).

This exercise has two steps. The first step involves learning through doing. Doing teaches the relevance of social construction theory by exposing students directly and concretely to the cultural ingredients of scripting. Manipulating material objects, participating in interpersonal interactions, and experiencing institutions that communicate the who, what, where, when, and why rules of human activity demonstrate to students that, indeed, "the world's a stage" (Shakespeare, *As You Like It*, 2:7). Although students cannot have sexual experiences in the classroom, dancing is an appropriate and striking analogue to teach them "sex is not a natural act" (Tiefer, 1995). Gagnon's (1977) script theory posits sex is not biologically determined, nor something people instinctively know how to perform. Rather, sex is composed of learned skills and preferences, which humans acquire the same way they acquire all other skills and preferences in life—by learning the requirements for performances deemed proper in their society (Gagnon, 1977).

The second step involves discerning how rules, absorbed bodily, convince people to accept particular roles and positions in their social hierarchy. Students' reflections in class upon the dances they dance, upon the societal values communicated by each dance, and upon how this translates to sexuality are achieved in this step.

Dancing in class involves performing a powwow two-step (Barry & Conlon, 2003), a ballroom waltz, and grinding, for instance, and analyzing the embodied messages each dance imparts. The exercise demonstrates how universal human activity functions disparately in different social contexts and for different reasons, which encourages students to cast skeptical eyes upon "gene" arguments, whether "selfish" (Dawkins, 1976) or "gay" (Hamer, 1995). Script theory is a useful tool for unpacking social constructions, "man-made" social arrangements people can remake to suit changing desires and interests.

Preparing for the Activity

1. Ask students to e-mail their favorite dance music or dance songs the week before you plan to use this activity. Select two or three examples that would be appropriate for contrasting kinds of dancing. Feel free to add some of your own music choices. Dancing styles leading to good discussions include Native American powwow, ballroom, Charleston, samba, tango, rock and roll, the twist, and grinding.

2. Prepare the music so you can play it using your classroom's audiovisual technology at sufficient volume for dancing. It may be convenient to prepare a playlist of the music you will use in class so you can seamlessly move from piece to piece. Practice in advance so playback goes smoothly.

3. Bring props that may be useful in performing the dances. For instance, drums and shakers or rattles are useful in performing Native American music. Dance cards and small pencils, used to reserve different partners, are helpful in demonstrating scripts for an evening of ballroom dancing. Empty beer cans and red cups are appropriate props for grinding.

4. Research each style you plan to analyze in class for dance theorists' insights into the meanings of dancers' gestures, costumes, relationship to audience, mode of moving, and relationship to each other, among others. Consider different uses of dance: as an art form, as a social activity, as entertainment, for courting, for sexual expression, and for religious observance.

Facilitating the Activity

1. As students arrive, have music playing to signal a different kind of class is about to take place. Once all have arrived, turn off the music and introduce the exercise: "Today we will be dancing in class to see what we learn about embodied experience." Then begin the first dance exercise.
2. Using Native American music and Barry and Conlon's (2003) suggestions for powwow dancing, direct some of the students to take male roles and to beat to the rhythm of the drumming music you are playing. Have other "men" perform a two-step dance in a circle and the "women" dance or clap in an outer circle. Continue for at least four minutes.
3. Next ask students to participate in ballroom dancing, including using a dance card to select partners, dancing, changing partners, and concluding the dance. Play "big band" music. Do not worry if students are not sure how to proceed. Their confusion is grist for your discussion about changing cultural expectations. The ballroom exercise should include at least two different dances so that students can experience changing partners. You need not play the pieces of music in their entirety. Using 2–3 minute selections keeps the exercise from dragging.
4. Ask students to dance in ways they would at a party or club. Play hip-hop or other contemporary dance music. Some of these may be some of the students' suggested music selections.
5. Ask students to return to their desks and process the activity with the provided discussion questions. Be sure to remind students to provide evidence for all claims they make.

Discussion Questions

-   How did you feel performing each dance?
-   What were some of the feelings you experienced while you performed each part of each dance?
-   Explain the who, what, where, when, and why rules for each dance.
-   What are some examples of the intrapsychic, interpersonal, and cultural scripts shaping each dance?
-   Describe the gender role you chose for yourself in each dance.
-   How did men's and women's performances compare to one another for each dance?
-   Who, if anyone, was privileged or disadvantaged in any dance? Why/why not?
-   How was your body disciplined or liberated by each dance?

- How, if at all, can you speculate about the values of the group of people who usually perform this dance from the characteristics of the dance?
- How are dance and sexuality similar?
- How might the society that dances this dance experience and express sexuality?
- How important is sexuality in each culture?
- How does sexuality function in each culture?
- What are ideal sexual citizens like in each culture?
- What other social rituals can you think of that shape your body to shape your mind?
- What did you learn from experiencing this exercise?
- What did you find most interesting in your own reactions to the scripted interactions?
- How did the exercise affect how you see sexuality?

Typical Results

- This exercise complicates students' understandings of gender and sexuality, sharpens their intellectual curiosity, and teaches them that getting out of their heads and into their bodies can lead to critical insight. Making the lesson fun helps to reduce student discomfort, defensiveness, and anxiety generated by the notion that sex and gender are socially constructed. Enjoyment also increases students' excitement over seeing their lives through a radically different framework.
- Attention to dancers' costumes, gestures, freedom to improvise, relationships to each other and any audience, preferred body shapes, rhythms, and flow of movement, among other variables, can yield insight into the dances' meanings, uses, and values. Students may note that the persistent beat of powwow music hypnotizes and merges the spiritual with the material. They may interpret circle dancers' complementary gender roles as constructing group solidarity, and they may see all these qualities as reinforcing Native American respect for the integrity of life. Students may conclude the manners of ballroom dancing, on the other hand, with men initiating all actions, leading, and even lifting their female partners off the ground, as demonstrating and enforcing polarized, dimorphic, patriarchal gender roles and heterosexuality. They may make the connection between the dance and its era: Heterosexual values prevailed in the twentieth century, boosted by romance and domesticity's synergy with market capitalism. Finally, students may deduce that grinding transforms sexuality into casual and easily available sensation, replaces romance with explicit genital contact, and parodies courting and the idealization of women. Some may see how these values are congruent with neoliberal consumerist values of disposability, fashion, fickleness, and pornification.
- Students learn that dancing choreographs power as they struggle to determine who leads, who follows, who can perform what actions, and which roles are more fun. Comparing and contrasting scripts implicit in dancing lead to questioning the "naturalness" of other human arrangements. Looking at scripts qua scripts helps students see that they may *vary* the scripts through dancing, but, nevertheless, they rarely make up the scripts entirely by themselves. Insights gleaned from dancing lead the way to students' analysis of the choreography of sexuality. These insights can lay firm groundwork for looking at feminist and queer theories about

gender and sexuality. Theories such as "compulsory heterosexuality" (Rich, 1978; 1993), "muted" group theory (Ardener, 1981), and hegemonic masculinity (Connell, 2005) come alive. Because "sex is more like dancing than digestion" (Tiefer, 2002), students recognize that sex programs some to lead, some to follow, and some to do their own thing.

- Students typically recall dancing in class as outrageous but convincing and unforgettable. In fact, they say it contributes to acquiring a new habit: closely scrutinizing all social rituals for deeper pattern and significance.

Limitations and Cautionary Advice

- Do not warn students in advance that they will be dancing in class. They may dread what they end up enjoying immensely.
- Do not worry unduly if students start the exercise with resistance. After a minute or two of groaning, with enthusiasm and assurance from their instructor that this is an academically salient exercise, they get into it. At first embarrassed, they end up delighted by this departure from their normal classroom decorum.
- Read Barry and Conlon's (2003) "Powwow in the Classroom" for advice on how to avoid ethnocentrism while engaging with Native American cultural artifacts in the classroom. Present some basic information about pre-encounter Native American culture, using information and suggestions from Paula Gunn Allen's *The Sacred Hoop*.
- Encourage students to connect dance details with cultural values.
- Introduce the exercise early in the semester. It sets the tone for an exciting semester.
- It is important to be cognizant of students' physical limitations and adapt appropriately.
- Be aware that "club" style dancing (or grinding) could lead to unwanted contact between individuals. Remind students of their right to decline dancing with others, but encourage them to continue to dance on their own.

Alternative Uses

- Some excellent follow-up readings include theoretical pieces by Plummer (2002) and Weeks (2010) and short stories such as "The Storm" by Kate Chopin (2004) and "Graduation" by Andre Dubus (1995). Ask students, "Using Gagnon's, Plummer's and Weeks' lenses of social construction, describe how the fictional societies in these short stories have choreographed sexuality and interpret the authors' attitudes about the sexual cultures they portray."
- Periodically have students analyze the lyrics of a song that has a theme you are teaching in class.

REFERENCES

Allen, P. (1986). *The sacred hoop: Recovering the feminine in American Indian traditions.* Boston, MA: Beacon Press.

Ardener, S. (1981). *Women and space: Ground rules and social maps.* London: Croom Helm.

Barry, N. H., & Conlon, P. (2003). Powwow in the classroom. *Music Educators Journal, 90*(2), 21–26.

Carpenter, L. (2010). Gendered sexuality over the life course: A conceptual framework. *Sociological Perspectives, 53*(2), 155–77.

Chopin, K. (1969). "The Storm." *The Complete Works of Kate Chopin.* Edited by Per Seyersted. Baton Rouge: Louisiana State University Press.

Connell, R. W. (2005) *Masculinities* (2nd ed.). Cambridge: Polity Press.

Dawkins, R. (1976). *The selfish gene.* New York: Oxford.

Dubus, A. (1999). "Graduation." *Adultery and Other Choices.* Boston, MA: David R. Godine.

Gagnon, J. (1977). *Human sexualities.* Glenview, IL: Scott, Foresman and Company.

Gardner, H. (2011). *Frames of mind: The theory of multiple intelligences* (3rd ed.). New York: Basic Books.

Hamer, D. H. (1995). *The science of desire.* Beaverton, OR: Touchstone.

Hanisch, C. (1969; 1970). The personal is political. In S. Firestone (Ed.), *Notes from the second year: Women's liberation.* New York: Radical Feminism.

H'Doubler, M. (1940). *Dance: A creative art experience.* Madison: University of Wisconsin Press.

Novack, C. J. (1990). *Sharing the dance: Contact improvisation and American culture.* Madison: University of Wisconsin Press.

Plummer, K. (2002). Symbolic interactionism and sexual conduct: An emergent perspective. In C. Williams & A. Stein (Eds.), *Sexuality and gender* (pp. 20–32). Oxford: Blackwell.

Rich, A. (1978; 1993). Compulsory heterosexuality and lesbian existence. In H. Abelove, M. A. Barale, & D. M. Halperin (Eds.), *The lesbian and gay studies reader* (pp. 227–54). New York: Routledge.

Tiefer, L. (Ed.). (1995). *Sex is not a natural act and other essays.* New York: Westview Press.

Tiefer, L. (2002). Sexual behaviour and its medicalisation: Many (especially economic) forces promote medicalisation. *British Medical Journal, 325*(7354), 452.

Vance, C. S. (1984). Pleasure and danger: Toward a politics of sexuality. In C. S. Vance (Ed.), *Pleasure and danger: Exploring female sexuality* (pp. 1–27). Boston: Routledge and Kegan Paul.

Weeks, J. (2010). *Sexuality.* New York: Routledge.

ADDITIONAL READINGS

Butler, J. (1990). *Gender trouble.* New York: Routledge.

Colosi, R. (Ed.). (2012). *Dirty dancing? An ethnography of lap-dancing. Crime Ethnography Series.* New York: Routledge.

Gergen, K. (2012) *Relational being: Beyond self and community.* Oxford: Oxford University Press.

Keeling, R. (1997). *North American Indian music: A guide to published sources and selected recordings. Garland Library of Music Ethnology.* New York: Routledge.

Seidman, S. (2003). *The social construction of sexuality.* New York: W. W. Norton.

Discussing Gender and Human Sexuality "Hot Button" Issues: Considering the Role of Religion and Religious Beliefs

Navita Cummings James, PhD
(University of South Florida)

Appropriate Course(s) and Level

Advanced undergraduate courses in women's/gender studies, communication studies, religious studies, cultural studies, anthropology, and sociology.

Appropriate Class Size

25–100 students or more.

Learning Goals

- To explore the diversity of viewpoints on hot button gender and human sexuality issues (e.g., abortion and gay marriage) among one's peers.
- To consider how, if at all, one's own and one's peers' faith beliefs (or non-faith beliefs) are related to positions taken on hot button gender and human sexuality issues.
- To discover the diversity of opinions of people-of-faith and others on hot button gender and sexuality issues by examining national opinion-poll data.
- To develop "civil discourse" speaking and listening skills that can be utilized in public discussions on hot button gender and human sexuality issues.

Estimated Time Required

The time needed to complete this assignment depends on the option selected. The full version can take 45 minutes when students first respond to a set of propositions related to a single hot button issue (see Handouts for a full list of suggested propositions) and then share their responses with the class. This is followed by a full class discussion. The "Be Counted" option, which works well with larger lecture classes, can take as little as 10 minutes when students are invited, but not required, to "show" to the class the specific position they take on a single, controversial, public policy issue (e.g., abortion) or selected proposition. This is then followed by a full-class discussion. In either option, to move students more quickly into a class discussion comparing their responses to the larger U.S. population, the facilitator can assign homework readings on relevant national opinion-poll data.

Required Materials

- Propositional statements on hot button gender and sexuality topics (see Handouts).
- Pew Forum on Religious & Public Life (www.pewforum.org) or similar source with current public-opinion results on topics related to religion and sexuality issues. The Pew website has specific sections on abortion and homosexuality, while the website's U.S. Religious Landscape Survey (35,000 U.S. adults) section has comparisons of the positions that self-identified religious and unaffiliated people take on social and political issues including abortion and homosexuality.

Rationale

A liberal arts college education should help prepare students to become informed citizens who can engage in rational, civil discourse and vote responsibly. Unfortunately, the public models for discussion of controversial topics often dissolve into name-calling shouting matches with little or no opportunity for the exploration or understanding of underlying issues. These practices of *un-civil* discourse are often exacerbated when religious assumptions and arguments are explicitly or implicitly used to support positions taken on issues related to gender and human sexuality. In the college classroom, to avoid this potential kind of conflict, many instructors may choose to shy away from the introduction of religion into discussions on gender and human sexuality controversies. This choice, however, may leave classroom discussions impoverished and students less well prepared to engage these topics in the context of an informed electorate. There are three pedagogical arguments for why students should be given the opportunity to discuss the intersections of gender and human sexuality hot button issues and religion in the college classroom.

- Religious Literacy and Human Sexuality. Religion is historically and contemporaneously a powerful shaper of gender identity, gender roles, and human sexuality. Ideally, college-educated students need to be equipped with at least some framework for understanding how to discuss and listen to human sexuality arguments influenced by religion. Prothero (2007) introduced the term "religious literacy" and suggested that it "refers to the ability to understand and use in one's day-to-day life the basic building blocks of religious tradition—their key terms, symbols, doctrines, practices, metaphors, and narratives" (pp. 1–12). It is important to note religious literacy as defined here does not suggest faculty are to teach students *to be* religious, but rather, faculty should help students understand how religion remains a major player in human life from the personal to the global. In the context of this exercise, religious literacy helps students appreciate that there is no one religious position on many of today's controversial human sexuality issues and that religious people can and do sometimes disagree.

- Dialogic Communication Skills. College students need to develop multiple communication skills to be able to participate effectively in discussions on controversial topics. One such skill is to be able to "listen to understand the other" in face-to-face dialogues. In controversial discussions, before attempting to understand what the other is saying, participants often argue, debate, and sometimes personally attack those with whom they disagree. The dialogic communication model recommended here discourages these behaviors and instead encourages, first, that students agree to respect one another and acknowledge reasonable people can and do disagree; and second, that students, without trying to persuade or be persuaded by the other, agree to listen to understand the complexity of the position taken by the other. In this exercise, neither the class nor the facilitator asserts that there is one right or wrong position to take on any of the propositions.
- Self-Reflexivity. Finally, since becoming adults, many college students may not have consciously considered how their "inherited" religious, spiritual, and/or anti-religious beliefs inform their current thinking and positions on gender and human sexuality issues. Key features of this exercise include giving students the opportunity to reflect thoughtfully on their current opinions and how those opinions compare to others' opinions on these topics.

This exercise gives students the opportunity to practice listening and talking about gender and human sexuality hot button issues in constructive and civil ways. It further offers them a rare opportunity in the college classroom to consider—without demonizing or being demonized—how religion and spirituality may inform and/or influence positions taken on these issues.

Preparing for the Activity

1. If you have not already developed a set of guidelines for having discussions on controversial topics, guidelines should be developed or pre-identified (see James, 1997, pp. 197–98). Consider using some or all of the following guidelines.
   - Engage in dialogue, not debate. Listen to understand the positions offered by others.
   - Seek "common ground." Acknowledge those places where agreement can occur.
   - Understand that reasonable people can and do disagree; people-of-faith can and do disagree.
   - Respect everyone's right to his or her own opinion. It is okay to agree to disagree.
   - Speak with "I" statements. Avoid trying to speak for all of any group (e.g., all Christians, all Muslims).
   - Do not attempt to persuade others to believe what you believe.
   Students can also be encouraged as a class to create their own set of guidelines.
2. Review national opinion-poll data on hot button gender and human sexuality issues by religious and nonreligious affiliation. National polls are periodically taken that assess how people of differing religious and nonreligious affiliation think

about controversial gender and human sexuality issues. Reviewing a selection of these data equips you and the students to connect student opinions within the context of the larger U.S. population.

3. Select propositions and/or public policy issues for class activity. In the full version of this exercise, you can choose from one of two proposition sets (see Handouts A and B). One set focuses on reproductive issues; the second focuses on gay marriage. You can tailor these lists to your classes and include additional propositions on topics taken from current-news headlines. Care should be taken to include both "conservatively" and "liberally" stated propositions. The "Be Counted" option is a quick way to assess and make known to the class where class members stand on a single, specific public policy. For this option, you need to select a current public policy issue (e.g., the legalization of gay marriage) and solicit student responses.

Facilitating the Activity

1. Review or create discussion guidelines (see Preparing for the Activity). Ask each student to abide by these guidelines for at least the duration of the exercise.

2. Instruct students that this exercise invites them to consider how people sometimes use religion, spirituality, and even nonreligious belief to inform positions taken on hot button gender and human sexuality issues. Emphatically emphasize that this exercise is not a referendum on the merits or demerits of religion and/or spirituality. Religion is a reality of human life that sometimes affects both the religious and nonreligious alike.

3. Inform students that in this exercise the standard for student religious, spiritual, or nonreligious/nonspiritual identity or affiliation will be "self-identification." This strategy is frequently used in national polls. The "self-identification" strategy helps avoid the controversy of some students trying to define who is or is not religious (i.e., Christian).

4. Give students an opportunity to self-assess their own positions on the propositions or the selected public policy issue. In the full version, this can be done by giving students printed copies of selected propositions in a handout that they can complete for homework or complete as an in-class, self-reflection activity prior to the class discussion. Another option is to let students discuss these printed propositions in dyads or small groups before the larger class discussion begins. In the "Be Counted" option, the facilitator announces the public policy issue, announces what the options will be, and then gives students a few seconds to reflect upon what their position will be.

5. After students have had the opportunity to consider their personal positions on the propositions or on a selected public policy issue, ask the students to share with the class their positions taken. For the full-version option, they can be asked to share their positions on selected propositions as follows: (1) Agree, (2) Disagree, (3) Not Sure, and (4) Would Prefer Not to Share. For the "Be Counted" option, students can be asked their position on the public policy issue. For example, on the issue of the legalization of gay marriage, position options can include (1) How many support it? (2) How many are against it? (3) How many are unsure? and (4)

How many would prefer not to share their position? Asking students to stand or raise their hand in response to these questions introduces a level of accountability and visibility. Soliciting anonymous responses via student use of clickers or other methods, however, is another option. If students publicly display their positions in class, ask them to look around the class to see how their peers are responding (see Limitations and Cautionary Advice). Finally, count and announce what portion of class takes what position (e.g., "It looks like at least two-thirds of the class agrees with or supports this position").

6. After the positions of class members are publicly assessed, invite students to share *why* they responded the way they did. Consider asking, "Who is willing to share why they took the position that they did?" Be sure to include students who take differing positions, including those who choose not to take or share their positions publicly.

7. Summarize or highlight some of the positions and reasons identified by students. If students did not offer religious "reasons" for why they took the positions that they did, ask them to reflect upon whether or not their religious, spiritual, or anti-religious beliefs influenced the positions they took. Ask for volunteers to share their assessments.

8. Next, visually project relevant websites or share other visual representations of poll data showing different positions on the selected hot button gender and human sexuality issues taken by people according to their faith beliefs or non-faith beliefs. Ask to what extent, if at all, the class's positions reflect national data. Reaffirm the argument that not all religious people—and in the case of the United States, not all self-identified Christians—agree or disagree on hot button gender and human sexuality issues. Optional: Identify the "official" positions taken by some religious denominations and group (see the Pew Forum website). Note how "self-identified" members within those religions groups (i.e., Roman Catholics) sometimes depart from the official positions taken by religious leadership.

Discussion Questions

- What, if anything, surprised (shocked, delighted, etc.) you the most about this exercise?
- What, if anything, reaffirmed what you already knew about hot button gender and human sexuality issues and related religious, spiritual, or nonreligious beliefs?
- What, if anything, challenged what you thought you knew about hot button gender and human sexuality issues and related religious, spiritual, or nonreligious beliefs?
- What, if anything, new did you learn about yourself or others in this class?
- What were any diversity related, discernible differences in how your peers responded to these propositions (i.e., differences between women-as-a-group and men-as-a-group)?
- What, if anything, new did you learn about how religion or your personal spirituality influences your personal beliefs about gender and human sexuality?
- What, if anything, would you like others in the class to know about why you think or believe the way you do or why you took the position you did on a given proposition?

• How do the opinions expressed by your peers in this class compare to local, state, national, or global national surveys on this topic?

Typical Results

• Students who disagree on gender and human sexuality issues learn to listen to one another and engage in civil discourse.
• The overwhelming majority of the college students today—including those who self-identify as religious or spiritual—still support a woman's right to choose, and a majority support gay marriage. However, in more religiously conservative colleges and universities, the majority of students may not support these positions.
• More religiously conservative students may fear that other students view them as "bigots."
• Some religious women and lesbian, gay, bisexual, transgender/transsexual, intersexed, and queer/questioning (LGBTIQ) students may feel devalued by the religions of their youth and report perceived devaluing as a reason why they are no longer religiously affiliated. When responding to these students, consider calling to their attention that their life experiences are valued and affirmed by at least some self-identified persons within their larger religious traditions. Use national survey data to help support this point. Also, in reference to the hot button topics of abortion and gay rights, let the students know about organizations of self-identified religious people who support a woman's right to choose (e.g., the Religious Coalition for Reproductive Rights) and who support LGBTIQ individuals (e.g., Dignity USA [Roman Catholic] and Integrity [Episcopalian]).
• Students from religious traditions such as Buddhism and Hinduism may be surprised by how the three Abrahamic religions—Judaism, Christianity, and Islam—treat human sexuality.
• Students who identify as "spiritual but not religious," agnostic, or atheist may be resentful of any mention of religion in politics and public policy. These students may believe this violates the "separation of church and state."
• Other students may be very angry with religion—period. Do not let their anger hijack the discussion. Remind students that this exercise is not a referendum on religion itself.

Limitations and Cautionary Advice

• Closeted Student LGBTIQ Identities: During discussions related to gender identity and sexual orientation and attraction, ask that students who have not previously "come out of the closet" as lesbian, gay, bisexual, transgendered and/or intersex, etc., do *not* choose to do so during this exercise. Although the facilitator may work hard to create a "safe" environment, no student should be allowed to assume coming-out-of-the-closet in a public situation is always safe.
• Facilitator's Religious Background and Knowledge: Typically, facilitators are not required to be "experts" in the topics they facilitate. Since the instructor assumes the role of facilitator in this exercise, the instructor does not have to be religious

or have a background in religion. The instructor is therefore not responsible for corroborating the veracity of student religious and nonreligious claims and may inform the class that this is not his or her role in the exercise. During the course of the class discussion, if the facilitator decides to divulge what position he or she takes on a given issue or proposition, the facilitator should model the spirit of this assignment (reasonable people can and do disagree) and suggest that in no way does the instructor want or expect the students to think as the instructor does. Students have to find their own way.

• Facilitator Classroom Management: Facilitators should have as their top priority the encouragement of a supportive and civil classroom environment. Consider publicly thanking students who have the courage to take positions counter to the class majority. Note the importance of being able to learn about different perspectives during this exercise. If you or any student detects an uncivil classroom environment beginning to develop, stop the class discussion. Have all students review and recommit to the class covenant or discussion guidelines. Then, return to the exercise.

REFERENCES

James, N. C. (1997). Classroom climate and teaching (about) racism: Notes from the trenches. In A. Arsenau Jones & S. P. Morreale (Eds.), *Proceedings of the National Communication Association Summer Conference on Racial and Ethnic Diversity in the Twenty-First Century* (pp. 195–201). Annandale, VA: National Communication Association.

Prothero, S. R. (2007). *Religious literacy: What every American needs to know—And doesn't.* New York: HarperOne.

HANDOUT A: SELECTED GENDER AND HUMAN SEXUALITY HOT BUTTON PROPOSITIONS

Directions: Agree or Disagree (some of these propositions may be experienced as offensive)

Set A Propositions: Reproductive Issues—Contraception and Abortion

1. Abortion is murder.
2. Any form of birth control that prevents an already fertilized egg from implanting in the uterus (e.g., birth control pills, the "morning after pill," and IUDs) should be made illegal.
3. *Roe v. Wade*, the U.S. Supreme Court case that gave women the right to a legal, safe abortion, should remain the law of the land and not be overturned.
4. Since God chose women to have babies, the decision to maintain or terminate a pregnancy should only be between the pregnant woman and her God.
5. All parents of minors should be notified before their daughters receive an abortion—even in cases of alleged incest.
6. Women should not have access to "late-term" abortions for any reason.
7. In the first six weeks of life, the rights of the fertilized egg/zygote/fetus to life should outweigh the right of a woman to have control of her own body.
8. Human life begins at conception and should be protected by "personhood" laws.
9. A human "baby" should only receive the full protection of the law when the baby becomes viable outside of the mother's womb and not sooner.
10. A man who impregnates a woman should have the right to prevent her from having an abortion if he is willing to be solely responsible for raising the child after he or she is born.
11. Women should be required to have a 24–48 hour waiting period before being able to go through with an abortion.
12. Before receiving an abortion, a woman should be required to undergo a sonogram that she should pay for herself—even if she chooses not to look at the results.

HANDOUT B: SELECTED GENDER AND
HUMAN SEXUALITY HOT BUTTON PROPOSITIONS

Directions: Agree or Disagree (some of these propositions may be experienced as offensive)

Set B Propositions: LGBTIQ Rights—Sex, Marriage, and Religious Roles

1. U.S. states should require all civil marriages be performed by public officials; churches, synagogues, mosques, etc., should only be authorized to perform *blessings* of civil marriages.
2. Openly gay men and lesbians in same-sex, loving, committed relationships should not expect to be permitted to marry in their home churches, synagogues, temples, mosques, etc.
3. All self-identified religious people condemn same-sex marriage.
4. Since God made some people LGBTIQ, God surely does not deny them the gift of sexuality or condemn the kind of sex that is natural for them.
5. There are some parts of religious texts (e.g., the Bible, the Qur'an) that appear to affirm—or at least not condemn—all same-sex, loving, committed relationships.
6. Openly gay men in same-sex, loving, committed relationships should be allowed to become priests, pastors, ministers, bishops, popes, rabbis, imams, gurus, etc.
7. Open lesbians in same-sex, loving, committed relationships should be allowed to become priests, pastors, ministers, bishops, popes, rabbis, imams, gurus, etc.
8. Openly transgendered and/or intersex people should not be allowed by their religious institutions to become priests, pastors, ministers, bishops, rabbis, imams, gurus, etc.
9. The Defense of Marriage Act (DOMA) should continue to be the law of the land and should be enforced.

III

FRIENDSHIPS AND ROMANTIC RELATIONSHIPS

Choose Your Own Adventure: Examining Social Exchange Theory and Gendered Relational Choices[1]

Elizabeth N. Ribarsky, PhD
(University of Illinois Springfield)

Appropriate Course(s) and Level

Interpersonal communication, relational communication, communication theory, psychology, and other courses that cover social exchange theory. Because of the simplicity of the activity, it is useful for even lower-level courses, but analysis of choices and theory application may be greater when used within higher-level courses.

Appropriate Class Size

10–100 students or more.

Learning Goals

- To explore the ways in which social exchange theory explains how individuals make choices as to whether to enter, continue, or terminate a relationship.
- To examine how gendered expectations influence the relational decision-making process.
- To assist students in practicing theory application.

Estimated Time Required

5–20 minutes, depending on the discussion that ensues.

Required Materials

- Hypothetical Dating Script (see Handout).

Rationale

To many students, theory can be confusing and difficult to retain. Therefore, instructors who put emphasis on theory in their courses and lectures must find new ways for students to connect to the sometimes obscure material. Through a hands-on approach to learning theory, students may be challenged to examine their own beliefs and knowledge (DeMulder & Eby, 1999). Ultimately, "engagement in learning involves formulating a deeper connection between the student and the material whereby a student develops an interest in the topic or retains learning beyond the short term" (Schussler, 2009, p. 115–16). To foster this form of engagement, this teaching activity encourages students to employ a pragmatic decision-making process of "choosing their own adventure" to examine how people make relational choices in light of social exchange theory.

Thibaut and Kelley (1959) argued from a social exchange perspective that most behaviors, including those within our interpersonal relationships, can be explained from a profit-motivated standpoint. Our "decisions are based upon our projections of the rewards and costs of a particular course of action" (Stafford, 2008, p. 377). Even within our romantic relationships, we often make choices and behave in a manner that we believe will reap the most rewards. However, what one individual may see as a reward, another person may not. Similarly, what a person sees as a reward at one time may not be seen as such at a later date. And many of these assessments of costs and rewards are based upon an individual's perception of gender and sex roles. Thus, what seems like a fairly simple economics-based perspective of relationships is actually much more complex. To tackle social exchange theory's complexity and important role in examining interpersonal relationships and the influence of gender on relational decisions, I developed the following activity. Through this activity, students are able to not only put this theory into practice but also to begin to critically think about the nuances of social exchange theory through discussion questions that address issues such as gender, age, and individuals' standpoints and their respective impact on cost/reward analysis.

Preparing for the Activity

1. Little to no preparation is needed for this activity because I most often use this activity *before* explaining social exchange theory, as it helps lead the class into a discussion about the theory, and oftentimes, the results serve as excellent examples of the theoretical tenets during lecture.
2. The only preparation needed is having the script ready and being prepared to discuss the intricacies of social exchange theory following the completion of the activity.

Facilitating the Activity

1. To start the activity, explain to the students that they are to listen carefully to the hypothetical dating scenarios (see Handout) and make decisions when prompted by the script but to keep these decisions to themselves for the time being. Emphasize that there are no right or wrong answers.

2. Once the three scenarios have been read, ask students to raise their hand to indicate whether they ultimately ended up choosing X, Y, or Z.

Discussion Questions

- Why did you ultimately choose X, Y, or Z?
  - What were the greatest benefits you imagine you would receive from your date selection?
  - What do you believe would be the greatest cost/risk of being in a relationship with your date selection?
- How, if at all, do you think your gender impacted the decision that you made?
  - From a gender-role perspective, what are the typical actions expected for men and women when asking for a date?
  - What do you think most men and women see as the greatest costs in romantic relationships?
  - What do you think most men and women see as the greatest rewards in romantic relationships?
  - How similar or different are the relational expectations between men and women?
  - How are these expectations created?
- How, if at all, would your decision have been impacted if you had been dating X for a longer period of time?
- How, if at all, do you think your choices would vary if you were currently at a different point and time in your life?
- Beyond the choices you made in this activity, how often do you believe you weigh the pros and cons of a relationship?
- What may make you more or less aware of this process of weighing the pros and cons of a relationship?

You can use this activity and the discussion generated to help exemplify the significance of this theory by showing how frequently the theory can be applied to our everyday interactions and relationships. Although the focus of the script is on dating relationships, remind students during your lecture on social exchange theory that we engage in a cost/benefit analysis in most, if not all, of our relationships—romantic or not. To emphasize how gender impacts even our friendship choices, feel free to add additional discussion questions that focus on gender-role expectations with friendship-based costs/rewards.

Typical Results

- Students typically engage in a lively discussion regarding the choices that they made, why they made the selections they did, and why they believe their decision was correct. Even if students are quiet or do not readily participate in the discussion, they have at least mentally gone through the exercise and internally have begun the application process. Therefore, this activity helps create engagement for the entire class.

- This activity makes clear ties to social exchange theory and its main tenets in four ways.
  - First, social exchange theory states that we continually weigh the costs and benefits of our relationships in order to determine if the relationship is worth entering or continuing to pursue. Thus, by having students choose which hypothetical relationship they want to pursue, they are actively engaging in this cost/benefit analysis.
  - Second, each scenario emphasizes a different possible cost and benefit: X stresses personality compatibility, Y focuses on physical attraction, and Z focuses on financial stability. Because each student is apt to desire different rewards and see different relational characteristics as costs, it demonstrates the theory's tenet that rewards and costs vary from individual to individual. I incorporated several different costs and rewards that may particularly be influenced by an individual's gender. For example, situation Z exemplifies this concept because it is a situation that many men do not feel is consistent with stereotypical sex/gender roles, and therefore, can serve as a significant point of discussion of how gender may impact what we view as rewards or costs in a relationship.
  - Third, by discussing if the length of time of the relationship would affect their choices, students are able to see how time/relational investment impacts the decision-making process.
  - Finally, the question regarding changes in decisions based upon the point and time in their life emphasizes that what individuals perceive as rewards/costs may vary over their lifetime.

Limitations and Cautionary Advice

- Every time I have done this activity, the students' discussion quickly turns into a debate. Therefore, the instructor must be prepared to moderate these debates and dissuade students from making any disparaging remarks.
- Because the script is gender neutral in its wording, it is specifically meant to avoid outing anyone's sexual orientation. Therefore, the focus of the activity should remain on gendered relational rewards and costs, not sexual preferences.
- Additionally, although students will engage in the decision-making process whether or not they engage in the discussion that follows, it is important to remain mindful of your more quiet students. If you perhaps have a larger number of shy students, you may want to consider doing this activity within small groups (see Alternative Uses).

Alternative Uses

- I thoroughly enjoy doing this activity as a class because there are few activities that instructors are able to conduct as an entire class, and this activity tends to generate significant discussion among the entire class. But this activity could easily be done within small groups. Each group could be given the hypothetical dating script and instructed to make their decisions as a small group. This approach may allow more-reserved students to feel more comfortable engaging in discussions with their group rather than the entire class. After completing the choices within their groups, the instructor could then open the discussion up to the entire class using the provided discussion questions.

REFERENCES

DeMulder, E. K., & Eby, K. K. (1999). Bridging troubled waters. *American Behavioral Scientist, 42*(5), 892–901.

Schussler, D. (2009). Beyond content: How teachers manage classrooms to facilitate intellectual engagement for disengaged students. *Theory into Practice, 48,* 114–21. doi: 10.1080/00405840902776376.

Stafford, L. (2008). Social exchange theories: Calculating the rewards and costs of personal relationships. In L. Baxter & D. Braithwaite (Eds.), *Engaging theories in interpersonal communication: Multiple perspectives* (pp. 377–89). Thousand Oaks, CA: Sage Publications.

Thibaut, J. W., & Kelley, H. H. (1959). *The social psychology of groups.* New York: Wiley.

HANDOUT: HYPOTHETICAL DATING SCENARIO SCRIPT

You have been dating X for a month now. You met through a mutual friend. Although you don't find X extremely attractive, you cannot help but have a good time with them. You share a lot of the same interests and find yourself frequently sharing a good laugh. And although you don't always agree on what constitutes a "good" movie, you usually have a lively discussion of why you enjoy certain movies.

One night, you are at a party with friends (and not X), and you are introduced to Y. You are immediately physically attracted to Y. However, you seem to have a difficult time holding a conversation with Y. You aren't sure that's because you are nervous or because Y just isn't very interesting or personable. Throughout the rest of the night, you continue to exchange flirtatious gazes with Y and get excited every time you catch Y's eye. At the end of the night, Y asks you out. Do you accept and go out with Y or stay with X?

A few weeks later, you are shopping at your favorite store. The line to make your purchase is quite long, so you strike up a conversation with Z who is in line behind you. Z is not your "typical" type but is attractive nonetheless. From your conversation, it seems as though Z is quite well-off financially. As you near the checkout counter, Z offers to pay for your purchase and invites you out on a seemingly luxurious and exciting date. Do you accept Z's offer or stay with your previous date?

NOTE

1. Portions of this activity have been previously published as "Choose Your Own Adventure: Examining Social Exchange Theory and Relational Choices" in *Communication Teacher* (2012), 27(1), 29–32.

Perceptions of Conversations and Gendered Language in Same- and Cross-Sex Friendships

Allison R. Thorson, PhD
(University of San Francisco)

Appropriate Course(s) and Level

Introduction to human communication, interpersonal communication, psychology of sex and gender, gender studies, culture studies.

Appropriate Class Size

Up to 40 students, in classrooms with space to allow for small-group work.

Learning Goals

- To help students better understand the connection between sex stereotypes and gendered communication in relationships.
- To explore students' perceptions of the connection between language, relationships, sex, and gender.
- To test students' accuracy and inaccuracy in identifying gendered language used in same- and/or cross-sex friendships.
- To better understand the difference between global versus interaction specific gender schemata.

Estimated Time Required

45 minutes. It can also be adapted for shorter or longer classes depending on how in depth a professor chooses to go in reviewing the related research before and after the activity.

Required Materials

- Excerpts from conversations between same- and cross-sex friends (see Handout for an example).
- A copy of Martin's (1997) article on the perceptions of conversation in same- and cross-sex friendships (or an article addressing similar material).
- A copy of the 1984 movie *When Harry Met Sally* (optional).

Rationale

Empirical research suggests that monogamous, cross-sex friendships are common, significant, and important relationships for individuals to maintain (Guerrero & Chavez, 2005; Monsour, 2002). Researchers have suggested, however, the discourses used among the sexes differ such that friendship expectations are higher for women than for men with regard to communion (e.g., intimacy), solidarity (e.g., mutual activities), and symmetrical reciprocity (e.g., loyalty; Hall, 2011). Specifically, compared to men's friendships, women's friendships are seen as more emotional (Duck & Wright, 1993), more confiding and disclosive (Parker & DeVries, 1993), and more mutually supportive and based on talking (Johnson, 1996). Researchers examining cross-sex friendships have also concluded both men and women are more likely to seek out a female friend for empathy and support because friendships with women are perceived as providing more acceptance, nurturance, and support than do friendships with men (Sapadin, 1988).

Despite these findings, students often assume that interactions among cross-sex heterosexual friends are predictable and involve some level of romantic intent. As such, they use anecdotal evidence to make assertions about the types of interactions that occur between same- and cross-sex friends based on sex stereotypes, cultural messages, or gendered beliefs and expectations. Martin (1997) argued that "direct investigations of the links between the semantic and episodic content of relational schemata" were especially valuable in studying friendships and important in understanding language and gender (p. 116). Thus, this activity tests students' accuracy, inaccuracy, and reliance on sex stereotypes when interpreting interactions using mediated examples (or actual examples—see Alternative Uses) to help them understand how global and interaction specific gender schemata influence their perceptions.

Preparing for the Activity

1. Before they come to class on the day you conduct this activity, students should read Martin's (1997) article "'Girls don't talk about garages!' Perceptions of conversation in same- and cross-sex friendships" or a similar article. Be sure to place this reading on the syllabus as a reminder to students.
2. Develop a brief lecture that reviews Martin's (1997) article and relevant research on sex and gender expectations in relation to language and everyday talk. For instance, be sure to
   - Discuss the limitations and contributions of this research as it relates to sex, gender, and language.

- Discuss the concepts of global and interaction specific gender schemata and how each influences perceptions.
- Address the fact that, despite these findings, individuals who simply analyze conversations (e.g., those who are not participants in the interaction) vary in the extent to which they can accurately distinguish between male-male, female-female, or male-female dyad interactions.
- Discuss how individuals vary in the extent to which they use gendered schemata to determine whether or not interactions took place between male-male, female-female, or male-female dyads.

3. Prepare a three-slide PowerPoint presentation with each slide depicting the transcription for each movie excerpt (see Handout) or print multiple copies of excerpts 1, 2, and 3 to hand out to students.
4. (Optional) Bring a copy of the movie *When Harry Met Sally* (1984) to class to show the actual footage of the conversations when reviewing answers:
   - Movie Excerpt 1: 35:30–36:25.
   - Movie Excerpt 2: 43:19–43:36.
   - Movie Excerpt 3: 55:00–55:30.

Facilitating the Activity

1. Review research for the class on sex, gender, language, and friendship using Martin's (1997) research as a guide.
2. Describe the purpose of the activity, such that even though there is a great deal of research on sex and gendered language, the extent to which sex and gender-based language can be perceived and identified varies from individual to individual. Thus, the purpose of this activity is to (a) determine how accurately students can differentiate between conversations taking place among same-sex and cross-sex friends, and (b) identify how students use global and/or interaction specific gender schemata to influence their perceptions.
3. Put students into groups of 2–4 individuals. Students must be able to sit close enough to each other to have a short discussion after reading each excerpt. In addition, you may require students to take notes on how they came to their conclusions as to whether an excerpt was an example of an interaction occurring between female-female, male-female, or male-male friends and what global and/or interaction specific gender schemata influenced their perceptions.
4. Share movie excerpt #1 with students. Present a PowerPoint slide depicting the transcript of movie excerpt #1 (see Handout) or print copies of this excerpt and hand a copy of it to each group. (Note: The answer key for movie excerpt #1 is that person A is a female and person B is a male.)
5. Provide roughly 10 minutes of small-group discussion time. After reading movie excerpt #1, each group should (a) determine whether the excerpt is representative of a discussion occurring between female-female, male-female, or male-male friends, (b) indicate the sex of person A and person B in the excerpt, and (c) articulate why they believe their perception is accurate. As part of step c, students should indicate what specific stereotypes they relied upon to come to their

decision, identify any specific words that led them to determine the sex of persons A and B, and highlight any topics which led them to these conclusions.

6. Repeat steps 4 and 5 above using movie excerpts #2 and #3. (Note: The answer key for movie excerpt #2 is that person A is a male and person B is a male. The answer key for movie excerpt #3 is that person A is a female and person B is a female.)

7. Discuss for roughly 15 minutes, as a class, students' perceptions, their decision-making process, and the actual sex makeup of the friends performing each movie excerpt using the discussion questions below. You may also choose to show excerpts of the actual film at this point.

Discussion Questions

• How accurate were you in differentiating among female-female, male-female, and male-male friendships using only the transcript provided?

• What, if any, sex specific stereotypes did you rely upon to come to your decision?

• What, if any, specific words led you to determine the sex of persons A and B in each transcript/excerpt?

• What, if any, topics led you to make these conclusions?

• What, if any, global gender schemata influenced your decision?

• What, if any, interaction specific gender schemata influenced your decision?

• For which dyad—female-female, male-female, and male-male—was it easiest to determine the sex of each friend? Why?

• For which dyad—female-female, male-female, and male-male—was it hardest to determine the sex of each friend? Why?

• How do your perceptions, and the perceptions of the class, reinforce or differ from those found in Martin's (1997) research?

• What, if any, role does the media play in developing our gender expectations of communication?

• How, if at all, do stereotypes of how men or women *should* communicate influence your everyday interactions?

• What are the strengths of relying on global and interaction specific gender schemata to determine the sex of individuals interacting in social situations?

• What are the limitations of relying on global and interaction specific gender schemata to determine the sex of individuals interacting in social situations?

Typical Results

• For most students, this exercise helps them understand how global and interaction specific gender schemata influence their perceptions of interpersonal relationships—and in some instances, it shows that their over-reliance on these gender schemata may lead to errors in their perceptions of same- and/or cross-sex friends' interactions.

Limitations and Cautionary Advice

- Students having a better grasp of the foundational concepts of global and interaction specific gender schemata will produce a deeper level of analysis. Those with little exposure or who only skimmed the course readings may struggle with this activity.

- As you conduct this activity, be prepared that one or more students may recognize the excerpts provided as being from the movie *When Harry Met Sally* (1984). If this occurs, ask these students to refrain from sharing their comments, opinions, and perceptions with others in the classroom until the class resumes its discussion of global and interaction specific gender schemata.

- The quotes from *When Harry Met Sally* (1984) are useful in pointing out students' reliance on cultural scripts to classify discourse. The movie excerpts were chosen from an older movie in order to limit the number of students who might be able to identify the characters of the script. Any instructor who finds this to be a limitation is encouraged to adapt this activity using a more recent film or sitcom (e.g., *Friends with Kids*; *The Hangover*; *Parks and Recreation*; *The Office*).

- In the instance that a student uses derogatory statements regarding how males and females *should* talk, have him/her reflect on the empirical research regarding cultural scripts and the inaccuracy of sex stereotypes.

Alternative Uses

- In replacement of, or in addition to, the movie excerpts provided, instructors may opt to use alternative or additional examples of same- and cross-sex friendship interactions when conducting this activity (see suggestions under Limitations and Cautionary Advice). In advanced classes, instructors may opt for students to collect their own data for analysis rather than relying on the excerpts provided. Specifically, instructors may request that their students record approximately 20 to 30 minutes of a face-to-face conversation with a good friend of either the same-sex or the opposite sex, complete a rough transcript of the conversation, and then turn in the transcript and the original recording as part of a class assignment. The instructor may then randomly select one 4-minute segment from a female-female, a male-female, and a male-male interaction to share with the class in order to conduct this activity. This procedure may benefit students' understanding, as it allows them to examine a non-mediated communication event occurring in everyday talk between same- and/or cross-sex friends and requires them to collect and analyze data in a way that mirrors the methods used by Martin (1997).

REFERENCES

Argyle, M., & Henderson, M. (1984). The rules of friendship. *Journal of Social and Personal Relationships, 1*, 211–37.

Duck, S., & Wright, P. H. (1993). Reexamining gender differences in same-gender friendships: A close look at two kinds of data. *Sex Roles, 28*, 709–27.

Guerrero, L. K., & Chavez, A. M. (2005). Relational maintenance in cross-sex friendships characterized by different types of romantic intent: An exploratory study. *Western Journal of Communication, 69*, 339–58.

Hall, J. A. (2011). Sex differences in friendship expectations: A meta-analysis. *Journal of Social and Personal Relationships, 28*, 723–47.

Johnson, F. (1996). Friendships among women: Closeness in dialogue. In J. Wood (Ed.), *Gendered relationships* (pp. 79–94). London: Mayfield.

Martin, R. (1997). "Girls don't talk about garages!" Perceptions of conversation in same- and cross-sex friendships. *Personal Relationships, 4*, 115–30.

Monsour, M. (2002). *Women and men as friends: Relationships across the lifespan in the 21st century.* Mahwah, NJ: Lawrence Erlbaum Associates.

Parker, S., & DeVries, B. (1993). Patterns of friendship for women and men in same- and cross-sex relationships. *Journal of Social and Personal Relationships, 10*, 617–26.

Reiner, R. (Director), Scheinman, A. (Producer), & Ephron, N. (Writer). (1984). *When Harry met Sally* [Film]. Los Angeles: Columbia Pictures.

Sapadin, L. A. (1988). Friendship and gender: Perspectives of professional men and women. *Journal of Social and Personal Relationships, 5*, 387–403.

ADDITIONAL READINGS

Afifi, W., Guerrero, L., & England, K. (1994, May). *Maintenance behaviors in same- and opposite sex friendships: Connections to gender, relational closeness, and equity issues.* Paper presented at the International Network on Personal Relationships Annual Conference, Iowa City, IA.

Aries, E. (1996). *Men and women in interaction: Reconsidering the differences.* New York: Oxford University Press.

Bischoping, K. (1993). Gender differences in conversation topics, 1922–1990. *Sex Roles, 28*, 1–18.

Booth, A., & Hess, E. (1974). Cross-sex friendship. *Journal of Marriage and the Family, 34*, 38–47.

Goldschmidt, O. T., & Weller, L. (2000). "Talking emotions": Gender differences in a variety of communication contexts. *Symbolic Interaction, 23*, 117–34.

Haas, A., & Sherman, M. A. (1982). Reported topics of conversation among same-sex adults. *Communication Quarterly, 30*, 332–42.

Hall, J. A., Larson, K. A., & Watts, A. (2011). Satisfying friendship maintenance expectations: The role of friendship standards and biological sex. *Human Communication Research, 37*, 529–52.

Hogg, M. A. (1985). Masculine and feminine speech in dyads and groups: A study of speech style and gender salience. *Journal of Language and Social Psychology, 4*, 99–112.

Hogg, M. A., & Reid, S. A. (2006). Social identity, self-categorization, and the communication of group norms. *Communication Theory, 16*, 7–30.

Hogg, M. A., & Turner, J. C. (1987). Intergroup behavior, self-stereotyping and the salience of social categories. *British Journal of Social Psychology, 26*, 325–40.

Janssen, A., & Murachver, T. (2004). The relationship between gender and topic in gender-preferential language use. *Written Communication, 21*, 344–67.

Lee, E. J. (2007). Effects of gendered language on gender stereotyping in computer-mediated communication: The moderating role of depersonalization and gender-role orientation. *Human Communication Research, 33*, 515–35.

Oliker, S. J. (1989). *Best friends and marriage: Exchange among women.* Berkeley: University of California Press.

Palomares, N. A. (2004). Gender schematicity, gender identity salience, and gender-linked language use. *Human Communication Research, 30*, 556–88.

Palomares, N. A. (2008). Explaining gender-based language use: Effects of gender identity salience on references to emotion and tentative language in intra- and intergroup contexts. *Human Communication Research, 34*, 263–86.

Palomares, N. A. (2009). Women are sort of more tentative than men, aren't they? How men and women use tentative language differently, similarly, and counterstereotypically as a function of gender salience. *Communication Research, 36*, 538–60.

Palomares, N. A., Bradac, J. J., & Kellermann, K. (2006). Conversational topic along a continuum of perspectives: Conceptual issues. In C. S. Beck (Ed.), *Communication yearbook 30* (pp. 45–97). Mahwah, NJ: Lawrence Erlbaum.

Palomares, N. A., Reid, S. A., & Bradac, J. J. (2004). A self-categorization perspective on gender and communication: Reconciling the gender-as-culture and dominance explanations. In S. H. Ng, C. N. Candlin, & C. Y. Chiu (Eds.), *Language matters: Communication, identity, and culture* (pp. 85–109). Hong Kong: City University of Hong Kong Press.

Thomson, R. (2006). The effect of topic of discussion on gendered language in computer-mediated communication discussion. *Journal of Language and Social Psychology, 25*, 167–78.

Chapter 12

HANDOUT: MOVIE EXCERPTS*

Movie Excerpt #1 (phone conversation)

Person A: Hello.

Person B: You sleeping?

Person A: No, I was watching *Casablanca.*

Person B: Channel please.

Person A: Eleven.

Person B: Thank you, got it. Now you're telling me you will be happier with *Casablanca* actor/actress A than *Casablanca* actor/actress B?

Person A: When did I say that?

Person B: When we drove to New York.

Person A: I never said that, I would never have said that.

Person B: Alright, fine. Have it your way. (Pause) Have you been sleeping?

Person A: Why?

Person B: Because I haven't been sleeping. I really miss (name of ex). (Pause) Maybe I'm coming down with something. Last night, I was up at four in the morning watching *Leave It to Beaver* in Spanish. *Buenos dias, Señor Cleaver. ¿Donde esta Wallace y Theodore?* I'm not well.

Person A: Well, I went to bed at 7:30 last night. I haven't done that since the third grade.

Person B: That's the good thing about depression. You get your rest.

Person A: I'm not depressed.

Person B: Oh, okay. Fine.

Movie Excerpt #2 (face-to-face)

Person A: I don't understand this relationship.

Person B: What do you mean?

Person A: You enjoy being with him/her?

Person B: Yes.

Person A: You find him/her attractive?

Person B: Yes.

Person A: And you're not sleeping with him/her?

Person B: No.

Person A: What are you afraid of? You're afraid to let yourself be happy.

Movie Excerpt #3 (face-to-face)

Person A: (Person A pulls Person B aside to get his/her attention)

Person B: Do you like him/her?

Person A: Person C? Yeah, he's/she's nice. But, how do you feel about Person D?

Person B: He/she seems okay. I could really get a sense of . . .

Person A: (interrupting) You think you'd go out with him/her?

Person B: I don't know. I mean . . .

Person A: . . . because I feel very comfortable with him/her.

Person B: You want to go out with Person D?

Person A: Would it be okay with you?

Person B: Sure. Sure. I'm just worried about Person C. He's/she's very sensitive. He's/she's going through a rough period, so don't, like, reject him/her, right now, you know?

Person A: Oh no, I wouldn't. I totally understand.

*Note: Any phrases or words that either directly or indirectly identified the sex of a conversation participant have been removed from or modified in the transcript.

Let's Talk about Sex: Teaching College Students How to Navigate Sexual Communication Conversations with Relational Partners

Jessica A. Nodulman, PhD
(University of New Mexico)

Appropriate Course(s) and Level

Interpersonal communication, health communication, family communication, gender and communication, human sexuality, and other gender-studies courses. Useful for both lower- and upper-level courses.

Appropriate Class Size

Optimal minimum class size is 15 students.

Learning Goals

- To discuss the importance of engaging in sexual communication in a variety of relationships across his/her lifetime.
- To analyze how gender and sex-role stereotypes influence sexual communication.
- To develop competent sexual communication strategies.
- To construct a sexual communication negotiation script.

Estimated Time Required

1–2 class periods depending on how much time you want to leave for class discussion.

Required Materials

- Negotiating Sexual Communication Worksheets (see Handouts).

Rationale

Americans experience numerous negative consequences from having poor sexual health. Statistics on unplanned pregnancies, abortions, and sexually transmitted infections (STIs) demonstrate people have not learned how to manage their sexual health. For example, data show more than half of women in the United States will experience an unintended pregnancy by the time they are 45, with unintended pregnancy rates highest among women 18–24, minority women, cohabitating women, and women of low-income (Guttmacher Institute [GI], 2012). It is estimated that 65 million people live with an STI, and each year there are approximately 19 million new cases of STIs—half of these cases among 15–24 year olds (GI, 2009). These statistics highlight why young adults need to be taught how to have effective sexual communication conversations. Since sex education underperforms or is not addressed in many schools, many young adults have never been given the tools to navigate negotiations around sex and sexuality. The negative consequences of risky sexual activity can be life-altering; therefore, educators should provide opportunities for students to learn how to effectively communicate about sexual situations they may encounter presently or in the future.

This activity introduces students to fundamental concepts from a variety of disciplines. First, this activity can be applied to social scripting theory. Much of the way people think and talk about sex is due to the sexual scripts they adhere to. As Gagnon and Simon (1973) discussed, three levels of sexual scripts—cultural, interpersonal, and intrapsychic—provide a blueprint for how people construct and organize sexual behavior. Scripts can be beneficial as they help to set expectations and reduce uncertainty. However, since people are unaccustomed to engaging in sexual communication, oftentimes their scripts for sexual behavior and communication are developed through stereotypical gender and sex roles or inaccurate or unqualified sources such as television shows, movies, or magazine articles (Noland, 2010; Wiederman, 2005). Therefore, classes that focus on the socialization of gender and sexuality and/or media literacy can easily implement this activity as it provides an opportunity to critique stereotypical gender and sex roles and media depictions of sexual communication.

Preparing for the Activity

1. Instructors must be familiar with sexual communication negotiation strategies—sample strategies are located in the instructor copies of the handouts. Carey Noland's (2010) *Sex Talk: The Role of Communication in Intimate Relationships* is a good resource to review prior to the activity. Instructors may also want to encourage students to review the scholarship located in References and Additional Readings.
2. Discuss with students the importance of sexual communication throughout their lifetime. Explain that you understand that they may or may not be in a sexual relationship right now. Remind students you are not privileging any experience, relationship status, or sexual orientation. However, as most adults will be involved in romantic relationships that will include sexual activity, learning how to have these discussions is important.

3. Facilitate a discussion examining why sexual communication is difficult for people to discuss. Encourage students to think of multiple contexts of sexual communication such as with romantic or sexual partners, family, friends, coworkers, and/or in healthcare patient-provider contexts. Some questions to get students thinking include

   • Are women taught to have different sexual communication strategies and/or scripts than men? How do they differ?

   • Why do so many people have trouble speaking to relational partners about sex despite the ubiquitous nature of sexual messages in our lives?

   • What are the consequences when individuals do not communicate effectively about sex and sexual activity? (Remember to include multiple gender identities, sexual orientations, and relationship contexts during these discussions.)

4. Teach key components to discussing sex (partly suggested by the Iowa Initiative to Reduce Unintended Pregnancies, 2012).

   a. Develop a clear goal. For example, if a woman wants her partner to start using protection, what kind of protection does she want to use?

   b. Strategize what communication (verbal and nonverbal) strategies would work best in this situation. For example, confirming versus disconfirming communication messages, using "I" statements versus "you" statements, or making sure you share the same sexual vocabulary as your partner.

   c. Plan the context. For example, it is best to participate in sexual communication privately and in situations that are void of tension or stress.

   d. Develop a script, and practice the important elements you want to communicate to your partner. For example, if a man wants to wait longer before initiating sex in the relationship, why does he want to do this? What is important to tell his partner about why he wants to wait?

   e. Remember to ask your partner for his/her opinion and feedback, but also be firm in your goals.

Facilitating the Activity

1. Display on a computer screen or post on a classroom board the sample scenario of Jack and Samantha (see Handout A). Read the scenario to the class. Give students 10 minutes to individually work on creating a sexual communication plan for this couple following the above-mentioned steps.

2. Reconvene the class. Discuss each step of the process. Have students share their examples. As students may feel apprehensive about discussing their answers, be sure to remind them there are no "correct" answers for this activity. You can supplement this discussion by sharing the sample answers listed in Handout A.

3. Next, place students in groups of 4 to 5 and pass out the Negotiating Sexual Communication Worksheet (see Handout B) for them to work on together during class time and develop a sexual communication script. Three worksheets covering three different sexual communication contexts (intimate partner, patient-provider, and family) are provided. An instructor copy with exemplars is provided follow-

ing each sexual communication context. If you have a large class, you may have multiple groups complete the same scenarios.

4. After 15 minutes, ask a member from each context group to read their scenario aloud to the class. Ask the group to discuss what they planned for each step. If multiple groups completed the same scenario, compare and contrast their answers. Encourage the rest of the class to also give feedback.

5. After each group has discussed what they created, debrief the activity by discussing the importance of sexual communication.

Discussion Questions

- What did you find useful about the examples shared in class?
- How do sexual stereotypes and gender roles influence sexual communication?
- What can people do to alleviate the apprehension they feel over sexual communication?
- What is the significance of planning a script for sexual communication negotiation episodes *before* they occur?
- How can feeling comfortable discussing sexual communication with your relational partner empower you?

Typical Results

- Students may be unaccustomed to discussing sex and sexuality in a public environment; therefore, be prepared for some students to be quiet or nonparticipants. However, if this activity is executed with respect, students should be able to gain crucial communication skills that may benefit them throughout their lives.

Limitations and Cautionary Advice

- Since college is a time where students may be experimenting sexually or trying to understand their sexual identity, the instructor should not privilege any sexual identity or allow any other students to create a hostile environment within the classroom. Students should only be required to share opinions if they feel comfortable doing so.
- This activity should be done within a class that has a healthy classroom climate. A healthy classroom climate is one where the instructor and students share mutual respect for one another, and where there is a good rapport among instructor and students. This activity is not recommended in a class where episodes of incivility are common.
- Instructors also need to be sure they can easily discuss sexual situations and will not be embarrassed by questions or comments students might raise during or after this activity.
- In the event that some students feel uncomfortable participating in this activity, instructors may want to notify students about this activity ahead of time.

Alternative Uses

- This in-class activity could be easily supplemented with a valuable homework assignment. For homework, students create their own sexual communication negotiation script that follows the guidelines discussed during class. Encourage students to create a real or hypothetical scenario that they believe will help them now or in the future.

REFERENCES

Gagnon, J. H., & Simon, W. (1973). *Sexual conduct: The social sources of human sexuality.* Chicago: Aldine.

Guttmacher Institute. (2009). In brief: Fact sheet. Facts on sexually transmitted infections in the United States. www.guttmacher.org/pubs/FIB_STI_US.html.

Guttmacher Institute. (2012). In brief: Fact sheet. Facts on unintended pregnancy in the United States. www.guttmacher.org/pubs/FB-Unintended-Pregnancy-US.html.

Iowa Initiative to Reduce Unintended Pregnancies. (2012). How do I talk to my partner about it? www.iowainitiative.org/women_and_partners/women_and_partners.php.

Noland, C. M. (2010). *Sex talk: The role of communication in intimate relationships.* Santa Barbara, CA: Praeger.

Wiederman, M. W. (2005). The gendered nature of sexual scripts. *Family Journal, 13*(4), 496–502.

ADDITIONAL READINGS

Broaddus, M. R., Morris, H., & Bryan, A. D. (2010). "It's not what you said, it's how you said it": Perceptions of condom proposers by gender and strategy. *Sex Roles, 62*(9/10), 603–14.

Greene, K., & Faulkner, S. L. (2005). Gender, belief in the sexual double standard, and sexual talk in heterosexual dating relationships. *Sex Roles, 53*(3/4), 239–51.

Noar, S. M., Carlyle, K., & Cole, C. (2006). Why communication is crucial: Meta-analysis of the relationship between safer sexual communication and condom use. *Journal of Health Communication, 11*, 365–90.

HANDOUT A: EXAMPLE FOR
INSTRUCTOR-LED IN-CLASS ACTIVITY

Jack and Samantha have been involved romantically for over two months. Samantha is concerned because they do not always use condoms when they have sex. Samantha is nervous about discussing this with Jack; however, she knows it is too important to ignore. How can Samantha communicate this to Jack?

a. Develop a clear goal:

Sample Answer: Have Jack agree to use condoms every time they are sexually intimate.

b. What communication strategies would work best:

Sample Answer: Explanation of consequences, assertive message format, and positive nonverbal communication.

c. Plan the context:

Sample Answer: Walking home after class.

d. Develop a script:

Sample Answer: "Jack, I really care about you and this relationship. There is something that has been on my mind for a while now, and I would like to talk to you about it. I really enjoy being intimate with you, but I am concerned that we are not using condoms. I am scared of the negative consequences of unprotected sex like STIs and pregnancy."

e. Ask for feedback:

Sample Answer: "It is important to me that we use condoms every time. Is this something that you can agree to?"

HANDOUT B: NEGOTIATING
SEXUAL COMMUNICATION, CASEY AND ALEX

Directions: Read the following scenario about Casey and Alex. In a small group or individually, plan a successful sexual communication negotiation scenario.

Scenario: Casey and Alex have been dating for three weeks. Casey knows that Alex would like to be intimate sexually; however, Casey is not ready for that step in their relationship. How can Casey communicate this to Alex?

Step One: Develop a Goal

Things to consider: What is Casey's goal in this situation?

Step Two: Strategize

Things to consider: What communication (verbal and nonverbal) strategies would work best in this situation?

Step Three: Plan the Context

Things to consider: When and where should this communication take place? Why?

Step Four: Write a Script

Things to consider: Using the first person, develop what Casey could say to Alex.

Step Five: Ask for Feedback

Things to consider: What can Casey say or ask of Alex in order to gain feedback?

NEGOTIATING SEXUAL COMMUNICATION:
CASEY AND ALEX (INSTRUCTOR COPY)

Directions: Read the following scenario about Casey and Alex. In a small group or individually, plan a successful sexual communication negotiation scenario.

Scenario: Casey and Alex have been dating for three weeks. Casey knows that Alex would like to be intimate sexually; however, Casey is not ready for that step in their relationship. How can Casey communicate this to Alex?

Step One: Develop a Goal

Things to consider: What is Casey's goal in this situation?

Casey does not want to have sex with Alex yet.

Step Two: Strategize

Things to consider: What communication (verbal and nonverbal) strategies would work best in this situation?

- *Condom negotiation strategies could be implemented in this scenario.*
- *Assertive message techniques are a valuable tool to implement in sexual communication scenarios.*
- *Positive nonverbal messages will be important.*
- *Relational partners should give confirming rather than disconfirming messages.*

Step Three: Plan the Context

Things to consider: When and where should this communication take place? Why?

Casey could discuss this with Alex after school when they walk to get coffee.

Step Four: Write a Script

Things to consider: Using the first person, develop what Casey could say to Alex.

Alex, I really am enjoying spending time with you, but I am not ready to go all the way sexually. We are only freshmen in college, and it is important to me to concentrate on school and band practice right now. Even if we were to use protection, I am not comfortable moving that fast right now. I don't want to move any further than we have already.

Step Five: Ask for Feedback

Things to consider: What can Casey say or ask of Alex in order to gain feedback?

Alex, how does this sound to you? Is this something that you will be comfortable with? I need to know how you honestly feel because this is something I am committed to.

NEGOTIATING SEXUAL COMMUNICATION:
JOHN AND DR. TAYLOR

Directions: Read the following scenario about John and Dr. Taylor. In a small group or individually, plan a successful sexual communication negotiation scenario.

Scenario: John is in his late thirties. He works 60 hours a week for a very demanding sales firm. For the past few months, he has become disinterested in sex, and this has caused many fights within his marriage. John thinks he is too young to have sexual dysfunction, and he is embarrassed to talk to his doctor about his problems. However, he decides to make an appointment with his doctor, Dr. Taylor, for a physical. John hopes maybe he will get the courage to talk to him about it. How can John talk to Dr. Taylor about his concern?

    Step One: Develop a Goal

        Things to consider: What is John's goal in this situation?

    Step Two: Strategize

        Things to consider: What communication (verbal and nonverbal) strategies would work best in this situation?

    Step Three: Plan the Context

        Things to consider: When and where should this communication take place? Why?

    Step Four: Write a Script

        Things to consider: Using the first person, develop what John could say to Dr. Taylor.

    Step Five: Ask for Feedback

        Things to consider: What can John say or ask of Dr. Taylor in order to gain feedback?

NEGOTIATING SEXUAL COMMUNICATION:
JOHN AND DR. TAYLOR (INSTRUCTOR COPY)

Directions: Read the following scenario about John and Dr. Taylor. In a small group or individually, plan a successful sexual communication negotiation script.

Scenario: John is in his late thirties. He works 60 hours a week for a very demanding sales firm. For the past few months, he has become disinterested in sex and this has caused many fights within his marriage. John thinks he is too young to have sexual dysfunction, and he is embarrassed to talk to his doctor about his problems. However, he decides to make an appointment with his doctor, Dr. Taylor, for a physical. John hopes maybe he will get the courage to talk to him about it. How can John talk to Dr. Taylor about his concern?

Step One: Develop a Goal

Things to consider: What is John's goal in this situation?

John's goal is to discuss his sexual problems with Dr. Taylor.

Step Two: Strategize

Things to consider: What communication (verbal and nonverbal) strategies would work best in this situation?

- *If the patient is too embarrassed to talk to the doctor about sexual issues, s/he may pass a list of questions to his/her doctor and ask the doctor to address them.*
- *A patient may want to ask the doctor his/her questions before an examination while s/he is fully clothed.*
- *Patients should remember that there are many qualified health professionals they can talk to. For example, some patients may feel more comfortable discussing issues with a nurse instead of a doctor (Noland, 2010).*

Step Three: Plan the Context

Things to consider: When and where should this communication take place? Why?

John should tell Dr. Taylor his concerns before his exam starts.

Step Four: Write a Script

Things to consider: Using the first person, develop what John could say to Dr. Taylor.

"Dr. Taylor, there is something that I wanted to check with you about. Lately, I haven't been as interested in sex."

Step Five: Ask for Feedback

Things to consider: What can John say or ask of Dr. Taylor in order to gain feedback?

"I just wanted to talk it over with you, Dr. Taylor. What do you think?"

NEGOTIATING SEXUAL COMMUNICATION:
DOTTIE AND KIERA

Directions: Read the following scenario about Dottie and Kiera. In a small group or individually, plan a successful sexual communication negotiation scenario.

Scenario: Dottie has a 15-year-old daughter, Kiera. Dottie gave Kiera the "birds and bees" talk when Kiera was 10 but since then hasn't spoken to Kiera about sex. Kiera has been going out with her boyfriend Adan for about a month. Dottie is concerned that Kiera is having sex with Adan without using protection. Although Dottie would prefer Kiera wait until she is older to have sex, she knows this may be unrealistic. Dottie feels embarrassed and nervous about talking to Kiera about sex. Dottie doesn't want Kiera to think she is "giving her permission" to have sex, but she also feels she must discuss with her daughter the importance of using protection. How can Dottie talk to her daughter about using protection during sex?

Step One: Develop a Goal

Things to consider: What is Dottie's goal in this situation?

Step Two: Strategize

Things to consider: What communication (verbal and nonverbal) strategies would work best in this situation?

Step Three: Plan the Context

Things to consider: When and where should this communication take place? Why?

Step Four: Write a Script

Things to consider: Using the first person, develop what Dottie could say to Kiera.

Step Five: Ask for Feedback

Things to consider: What can Dottie say or ask of Kiera in order to gain feedback from her?

NEGOTIATING SEXUAL COMMUNICATION:
DOTTIE AND KIERA (INSTRUCTOR COPY)

Directions: Read the following scenario about Dottie and Kiera. In a small group or individually, plan a successful sexual communication negotiation scenario.

Scenario: Dottie has a 15-year-old daughter, Kiera. Dottie gave Kiera the "birds and bees" talk when Kiera was 10 but since then hasn't spoken to Kiera about sex. Kiera has been going out with her boyfriend Adan for about a month. Dottie is concerned that Kiera is having sex with Adan without using protection. Although Dottie would prefer Kiera wait until she is older to have sex, she knows this may be unrealistic. Dottie feels embarrassed and nervous to talk to Kiera about sex. Dottie doesn't want Kiera to think she is "giving her permission" to have sex, but she also feels she must discuss with her daughter the importance of using protection. How can Dottie talk to her daughter about using protection during sex?

Step One: Develop a Goal

Things to consider: What is Dottie's goal in this situation?

Dottie's goal is to talk to her daughter about the importance of using protection during sex.

Step Two: Strategize

Things to consider: What communication (verbal and nonverbal) strategies would work best in this situation?

- *Parents must be familiar with the language their children use to discuss sex—without shared meaning there may not be a clear understanding.*
- *Expectations parents have about their children's sexual behavior should be openly and honestly discussed.*
- *Parents should avoid using controlling language; instead, they should help teens make autonomous decisions.*
- *Parents should remind their children that they want them to come to them when they want to discuss sex. If that is not possible or too uncomfortable for the parties, parents can recommend their children talk to a third party, such as a doctor or health professional, about sexual matters* (Noland, 2010).

Step Three: Plan the Context

Things to consider: When and where should this communication take place? Why?

At home while mother and daughter are preparing dinner.

Step Four: Write a Script

Things to consider: Using the first person, develop what Dottie could say to Kiera.

Kiera, I want to talk about you and Adan. I know your relationship has gotten pretty serious, and I would like to talk to you about being intimate with him. You know that I expect that you will not be sexually active until you are older. Being sexually active requires a lot of responsibility. When you are sexually active, you have to always think about the negative consequences that could happen like getting pregnant or getting an STI but also some of the emotional tolls that can come from having sex before you are ready. However, I also know you might feel you are ready to have sex or will be ready soon. I want you to be protected from those negative consequences we discussed, Kiera. So, that is why today I want to talk to you about the importance of using protection.

Step Five: Ask for Feedback

Things to consider: What can Dottie say or ask of Kiera in order to gain feedback from her?

Kiera, I know this is a tough thing to talk about. I love you so much, and I want to protect you. What can I do to make sure when you are ready to have sex, you always use protection?

IV

LITERATURE

Encouraging Reader Identification with LGBT Literary Characters through Role-Play

David Hennessee, PhD
(California Polytechnic State University, San Luis Obispo)

Appropriate Course(s) and Level

Gender studies, women's studies, LGBT studies, and English classes, across all levels.

Appropriate Class Size

Up to 50 students, in a classroom large enough for students to move around freely.

Learning Goals

- To review, in a collaborative, interactive way, characters and plot in preparation for more in-depth analysis of LGBT fiction.
- To help students relate to and connect with the experiences of LGBT individuals, as represented in fictional narratives.
- To help break down an us/them dichotomy that might exist in a class where LGBT texts are being taught to heterosexual students and closeted students.
- To encourage students to talk openly about LGBT experiences and issues, as represented in fictional narratives, without students having to self-identify as LGBT or heterosexual.
- To build a safe, accepting classroom community where frank discussion of LGBT issues can occur.

Estimated Time Required

A single class.

Required Materials

- Adhesive nametags.
- An LGBT-themed novel with a variety of characters (see Readings for suggestions).

Rationale

Because courses dealing with LGBT texts and topics are becoming more commonplace in college curricula, students who may have limited prior knowledge of LGBT issues are being asked to engage with, discuss, and write critically about them. Most students for LGBT-themed courses self select into them, with an above-average degree of interest in and understanding of the subject matter. Even so, texts dealing with LGBT issues can pose special challenges for students.

Every literature class—LGBT-themed or not—that includes a reading of a work of realist fiction requires a "willing suspension of disbelief." Fully experiencing such fiction requires a reader to imagine the plot really could have happened and the characters could be real, connecting emotionally with characters who are both like and unlike them. Readers with limited knowledge of LGBT experiences and issues may have difficulty imagining LGBT characters. They may have trouble connecting to the specific experiences being narrated, either through limited knowledge or lingering homophobic attitudes. In particular, students who are cisgendered (that is, those whose gender assignments at birth, their sense of gender identity, and their bodies all line up into either male or female categories) may have difficulty relating to what it would be like to feel out of place in the body one was born into. At worst, students may express open hostility to and invalidation of transgender identity.

To deal with these problems, I developed this activity for the first day of discussing Leslie Feinberg's (2003) novel *Stone Butch Blues*. This extraordinary novel compels with its emotional intensity and gritty, realistic depictions of coming-of-age in the butch/femme culture of the 1950s and 1960s. The narrator Jess encounters a broad range of other characters: butches, femmes, drag queens, straight men and women, FtMs (female-to-male transgender/transsexual), and MtFs (male-to-female transgender/transsexual). This variety offers a widely representative panorama of lesbian and trans experience of its time. However, this activity would be of value in teaching any number of LGBT texts, especially those with a wide variety of characters and intricate plots, or whose plotlines might be difficult for some students to relate to because it is outside their realm of experience or represents more explicit aspects of LGBT lives.

How this activity encourages students to identify with LGBT experiences is through role-playing as characters in a novel. Additionally, students are invited to discuss LGBT issues and experiences in very detailed ways without being required to out themselves in the classroom.

Preparing for the Activity

1. For this activity, it is suggested you have students read or view material on gender variance, such as Bornstein's (1995) *Gender Outlaw.*

2. Students should have read the required text in its entirety. A reading-check quiz will encourage them to do so. It is advisable to plan a reading quiz, as the activity is most successful when students have completed the reading.
3. Prepare nametags with several of the characters' names written on them.

Facilitating the Activity

1. Explain the goals of the activity are to review characters and plot and to help students to relate to and figure out which character they "are."
2. Attach the prepared nametags to the back or forehead of approximately half of the students.
3. Instruct students that they can ask only "Yes/No" questions about their character. Encourage them to move around the class, asking different groups of peers their questions. They are only allowed to ask the same person three questions before moving on to someone new (this encourages students to interact with a variety of their peers).
4. Once they figure out who they "are," they are to put their nametag in its usual place on their chests.
5. When everyone is finished, each person should introduce him/herself as their character, using first-person pronouns. Instruct them to describe their character's main traits and contributions to the plot, especially as they interact with the novel's protagonist and add to the novel's main themes.
6. The instructor should make a list of character names on the board, grouped into different categories as appropriate. For example, in *Stone Butch Blues*, the characters break down into "butches," "femmes," "straight men," "straight women," and "drag queens." You can then begin further exploring plot and character information.
7. Then, process the experience with the Discussion Questions.

Discussion Questions

- For those of you with nametags, how did you feel trying to figure out who you were?
  - What questions were least helpful to use?
  - What types of assumptions did you jump to when receiving answers?
  - How did you feel once you discovered who you were?
- For those of you without nametags, what questions were easier to answer? Which were more difficult? Why?
- How, if at all, do your experiences in discovering the various characters relate to how we construct our gender and sexual identities?

Typical Results

- Usually, it takes students about 20 minutes to figure out who they "are," leaving the bulk of class time for discussion of the characters and the students' experiences.

- Students move around, interacting with other students, laughing and smiling. They enjoy the game aspect of the exercise and the chance to break from more traditional class discussions and activities.
- Often, students display some embarrassment as they introduce who they "are" in the novel (for example, a gender-normative man describing himself as a femme lesbian). This discomfort usually dissipates as the students grow more comfortable discussing the traits and experiences of their characters.

Limitations and Cautionary Advice

- It is important that students with nametags have completed the reading. Suggest to the class (in a nonjudgmental tone) only students who have done so should take a nametag.
- In my classes, I have never encountered students' resisting this activity or having strongly negative emotional reactions to it. We do the activity late in the term when the students are comfortable talking about LGBT texts. To avoid possible resistance and negative reactions, framing the activity as simply a way to review plot and characters will set the activity up as having a practical value.
- Suggesting to students up front it is hoped they will relate to the characters can prompt resistance to doing so. It is better to let identification happen naturally.

Alternative Uses

- This activity could also be done by distributing nametags to everyone in the class. Students may end up with duplicate characters, but this may help the students explore how their experiences may be different even with the same character.
- As previously discussed, this activity would work for any LGBT narrative fiction with a variety of characters (see Readings).

READINGS

Allison, D. (1993). *Bastard out of Carolina*. New York: Plume.

Bechdel, A. (2007). *Fun home*. Boston: Houghton Mifflin.

Bornstein, K. (1995). *Gender outlaw*. New York: Routledge.

Brown, R. M. (1983). *Rubyfruit jungle*. New York: Bantam.

Feinberg, L. (2003). *Stone butch blues*. New York: Alyson Books.

Fierstein, R. K. (Producer), & Bogart, P. (Director). (1988). *Torch song trilogy*. United States: New Line Cinema.

Forster, E. M. (1971). *Maurice*. New York: Norton.

Holleran, A. (1986). *Dancer from the dance*. New York: Penguin.

Livingstone, J. (Producer & Director). (1991). *Paris is burning*. United States: Miramax.

Rechy, J. (1963). *City of night*. New York: Grove Press.

15

Designing Utopia: Teaching Gender through the Creation of "Hisland"

Christin L. Munsch, PhD
(Stanford University)

Appropriate Course(s) and Level

Introductory and advanced courses in sociology, literature, women's/gender studies, philosophy, government, and public policy.

Appropriate Class Size

Up to 35 students, in classrooms with enough space to allow for small-group work. Activity can be modified for use in large classes (see Alternative Uses).

Learning Goals

- To identify cultural expectations and stereotypes of men and women.
- To understand men and women are not inherently all that different from one another, but rather, gender is a social construction that varies across time and space.
- To explore the ways in which institutions are gendered.

Estimated Time Required

50–90 minutes depending on the discussion that ensues.

Required Materials

- Hisland Handout (see below).
- Charlotte Perkins Gilman's novel *Herland* or another utopian work (optional).

Rationale

Gender has now secured a legitimate (albeit marginalized) status within the academy, and some facet of gender or feminism can be found in the majority of syllabi within the humanities and social sciences. For example, contemporary introductory sociology textbooks contain more pictures of women (Clarke & Nunes, 2008) and more text devoted to topics specifically relevant to women (Manza & Van Schyndel, 2000) than ever before. Although gender research and theory is extensive and complex, instructors tend to highlight socialization processes while ignoring some of the most fundamental contributions to the study of gender (Ferree & Hall, 1996; Manza & Van Schyndel, 2000).

This limited focus is problematic for several reasons. First, socialization narratives emphasize difference, not similarity. Yet men and women are overwhelmingly similar. According to the gender similarities hypothesis, men and women are remarkably similar, yet gender differences are overemphasized (Hyde, 2005). This overemphasis leads to exaggerated beliefs about men and women and the incompatibility of the two (Epstein, 1988).

Second, an emphasis on socialization hinders students' understanding of gender as a social construction. Gender theorists emphasize the social construction of gender and suggest gender and gender differences between men and women are actually created (and re-created) by individuals within a particular culture or society (Connell, 2005; Kessler, 1990; Kimmel, 2004; Lorber, 1994; West & Zimmerman, 1987). In other words, nothing (or very little) is inherent in these constructions. The socialization approach suggests attributes associated with gender are relatively fixed, particularly by adulthood (Risman, 1999). In so doing, this interpretation ignores the changing nature of gender over time and the many ways people challenge gender stereotypes and mold and shape gender throughout their lives.

Third, the sex-role socialization approach ignores macro-level social processes. Socialization accounts are individual-level explanations, meaning they rely on factors that exist within—as opposed to outside of—individuals (Lopata & Thorne, 1978). For example, a socialization account of occupational segregation suggests boys are socialized to be assertive and girls are socialized to be nurturing. Thus, men choose certain careers (e.g., management) while women choose others (e.g., nursing). Although this may be true, this account fails to acknowledge the effect of structural arrangements on individuals (Ferree & Hall, 1996). For example, organizational components such as workplace norms, job descriptions, and performance expectations are not gender neutral. Rather, they steer men and women into different occupations (Acker, 1990; Britton, 2000; Dellinger, 2004; Martin, 2003; Pierce, 1995).

Fourth, socialization accounts encourage victim-blaming (Ferree & Hall, 1996). Because of their individual-level focus, they suggest problems and solutions lie within—as opposed to outside of—individuals. For example, if differential career outcomes are the result of men's assertiveness and women's passivity, it follows that if women were more assertive there would be more gender parity within occupations. This perspective makes individual women responsible for the problem, and the solution, hiding the need for institutional change (Rhode, 1997).

This activity helps students move away from overstressed socialization accounts toward more complex explanations for gender difference and inequality. Namely, students are asked to outline an all-male, utopian society. The key to the exercise is it allows students to think about the construction of social institutions in the absence of gender. Masculinity and femininity exist in relation to—and in opposition to—one another. Thus, without women (or without men), there can be no characteristics associated with women (or men). In other words, the students create genderless societies. The creation of a genderless society helps students recognize the overwhelming similarities between men and women, understand gender differences as largely constructed, and begin to think about the ways in which cultural ideas about gender permeate social institutions. The activity also helps students identify gender stereotypes.

Typically, I have students read Charlotte Perkins Gilman's *Herland* (1915; 1992), but it is not required to conduct the activity. The story follows the adventures of three men (Terry, Jeff, and Van) who discover Herland, a society that consists entirely of women. Prior to their discovery, the three men imagine what they might find in an all-female society. Terry views women as objects and anticipates seducing the inhabitants and becoming king; Jeff views women idealistically, believing them to be delicate, kind, and in need of chivalrous attention; Van believes men and women are innately different and simply asserts Herland will differ greatly from both patriarchal and all-male societies. All three men are surprised when they meet the women of Herland. The women are neither sexually available nor conventionally attractive. They possess many positive, stereotypically masculine attributes like intelligence, courage, and strength. And they have developed sophisticated social institutions and conventions to educate the young, care for the elderly, and rehabilitate criminals. The story follows the three men during their stay in Herland; however, like most utopian works, the story predominantly serves to transition between extended descriptions of the set-up and regulation of Herland's social structure. In this way, another utopian work—or a more general introduction to utopian writing—would suffice to prepare students for the activity.

Preparing for the Activity

1. It is helpful to introduce students to the concept of utopia and utopian literature.
2. If students are reading a utopian work, ask students to complete the reading prior to class. If you do not plan on assigning a utopian literature piece, the Hisland Handout (see Handout) provides a brief summary of *Herland* which should provide sufficient background information to guide students in this activity.
3. Instructors may prepare an introductory lecture in order to place Charlotte Perkins Gilman and her work in historical context (optional).
4. Make one copy of the Hisland Handout for each student.

Facilitating the Activity

1. Divide the class into small working groups. I suggest no more than 4 students per group in order to involve all students and move through the questions expeditiously.
2. Distribute the Hisland Handout and briefly introduce the task at hand. Answer any questions.

3. Allow groups to work collaboratively in the creation of a hypothetical utopian community named "Hisland" by answering the questions on the Hisland Handout.

4. Circulate among groups to monitor progress. Spend time with each group, probing students to think deeply, particularly about the design of Hisland's institutions.

5. After the groups appear to have wrapped up their discussions, ask groups to report their findings to the class. Have each group report their answers to one question before moving to the next. This method provides an opportunity for the instructor to ask insightful questions that stress the activity objectives.

Discussion Questions

- Describe for me your women visitors.
- What do you think the women anticipated seeing in Hisland?
- What overlap existed between your expectations and other groups (or other group members' expectations)? Did you draw on certain archetypes to create the characters? What were these?
- Where do you think these conceptions came from? How representative are these archetypes of actual people?
- How, if at all, do the Hisland men represent some heightened form of masculinity?
- What do you think would have happened if the interaction you described (the women's reaction to the men dancing, baking, or sewing; the men's reaction to the women's reaction) had taken place in contemporary, Western society?
- How do the men of Hisland balance work and family responsibilities?
- How does contemporary Western society characterize men's and women's task?
- How, if at all, do you think we could promote a genderless society?

Typical Results

- This activity facilitates an understanding of gender stereotypes. In response to the first question on the Handout, multiple groups create a "feminist" and/or "masculine" female character. My students have referred to such characters as "the feminist" "the angry feminist," "the feminazi," "the masculine one," and the "butch lesbian." Students usually create a hyper-feminine character as well. My students have referred to this character as "Barbie," "the bitch," and the one who "uses her feminine wiles to get what she wants." Students have also created tropes such as "the slut," "the mother," and "the girl next door." I use this time to help students identify cultural stereotypes about women and identify them as such.

- Similarly, assumptions about what the three women anticipate prior to their arrival in Hisland (question 2 in the Handout) shed light on masculine stereotypes. My students have stated that the women expect to find drunken slobs, sex-starved Neanderthals, excessively violent military men, and chivalrous gentlemen. Although students often find these depictions humorous, I ask students to elaborate upon these archetypes and to think about where these stereotypes come from and how representative they are of actual people. This enables students to recognize stereotypes are often inaccurate and overly hostile.

- This activity helps students understand that men and women are not vastly and inherently different. Rather, it aids in a more constructionist understanding of gender. When students describe the men of Hisland (question 3 in Handout), inevitably they describe men who look and act somewhat androgynously, or they describe tremendous variation among the men with some taking on "feminine" characteristics and others taking on "masculine" characteristics. Rarely do the men of Hisland represent some heightened form of masculinity, particularly if the students have read *Herland*. This is because a society devoid of feminine-typed tasks is unlikely to thrive. The same tasks that we currently associate with femininity (e.g., baking, sewing) will also need done in Hisland, and the same things that humans think are fun in heterosexual groups (e.g., dancing), the men of Hisland will likely find fun in homogenous groups. This discussion allows students to see, in the absence of a binary system, both men and women can perform the same tasks, enjoy the same activities, and even look somewhat similar. Students typically state that three women visitors accustomed to a binary system would be surprised to find a cohesive group of men doing feminine-typed tasks (question 4 in Handout). Students typically envision the three women staring at, making fun of, or laughing at the dancing men. Ultimately, however, they can see how the men of Hisland might transform the women's conceptions of "appropriate" behavior. To push students further, I ask them how the interaction they described would differ if it took place in contemporary, Western society, as opposed to in Hisland. Under different circumstances, they can see how men might hide such activities and react to the women's judgment with embarrassment, shame, or anger. This discussion allows students to see how behaviors become constructed as masculine or feminine and how individuals are held accountable when they engage in behavior deemed "inappropriate" for their gender—one of the most powerful ways social constructions of gender get reproduced.
- Another way to demonstrate the social construction of gender is to ask the students how the men of Hisland react to the women visitors (question 5 in Handout). Students typically describe reactions that range from fear to disinterest. Again, the class finds this funny; however, students can easily see why the men might be afraid. Femininity has been constructed as weak and unimposing. Masculinity has been constructed as strong and fearless. Without these constructions, the women aren't weak. Rather, they are intruders. I use this opportunity to give historical examples of masculinity construction. For example, I point out that in upper-class seventeenth-century France, men wore high-heeled patent leather shoes, red velvet jackets, frilly white shirts and makeup (Kimmel & Messner, 1998).
- For many students, the activity helps them understand how cultural beliefs about gender are built into institutions and organizations. Students usually understand that institutional structures affect individuals; however, they are less likely to understand how institutions themselves are gendered. To facilitate this conversation, I have students report who performs the childcare in Hisland and how it is compensated (question 6 in the Handout). I then follow up by questioning how the men of Hisland balance work and family responsibilities like childcare. Can these men have children and a job? How? Is this arrangement particularly time-consuming? This line of questions typically yields one of two responses. Some report that work

doesn't look like it does in the United States. Rather, the inhabitants of Hisland work several hours a day and have plenty of time for other activities. This is the perfect opportunity to point out workplaces share organizational norms, ideologies, and policies based on the "ideal worker" (Williams, 2000). The ideal worker is someone who works at least 40 hours a week, year round, and is committed, above all else, to the corporation. Long hours and near complete devotion is easier for men than it is for women given that women are expected to perform the majority of the childcare and household duties within the family. This line of inquiry reveals how assumptions about masculinity and femininity have shaped the way in which two institutions—the modern industry and the family—are configured and how these configurations differentially affect men and women. Question 8 on the Handout allows students to think about what can be done about such inequalities. The question asks students to entertain the idea of *altering institutions*, instead of individuals, to combat inequality. In response to the question, one student noted, "The kids [of Hisland] need taken care of, and this can't interfere with people's jobs. But if a guy has a kid, it doesn't mean he has to be the one taking care of it all the time. Some sort of universal childcare system would be helpful." The student could have pointed to solutions that rely on innovative individuals (e.g., "The men need to figure out how to balance their time better"), but instead, the student pointed to an institutional-level solution, universal childcare, and suggested that caretakers in this system be well compensated.

Limitations and Cautionary Advice

1. Because the students are creating an entire society, be prepared for students to bring up a number of tangentially related topics. On the one hand, tangents might foster creativity and serve to introduce important ideas and concepts; however, on the other hand, the activity requires some occasional steering of conversation to keep the discussion on topic.

2. Some students will be inclined to rely heavily on technological innovations that have yet to be developed (e.g., "Robots do all the housework") in order to avoid having to think deeply about the social construction of institutions. Do not allow students to take this route. Stress the importance of coming up with plausible, workable solutions as opposed to a fantasy unrestricted by reality.

3. The most significant limitation of this activity is that it rarely gives rise to interlocking systems of oppression. Some women occupy positions of higher status by virtue of their race, class, or sexuality; yet issues of race, ethnicity, and class are notably absent in *Herland* and the constructed modern-day Hislands. I specifically address this omission by asking students if they thought about race or not. The majority of students have not. Why? What assumptions did they make? In the same way that we saw how institutions appear gender-neutral but actually are heavily gendered, might institutions also be racialized? How? How might gender and race work together to the advantage of some individuals and the disadvantage of others?

Alternative Uses

- Instructors may wish to make several adaptations, particularly instructors of large classes. For example, instructors may continue the discussion on a second day to allow more groups to share, or instructors can assign the activity (or a portion of the activity) to be completed outside of class.
- Instead of answering the Handout questions, students can write a short story based on the prompts and address the answers to the questions throughout their narrative, or they can write a script and act out interactions within their constructed utopia.
- Although I have my students read *Herland*, it is not necessary to require any reading. If the instructor does wish to combine the activity with course reading, any utopian or dystopian work will suffice. Like Gilman's *Herland*, such texts criticize political and social arrangements and suggest alternatives. As a result, exposure to such works will similarly prime students to think about the way individuals shape social institutions and vice versa. Students could read the considerably shorter novel after which the genre was named, Sir Thomas More's (1516/1995) work *Utopia,* or one of the more popular dystopian novels like Aldous Huxley's (1932) *Brave New World* or George Orwell's (1949/1981) *Nineteen Eighty-Four*. Alternatively, some science fiction novels—like Ursula K. Le Guin's (1969) *The Left Hand of Darkness* or Margaret Atwood's (1985) *The Handmaid's Tale*—would serve a similar purpose.

REFERENCES

Acker, J. (1990). Hierarchies, jobs, bodies: A theory of gendered organizations. *Gender & Society, 4*(2), 139–58.

Atwood, M. (1985). *The handmaid's tale.* Toronto: McClelland & Stewart.

Britton, D. M. (2000). The epistemology of the gendered organization. *Gender & Society, 14*(3), 418–34.

Clarke, R., & Nunes, A. (2008). The face of society: Gender and race in introductory sociology books revisited. *Teaching Sociology, 36*(3), 227–39.

Connell, R. W. (2005). *Masculinities. Revised edition.* Berkeley: University of California.

Dellinger, K. (2004). Masculinities in "safe" and "embattled" organizations: Accounting for pornographic and feminist magazines. *Gender & Society, 18*(5), 545–65.

Epstein, C. F. (1988). *Deceptive distinctions: Sex, gender and the social order.* New Haven, CT: Yale University Press.

Ferree, M. M., & Hall, E. J. (1996). Rethinking stratification from a feminist perspective: Gender, race, and class in mainstream textbooks. *American Sociological Review, 61*(6), 929–50.

Gilman, C. P. (1915/1992). *Herland and selected stories by Charlotte Perkins Gilman.* New York: Signet Classic. (Original work published 1915).

Huxley, A. (1932). *Brave new world.* London: Chatto & Windus.

Hyde, J. S. (2005). The gender similarities hypothesis. *American Psychologist, 60*(6), 581–92.

Kessler, S. J. (1990). The medical construction of gender: Case management of intersexed infants. *Signs: Journal of Women in Culture and Society, 16*(1), 3–26.

Kimmel, M. S. (2004). Spanning the world: Cross-cultural construction of gender. In *The gendered society* (2nd ed.) (pp. 52–71). New York: Oxford University Press.

Kimmel, M. S., & Messner, M. A. (1998). Introduction. In M. S. Kimmel & M. A. Messner (Eds.), *Men's lives* (4th ed.) (pp. xii–xxii). Boston: Allyn & Bacon.

Le Guin, U. K. (1969). *The left hand of darkness.* New York: Walker.

Lopata, H. Z., & Thorne. B. (1978). On the term "sex roles." *Signs: Journal of Women in Culture and Society, 3*(3), 718–21.

Lorber, J. (1994). *Paradoxes of gender.* New Haven, CT: Yale University Press.

Manza, J., & Van Schyndel, D. (2000). Still the missing feminist revolution? Inequalities of race, class, and gender in introductory sociology textbooks. *American Sociological Review, 65*(3), 468–75.

Martin, P. Y. (2003). "Said and done" vs. "saying and doing": Gendering practices, practicing gender at work. *Gender & Society, 17*(3), 342–66.

More, T. (1516/1995). *Utopia: Latin text and English translation.* (G. M. Logan, R. M. Adamas, & C. H. Miller, Trans.). Cambridge: Cambridge University Press. (Original work published 1516).

Orwell, G. (1949/1981). *Nineteen eighty-four.* New York: New American Library, 1981. (Original work published 1949).

Pierce, J. L. (1995). *Gender trials: Emotional lives in contemporary law firms.* Berkeley: University of California Press.

Rhode, D. (1997). "The 'no problem' problem" in *Speaking of sex: The denial of gender inequality* (pp. 1–20). London: Cambridge University Press.

Risman, B. J. (1999). *Gender vertigo: American families in transition.* New Haven, CT: Yale University Press.

West, C., & Zimmerman, D. (1987). Doing gender. *Gender & Society, 1*(2), 125–51.

Williams, J. (2000). *Unbending gender: Why family and work conflict and what to do about it.* New York: Oxford University Press.

HANDOUT: CONSTRUCTING HISLAND

In 1915, Charlotte Perkins Gilman penned the utopian novel *Herland* about an isolated society comprised entirely of women. The women are able to reproduce without men, and their offspring are all female. The story is told from the perspective of Van, who, along with two friends (Terry and Jeff), sets out to find the rumored society. Before arriving, the men speculate about what a society of women would be like based on their beliefs about women in the early nineteenth century. For example, Jeff regards the women as worthy of (and in need of) protection whereas Terry regards them as potential sex partners with which he can have his way. Upon arrival, the men are seized and held captive; yet they are given clean clothes, food, and tutoring to learn the language. The women are strong, agile, brave, intelligent, and pragmatic, as well as patient and kind. They have well-made, yet aesthetic, homes and buildings. They have very little crime yet have an effective justice system in place to deal with delinquents. They have no conception of marriage or what it means to be a wife.

For this assignment, suppose that you are charged with writing a modern-day novel/play/sitcom titled *Hisland.* The premise of your novel/play/sitcom is a society comprised of only men, the men are able to reproduce without women, and their offspring are all male. Three women discover the land and the men who live there. In your small groups, answer the following questions.

1. Describe the three women visitors. What personality characteristics do each of these women have?
2. Upon hearing about *Hisland,* what do the three women visitors expect to find? Describe their expectations about *Hisland* and their assumptions regarding the men who live there.
3. What do the women actually find? Describe the men of Hisland. What do they look like and how do they act? In what ways are the men largely similar? In what ways is there variation?
4. Describe the women's reaction the first time they see men dancing, baking, or sewing. What do they say or do? How do the men react to this reaction?
5. How do the Hisland men react to the women visitors? With heterosexual anticipation? Fear?
6. Describe in detail how children are cared for in this society. Who performs the childcare in Hisland? How are childcare providers compensated?
7. Within any society, some things need to get accomplished for survival. Below is a list of occupations and tasks that fulfill certain societal needs. Arrange the items below in order from the most important to the least important for the survival of Hisland.

clergy
emergency responders—police,
    firefighters
caring for the sick or elderly
teachers
waste removal
road construction, paving
textile knitting and weaving

construction
day care attendants
doctors
farming
lawyers, judges
maids and housekeeping
artists, musicians

8. Pick one of the above occupations or tasks. Outline how your utopian society ensures the need associated with the task gets met. For example, if you choose "construction," how does your society make sure that new buildings get constructed and old buildings get repaired? Try to describe a way in which the need can be met—without relying on technological innovation that has yet to be developed—that differs from the way in which we, in contemporary Western society, organize this task.

16

The Big Bad Wolf Carries a Purse: Restorying Gender Roles in Popular Children's Stories

Stacy Tye-Williams, PhD
(Iowa State University)

Appropriate Course(s) and Level

Appropriate for introductory and advanced courses in women's and gender studies, cultural studies, and communication.

Appropriate Class Size

Up to 35 students. The classroom needs to be able to accommodate small-group work.

Learning Goals

- To examine the impact of gender roles on men and women.
- To explore taking a feminist perspective.
- To encourage students to think creatively about gender and feminism.
- To critically reflect upon the role of literature and media in constructing gender-role expectations.

Estimated Time Required

50 to 120 minutes. If this activity is to be completed in 50 minutes, provide students with a short story and ask them to rewrite it in 20 minutes. Discuss their stories and cover discussion questions with the 30 minutes of class time remaining. This activity could be extended over multiple class periods. For example, allow students to rewrite a story during one 50-minute class period. Discuss their stories and synthesis questions during the next class period.

Required Materials

- Edited volume of classic children's short stories for you or your students to select a story from or allow students to bring in their favorite children's story to rewrite. Children's stories can easily be found both online and through the local library. There are also several suggestions included under Additional Readings.
- Notebooks and writing utensils.

Rationale

The shaping of notions about what it means to be a man or a woman in society begins at a very young age. Something as seemingly benign as a children's story has profound influences on perceptions of what it means to perform appropriate gender roles for men and women. However, the influences that shape understandings of what is masculine and what is feminine often go unnoticed. This activity aids students in developing a better understanding of how gender is socially constructed through the stories that get told about boys and girls and women and men. It also allows for greater awareness of how entrenched we become in "doing gender" appropriately that it becomes difficult to develop alternatives to traditional notions of the roles men and women take in society along with the stereotypes which often constrain both men and women (West & Zimmerman, 1987).

Women are typically thought to be nurturing, caring, emotional, and weak; whereas men are stereotyped as being rational and strong (Wood, 2011). These stereotypes limit women and men by placing them in binary categories. If a woman displays assertiveness, she is not doing gender properly and thus might be sanctioned by statements about not demonstrating ladylike behavior. Similarly, if a man shares his feelings or emotions, he may be deemed feminine. These stereotypes can be easily found in children's literature. For example, Little Red Riding Hood is saved from the big, bad wolf by strong, woodcutters who are all men. Fair Snow White is rescued from her slumber by a brave prince. Cinderella is also rescued by a handsome prince. Time and time again, women in children's stories are rescued by men. When we are read these stories as young children, we begin to internalize appropriate roles for women and men. Storytelling is a powerful force in the formation of societal norms such as gender roles. According to Fisher (1987), we make sense of the world through telling stories. Ultimately, a primary way we communicate how to be and behave in society is through the telling of stories. These stories and many others like them portray women as victims who must be saved by men. It is important to examine and question how these stories contribute to the empowerment and disempowerment of both women and men. Additionally, the role of stories in reflecting a world where men and women hold equal roles in society needs to be examined.

At the heart of feminism is a desire for equality between women and men (Wood, 2011). However, children's stories oftentimes place women and men in limiting roles. A useful theory to examine the impact of communication with others on identifying appropriate gender roles is cognitive development theory (Bussey & Bandura, 1999; Martin, Ruble, & Szkrybalo, 2002) which posits children learn appropriate gender roles through their interactions with others. According to cognitive development theory, this is an active process whereby children seek out others to emulate in order to behave in ways appropriate for their gender. Some interactions very specifically highlight how boys and girls should act. For example, getting dirty is not ladylike and boys don't cry. As was discussed earlier, the stories that are read to girls and boys reinforce societal norms for how boys and girls should act. Ultimately, cognitive development theory is a useful way to examine the impact of early experiences such as being read children's stories on establishing gender roles.

Children's stories also portray relationships in hetero-normative ways. The beautiful (female) princess is rescued by the handsome (male) prince, and then they marry and live happily ever after. Same-sex relationships are left out of most children's literature (for exceptions see de Haan & Nijland, 2000). Queer performative theory is a useful theoretical approach to utilize when working to break out of binary views of gender and sexuality (Sloop, 2006). The essence of queer performative theory is to think more fluidly about identity. People are not just women or men or gay or straight. Focusing only on these aspects of identity leaves out a myriad of other layers that ultimately define who we are. Additionally, queer performative theory posits that gender is a performance. Ultimately, we "do" gender by acting in ways that are in line with our biological sex.

Students often find it difficult to imagine the world in new and different ways, especially ones that may challenge long-held beliefs. This activity gives them an opportunity to break out of these traditional storylines to rewrite the script. Students are challenged to imagine a world in which women and men play different roles in the story. This activity allows them a safe space to examine and explore revised gender roles.

Preparing for the Activity

1. Discuss traditional gender roles of men and women along with ways we come to understand appropriate ways to perform gender. As you finish this discussion, ask students to think about the constraints these perceptions have for women and men and have them imagine what it would be like if the norms for gender roles were transformed. For example, how could men and women be framed as equal partners working together?
2. You may either give students a list of stories to select a story from or assign them a story to read prior to coming to class the day of the activity. It is useful to provide students with a copy of the story to aid them in the activity. Stories that work well include but certainly are not limited to "Little Red Riding Hood," "Snow White," "Sleeping Beauty," and "Cinderella."

Facilitating the Activity

1. Break students into small groups of 4–5 students.
2. Have students identify the traditional gender norms for men and women that are depicted within their story. Then instruct students to rewrite their assigned story, paying careful attention to thinking beyond traditional gender roles. You might consider brainstorming with students what it would mean to step outside of traditional roles and place characters in a collaborative process of overcoming obstacles. Ask students to rewrite the entire story. Tell them to be creative

as they rewrite the story. Additionally, they can change anything about the story they want—characters, plot, scene, everything in the story can be altered. Give students guidance; however, refrain from telling them exactly how to rewrite the story. Part of the learning opportunity of this activity is getting students to think differently about gender roles.

3. If you allotted 50 minutes to this activity, give students about 20 minutes to rewrite their story. If you have more time, give them extra time.
4. Have each group share an abridged version of their new story with the rest of the class.
5. Engage the students in a discussion of the activity.

Discussion Questions

- How do children's stories we are told and the media we encounter as children shape our notions of how to behave in gender appropriate ways?
- What did you find challenging about completing this activity?
- What changes would you make to your classmates' stories, if any?
- Did any of you just flip flop the roles of men and women in your stories? How does this reflect a feminist perspective, if at all?
- One way to reflect a feminist perspective to storytelling would be to portray men and women working together to overcome obstacles. Discuss how you incorporated collaboration in your stories. If you did not focus on collaboration, how might you change it to portray men and women working together collaboratively?
- What impact do you think restorying children's literature might have on perceptions of gender/sexuality?
- You rewrote fictional stories. Do you think we are capable of changing notions of the roles men and women should play in everyday life? Why or why not? How, if at all, could these notions begin to be changed?

Typical Results

- Students often find it difficult to envision men and women enacting different roles. One approach students often use is to merely take women and replace them with men in the story and vice versa. Explain that while it does typically put women in more independent roles, it doesn't fully represent a feminist perspective of equality for everyone as the limiting position the woman played in the original story becomes limiting for the man. Ask students to think of how all characters can collaborate together to overcome obstacles rather than thinking in terms of the need for one gender to save the other.
- Ultimately students find this activity useful because it helps them think in more creative ways about the roles of men and women in society.

Limitations and Cautionary Advice

- Students may have trouble rewriting these stories. It is sometimes necessary to do a quick brainstorming session with them to get their creativity flowing. Brainstorm about what it means for men and women to embody nontraditional gender roles. Encourage them to be creative and think outside of the box.

- If students remain "stuck," ask them how the roles the characters in the story take reflect traditional notions of how men and women should act. Then challenge them to think about alternative roles men and women could take in the story.
- Students may argue that it is impossible to portray men and women in stories as having equal roles due to story conventions. In stories, there is typically a protagonist(s) who works to overcome an antagonist. As such, something has to be "conquered" in order for the story to move into resolution. Focusing on collaboration is one way to address this argument. For example, in "Little Red Riding Hood," perhaps Little Red Riding Hood could engage in dialogue with the Big Bad Wolf to bring about an understanding of how the wolf could become a better citizen of the social world by committing to not doing harm to others.

Alternative Uses

- This activity can move beyond roles of men and women to also include roles of gay, lesbian, bisexual, and transgender characters. This approach brings about interesting discussions of what should and should not be included in children's literature. When including sexuality in the restorying process, consider having students read the story "King and King" (de Haan & Nijland, 2000).
- This activity can also be turned into a take-home assignment. Individually or in groups, students can rewrite these stories and turn them in for credit. The same discussion questions apply and can be discussed as a class on the day the stories are due.

REFERENCES

Bussey, K., & Bandura, A. (1999). Social cognitive theory of gender development and differentiation. *Psychological Review, 106*, 676–713.

de Haan, L., & Nijland, S. (2000). *King and king.* Berkeley, CA: Tricycle Press.

Fisher, W. R. (1987). *Human communication as narration: Toward a philosophy of reason, value, and action.* Columbia: University of South Carolina Press.

Martin, C. L., Ruble, D. N., & Szkrybalo, J. (2002). Cognitive theories of early gender development. *Psychological Bulletin, 128*, 903–33.

Sloop, J. (2006). Critical studies in gender/sexuality and media. In B. Dow & J. T. Wood (Eds.), *Handbook of gender and communication* (pp. 319–33). Thousand Oaks, CA: Sage Publications.

West, C., & Zimmerman, D. H. (1987). Doing gender. *Gender and Society, 1*, 125–51.

Wood, J. T. (2011). *Gendered lives: Communication, gender, & culture* (9th ed.). Boston: Wadsworth.

ADDITIONAL READINGS

Eisen, A. (1992). *A treasury of children's literature.* New York: Houghton.

Kilodavis, C. (2009). *My princess boy.* New York: Aladdin.

Richardson, J., & Parnell, P. (2005). *And Tango makes three.* New York: Simon & Schuster.

Walker, B. (1996). *Feminist fairy tales.* New York: HarperCollins.

HANDOUT: RESTORYING GENDER

1. Fully read the assigned story.
2. Examine the men and women in the story. Pay special attention to how characters reflect traditional gender roles of men and women. What are the characters wearing? What are the characters doing? What are their expectations? Who is the hero? Who is the villain? How would you describe the personalities of the men and women in the story?
3. Rewrite the story by challenging traditional gender roles throughout. For example, Snow White could potentially avoid the spell in the first place by launching an awareness campaign highlighting the importance of brains rather than beauty that alters the queen's obsession with being the fairest of them all. Try to avoid merely replacing women's roles with men and vice versa.
4. You have free rein to change the plot, characters, scene, and outcome of the story, so be creative.
5. Be prepared to share your story with the class.

V

MEDIA AND ARTIFACTS

Marlboro Men, Virginia Slims, and Lucky Strikes: The Social Construction of Reality in Tobacco Advertising

Amie D. Kincaid, PhD
(University of Illinois Springfield)

Appropriate Course(s) and Level

Introductory to advanced courses in women's/gender studies, media studies, communication studies, cultural studies, sociocultural studies, American studies, psychology, marketing/advertising, and educational foundations, as well as other courses that may cover social construction.

Appropriate Class Size

10–40 students.

Learning Goals

- To understand the social construction of gender, sexual orientation, sexuality, etc., by showing how the mass media has marketed cigarettes from generation to generation.
- To understand how the social construction of reality and stereotyping are inextricably linked—specifically, in regard to gender, sexual orientation, and sexuality.
- To understand that our social constructions and stereotypes of gender, sexual orientation, and sexuality are often perpetuated by the pervasiveness of the mass media.
- To understand how our social constructions and stereotypes can change over time and are often influenced by power structures and social movements.
- To practice analytical, descriptive, and critical-thinking skills.

Estimated Time Required

A minimum of a 75-minute class.

Required Materials

- Laptop or desktop computers and/or smartphones with Internet access.
- Projector (optional).
- Handout (see below).

Rationale

Why am I the way I am? Why do I view the world the way I do? Is it nature, nurture, or a combination? When we are covering topics regarding identity, these questions likely become part of almost any learning environment. Although biological accounts, or specifically, genetic influences, on our patterns of human communication have been well accounted for over the years (Ayers, 2000; Beatty, McCroskey, & Valencic, 2001; Cappella, 1996; Craig & Muller, 2007; Sherry, 2004; Teboul & Cole, 2005;), there still remains a strong argument that maintaining the nature of the world is not as important as the symbols or the nurturing we use to inhabit that world (Berger & Luckmann, 1966; Schutz, 1967). This activity seeks to engage learners in a sustained conversation where they may explore the power of symbols in regard to gender, sexual orientation, and sexuality. After all, symbols are what help us bring meaning to colors, bodily gestures, food, race, gender, sexuality, and so forth. Meaning does not come out of nowhere; it comes from people using symbols to make claims about "reality," which is a process that is highly culturalized (Martin & Nakayama, 2011).

According to Berger and Luckmann (1966), the social construction of reality explains that humans create a human environment together by using both sociocultural and psychological formations (in other words, the social and cultural factors that influence our cognitive development). These formations cannot be understood solely as products of biology, which "provides only the outer limits for human productive activity" (p. 51). Furthermore, "just as it is impossible for man to develop as man in isolation, so it is impossible for man in isolation to produce a human environment. . . . As soon as one deserves phenomena that are specifically human, one enters the realm of the social. Man's specific humanity and his sociality are inextricably intertwined" (p. 51).

From the aforementioned quote, Berger and Luckmann's (1966) social construction of reality, later termed "social constructionism" by Gergen (1985), helps to bring the nature/nurture argument together in a manner allowing students to begin to focus on how our use of symbols in human interactions impacts our way of being. In other words, our gender may be determined by biology/nature; however, how we enact that gender is largely dependent upon the people and symbols used to make up the society we encounter on a daily basis. What learners sometimes struggle with, though, is the overwhelming presence of symbols within society and how these symbols are used to help us construct our realities regarding what it means to be female, male, heterosexual, homosexual, etc. For instance, the clothes a woman wears in the United States to express what it means to be sexy and/or feminine are different from what a woman wears in the Middle East to express the same thing. Similarly, what counts as masculinity in the United States may differ from what constitutes masculinity in other parts of the world. Both of these simple examples begin to not only show how we use symbols to construct reality but also how symbols used in this way normalize a taken-for-granted reality that is a product of our specific culture.

Another area rife with examples of how symbols are used to socially construct reality is that of the mass media. According to Gamson, Croteau, Hoynes, and Sasson (1992),

> We walk around with media-generated images of the world, using them to construct meaning about political and social issues. And the special genius of this system [the media] is to make the whole process seem so normal and natural that the very art of social construction is invisible. (p. 374)

Because we are constantly encountering messages from the mass media that feed into our social constructions of reality and that often feed our stereotypical thinking about what it means to be female, male, feminine, masculine, sexual, etc., focus on the mass media (specifically, commercials and advertising) for the current activity allows for an in-depth analysis.

A large number of media advertising resources focus on studying audiences and trying to figure out how they can get their messages to resonate with consumers. For years, much criticism has been given to these efforts by complaining specifically about the stereotypes being perpetuated in mainstream media (Campbell, Martin, & Fabos, 2012). Stereotyping is a social construction process which enables us to assign a person or a group to categories. It is important to note, however, that not all stereotypes represent a negative connotation. In fact, some can be quite positive. Regardless, no matter if they are positive or negative, they still have the power to make the same "judgment over and over again, failing to consider the uniqueness of individuals, groups, or events" (Beebe, Beebe, & Ivy, 2013, p. 156). Throughout advertising history, men and women have been stereotyped. In addition, throughout history, there has also been something known as invisible stereotyping, which occurs when segments of a population are ignored (Campbell, Martin, & Fabos, 2012). For instance, in the 1960s, network television was comprised of shows like *Gunsmoke*, *Dennis the Menace*, and *My Three Sons*, making it appear as if white people were the only people in the United States and leading some individuals to perhaps ask who was not being represented and why they were not represented. Looking at how the media goes about (re)constructing stereotypes from generation to generation—specifically, through the use of cigarette commercials and advertisements—can be very telling of the symbols being used to help us socially construct our realities.

In addition to allowing a generational comparison regarding social constructions, a specific focus on cigarette ads allows students to analyze the use of stereotypes in the social construction of reality in the tobacco industry as it has changed over time (James & Olstad, 2009). Once able to advertise almost free of regulation, tobacco advertisers are now highly regulated by the government. Studying changes in such advertisements allows students to assess the social construction of reality as power structures change and how this change in power structures impacts the representations of gender and sexuality. Finally, an analysis of cigarette commercials and/or advertisements allows an opportunity for learners to see why it is important for us to continually assess the social constructions and stereotypes present in the mass media.

Preparing for the Activity

For this activity, there is little to no preparation because it is generally more impactful to use this activity *before* explaining social constructionism as the activity can help lead the class into a discussion with very rich and concrete examples. Therefore, the only preparation needed is to

1. Place on the syllabus and remind students before class to bring a laptop and/or smartphone with Internet capability to class on the day(s) they will conduct the analysis. (Another option would be to reserve a computer lab, as we should not assume everyone will have a laptop and/or a smartphone with Internet access.)
2. Have copies of the Handout available that accompanies the current activity (see below).
3. Have a projector available to show specific commercials and/or advertisements to the entire class (optional). (I will sometimes use a projector, depending upon time, to show pre-selected commercials and/or advertisements I feel embody particular identity elements the class should be finding to jumpstart discussion and/or to let students show some of their favorite advertisements and/or commercials.)
4. For personal preparation, in addition to being familiar withsome of the basic components of the social construction of reality (see Berger & Luckmann, 1966), it may also be useful to read a very simple article on the history of cigarette advertising (see James & Olstad, 2009).

Facilitating the Activity

1. Depending upon class size, divide the class into small groups of 3–5 students. I find groups of no more than 5 students will involve all students, allowing them to move through the questions in the allotted time. Each group should have at least one computer or smartphone with Internet access for easy viewing of the chosen commercials and advertisements.
2. Distribute and review the Handout (see below) and answer any questions the class may have.
3. Allow groups to analyze their chosen commercials and/or advertisements using the steps on the Handout (35–45 min.).
   - I find it helpful to check in with the class as a whole every 5 minutes or so to make sure they are moving at a good pace through each decade (generally, I allow 5–7 minutes for each decade).
   - Circulate among groups to monitor progress and push students to move beyond the obvious big-picture elements of the commercials and/or advertisements. For instance, if you have a group that is struggling, ask them who and what is present in the commercials and/or advertisements? Why are they doing what they are doing? Is this an accident, or is this planned? Why would the creators of this commercial and/or advertisement make these choices? What seems to be absent from the commercials and/or advertisements? What's not said but, perhaps, only implied?

4. Bring the class back together as a whole. Get a quick debriefing from each group by asking each group to report some of the most interesting findings they discovered in their critical inquiry to the class as a whole. Allow at least 10–15 minutes for all groups to debrief to the whole class.

5. Once groups have reported their general findings, lead the class through the Discussion Questions.

Discussion Questions

- What general characteristics were uncovered about representations of gender (masculinity and femininity) and sexuality through your analyses? (Write these on the board in categories that match the generation they belong to so you can help students attempt to derive some trends and themes. I generally just write key words or phrases regarding what students are seeing for each generation. This will allow input from all groups/individuals as well as a visual example that will enable the class to see similar words and/or phrases from generation to generation.)
- When do you see the major shifts happening regarding gender and sexuality?
  - Why do you think we are seeing these shifts at this point?
  - Does this reveal something about how our culture is changing? Or perhaps how the power structures are changing? Why or why not?
- Why do you think some of the themes and/or representations in cigarette commercials and advertising remain relatively consistent? What does this say about how we use media to help us socially construct our realities?
- How do you think the gender and sexual representations within these commercials impact consumers' buying decisions?
- Why do you suppose consumers still buy cigarettes? (This question usually helps students develop a conversation regarding the idea that even if something is bad for our health, the media can construct a product in a way that makes us forget about our health.)
- How do representations of gender and sexuality in cigarette commercials and advertising relate to larger social issues like equality, health, success, and governmental control?
- How do you think generational representations of gender, sexual orientation, race, health, success, etc., have impacted social perceptions of cigarette use?
- Who and/or what do we *not* see represented in cigarette commercials and/or advertisements? Why do you suppose these representations might be lacking?
- Why should we question mass media images/advertisements in this way?

Typical Results

- For many students, this exercise helps them understand how we are consistently encountering and using symbols to make sense of what it means to be gendered, sexual, and/or successful.
- Students acquire new respect for the pervasiveness of such symbols and gain a deeper understanding of how gender, sexual orientation, etc., can be larger than individual psychology or biology.

- Students also begin to understand how these components of our identities can, and do, change over time for both individuals and society as a whole.
- Finally, students begin to appreciate and understand the mass media's role in helping to (re)construct identity.

Limitations and Cautionary Advice

- As you monitor student work, be prepared to advise students in their choice of which commercials and advertisements to analyze. If you have a good idea of what commercials and advertisements will appear first in their Google and YouTube searches, you can use this information to help point students in the right direction. In addition, you can also make sure students are accessing varying commercials/advertisements.
- Be prepared for some students to disagree with the advertisements' stereotypical representations and how they are used. Acknowledge that, yes, individual beliefs and behaviors can vary, but varying individual beliefs and behaviors only show that we, in fact, do socially create our realities. It is important to acknowledge students' individual perspectives while encouraging them to think in terms of *widely held* and *enduring* cultural beliefs.

Alternative Uses

- If it is a larger class, instead of going through what each group has individually uncovered, use think-pair-share, which requires the groups to think about what they are being asked to do, group up with designated members to discuss, then share their general results with the class. I find this model enables the facilitator to go easily from group to group and to simply build upon previously stated ideas by asking them if they agree and/or found anything different or also worth sharing.
- This activity can be applied to analysis of most any form of commercial and/or advertisement. In addition, the process outline in the Handout could be applied to the social construction of race, class, education, success, etc., for intersectional analysis.

REFERENCES

Ayers, J. (Ed.). (2000). Special focus: The nature/nurture balance. *Communication Education, 49*(1), vii–98.

Beatty, M. J., McCroskey, J. C., & Valencic, K. M. (2001). *The biology of communication: A communibiological perspective.* Cresskill, NJ: Hampton Press.

Beebe, S. A., Beebe, S. J., & Ivy, D. K. (2013). *Communication principles for a lifetime.* (5th ed.). Boston, MA: Pearson.

Berger, P. L., & Luckmann, T. (1966). *The social construction of reality: A treatise in the sociology of knowledge.* New York: Doubleday.

Campbell, R., Martin, R. C., & Fabos, B. (2012). *Media & culture: An introduction to mass communication* (8th ed.). New York: Bedford/St. Martin's.

Cappella, J. N. (Ed.). (1996). Symposium: Biology and communication. *Journal of Communication, 46*(3), 4–84.

Craig, R. T., & Muller, H. L. (Eds.). (2007). *Theorizing communication: Readings across traditions.* Los Angeles: Sage Publications.

Gamson, W. A., Croteau, D., Hoynes, W., & Sasson, T. (1992). Media images and the social construction of reality. *Annual Review of Sociology, 18*, 373–93.

Gergen, K. J. (1985). The social constructionist movement in modern psychology. *American Psychologist, 40*, 266–75.

James, R., & Olstad, S. (2009). Cigarette advertising. *Time Magazine.* www.time.com/time/magazine/article/0,9171,1905530,00.html.

Martin, J. N., & Nakayama, T. K. (2011). *Experiencing intercultural communication: An introduction* (4th ed.). New York: McGraw-Hill.

Shutz, A. *The Phenomenology of the Social World.* Translated by George Walsh and Frederick Lehnert. Evanston, IL: Northwestern University Press, 1967.

Sherry, J. L. (2004). Media effects theory and the nature/nurture debate: A historical overview and directions for future research. *Media Psychology, 6*(1), 83–109.

Teboul, J. C. B., & Cole, T. (2005). Relationship development and workplace integration: An evolutionary perspective. *Communication Theory, 15*(4), 389–413.

HANDOUT: MARLBORO MEN,
VIRGINIA SLIMS, & LUCKY STRIKES[1]

Purpose

The purpose of this activity/discussion is to get us thinking about some of the working principles foundational to understanding dominant identity representations.

Pre-Exercise Question

What do cigarette commercials and/or advertisements tell us about gender, sexuality, and success from generation to generation?

Your Task

1. Group-up with 3–5 of your classmates. Designate a note taker. Use your computer and/or smartphone to
   a. Do a Google and/or YouTube search on cigarette commercials and/or advertisements from the 1950s, 1960s, 1970s, 1980s, 1990s, and 2000s.
   b. Select from each decade a commercial and/or advertisement that your group finds interesting.
2. Proceed with a critical inquiry:
   c. Description. Isolate the major elements uncovered from generation to generation. How is gender represented from generation to generation? Sexual orientation? Sexuality? Race? Ethnicity? Education? Socioeconomics? Etc.? (Note what is happening across each generation.)
   d. Analysis. Compare the commercial and/or advertisement elements. Do any patterns of representation emerge from generation to generation? What types of differences are emerging from generation to generation?
   e. Interpretation. What do these representations mean to the sale and acceptance of cigarettes within the United States? What do these representations say about our culture?
   f. Evaluation. What do you think about the representations displayed in these commercials and/or advertisements from generation to generation? Do you feel they are accurate representations of accepted ideas regarding gender, sexual orientation, and success? Do you feel we, as a culture, put excessive value on what someone looks like and/or acts like to decide if something is (un)desirable? Why or why not? How do you think generational representations of gender, sexual orientation, race, health, success, etc., have impacted social perceptions of cigarette use?
   g. Engagement. Make some predictions about how the mass media will use gender, sexual orientation, race, health, and success to continue to market cigarettes to future generations.
3. Debrief and discuss findings with the class.

NOTE

1. Adapted from Campbell, R., Martin, R. C., & Fabos, B. (2012). *Media & culture: An introduction to mass communication* (8th ed.). New York: Bedford/St. Martin's. The questions in each of these steps were constructed by A. D. Kincaid.

18

Writing a Nonsexist Television Advertisement

David Bobbitt, PhD
(Wesleyan College)

Appropriate Course(s) and Level

Appropriate for introductory to advanced courses in media studies, women's/gender studies, cultural studies, and advertising.

Appropriate Class Size

Up to 25 students.

Learning Goals

- To understand how advertising constructs our notions of gender and sexuality.
- To understand the degree to which sexual appeals have become normalized as a mode of discourse in advertising.
- To develop skills in writing a nonsexist advertisement that does not depend on sexual stereotypes or sexual appeals.
- To develop creative skills in constructing advertising texts.

Estimated Time Required

50–75 minutes depending on how much time students are given to write scripts and how much time is allotted for discussion.

Required Materials

- Writing a Nonsexist Television Advertisement Handout (see below).

Rationale

Sexuality has become a pervasive aspect of American popular culture (Streitmatter, 2004). Popular culture is saturated with advertisements using sexual imagery, sexual stereotypes, and objectification of women to sell products (Cortese, 2007). This is especially true with regard to advertisements designed to sell personal-care products that promise women and men the product will make them more physically attractive or sexy.

Jhally (2009) argued advertising influences our normative ideas about what constitutes femininity and masculinity. Sexist advertising can have deleterious effects on the self-image of viewers. For example, Lavine, Sweeney, and Wagner (1999) found exposure to television advertising depicting women as sex objects increased women's dissatisfaction with their bodies as compared to women exposed to nonsexist advertisements.

Requiring students to write a nonsexist television advertisement makes students more aware of the extent to which sexual stereotyping and objectification have become normalized in advertising. This activity helps students understand not only how to design and pitch a television advertisement but also how to design one without falling into the normal routine of using appeals to sexuality or physical attractiveness.

Preparing for the Activity

Instructors should assign Caputi (2008) or a similar reading and possibly have the students watch and discuss Kilbourne's (2010) *Killing Us Softly 4* video in class the day previous to the assignment. These texts document the use of sexist appeals in advertising's images of women, so they provide a context for explaining the necessity to develop advertising messages that do not degrade women or men.

Facilitating the Activity

1. Hand out the assignment (see Handout), and go over it at the beginning of the class period.
2. Divide students into small groups of 4–5 students and give them 30–45 minutes to prepare their script. Students are to write a visual and sound script for a 30-second television advertisement for a personal-care product that avoids using any appeals to sexuality or the physical attractiveness of the characters. Personal-care products, such as perfume and shampoo, are used for this assignment because these are the types of products for which advertisers frequently use appeals to sexuality or gender stereotyping—thus, the contrast with nonsexist advertising is more conscious and clear in the minds of students. A formal script or knowledge of professional scriptwriting techniques is not required for this assignment. Explain to students that the visual script should list, in order, all action and images the audience would see. The sound script should list, alongside the visual script, all corresponding sound, music, dialogue, or announcer's words. A 30-second script of this type would typically be about two pages long with appropriate spacing for ease of use. Students are not required to hand in their script but to perform it for the class.
3. Once the class has finished their scripts, have students perform their scripts. Students can use whatever materials they have at hand (paper, pens, chairs, white

boards, smartphones to play music, etc.). Visuals that cannot be depicted can be described. Everyone in the group should have some role in the enactment.

4. Be sure the class creates a supportive environment by clapping at the end of presentations (the instructor can usually take the lead on this). After going through all the commercials, process with the provided Discussion Questions.

Discussion Questions

- Why do you think advertisers rely so frequently upon sexual appeals to sell their products?
- How difficult, at first, was it to write a script that avoided sexual appeal? Why or why not?
- What type of nonsexual appeals did you choose or consider in writing your script?
- Even with attempts to remove sexual appeals, they often creep in. What sexual appeals did you note that were still existent in yours or others' presentations?
- How effective are nonsexual appeals when compared to sexual appeals?
- Do advertisers have a moral obligation to eliminate the use of sexism and sexual stereotyping in their advertisements? Explain your reasoning.

Typical Results

- My experience has been that students take to this activity easily, so I have had very few problems with it. Students are so familiar with the conventions of television advertising that they can usually put together a basic script for a commercial with no formal training in writing advertising copy. Also, students are generally familiar with the concept of sexism in advertising, so they implicitly understand how to create a nonsexist advertisement once asked to do so.
- Students typically find this activity not only gives them a sense of how to design a television advertisement but also provides a greater awareness of how commonly advertisers use appeals to sexuality.
- Many students are interested in careers in advertising, or media in general, so they see this as the type of work they want to do after graduation and tend to be very interested in completing this activity.

Limitations and Cautionary Advice

- I find that group sizes of 4–5 students work best for this activity. A group of fewer than 4 may not generate a variety of creative ideas or have enough people to play all the roles in the performance of the script. A group of more than 5 will usually be too many to give every student a meaningful role in the writing and performing process.
- If possible, allow each group to work in separate rooms while writing and rehearsing their script. The instructor should visit each group as they work to see if they have any questions.

Alternative Uses

- This is a very flexible assignment. This activity could also work by giving students the assignment ahead of time and having them work in groups outside of class to write the script and then present/perform the script in class on the assigned day.
- It could also be extended to writing and turning in a professional-quality script or even shooting, editing, and showing the commercial in class. If students are asked to write and submit a formal script, they will need instructions on how to do that (see Hose [2012] for a good online resource). If students are to film and edit the scripts, they will need the necessary equipment, facilities, and instructions.
- This assignment could also be adapted to writing an advertisement for radio or the Internet.

REFERENCES

Caputi, J. (2008). A (bad) habit of thinking: Challenging and changing the pornographic world-view. In M. Meyers (Ed.), *Women in popular culture: Representation and meaning* (pp. 29–55). Cresskill, NJ: Hampton Press.

Cortese, A. J. (2007). *Provocateur: Images of women and minorities in advertising.* (3rd. ed.). Lanham, MD: Rowman & Littlefield.

Hose, C. (2012). How to write an advertising script. www.ehow.com/how_5022258_write-advertising-script.html.

Jhally, S. (2009). *The codes of gender: Identity and performance in pop culture.* Media Education Foundation.

Kilbourne, J. (2010), *Killing us softly 4: Advertising's image of women.* Media Education Foundation.

LaFrance, E. (1995). *Men, media and masculinity.* Dubuque, IA: Kendall/Hunt.

Lavine, H., Sweeney, D., & Wagner, S. H. (1999). Depicting women as sex objects in television advertising: Effects on body dissatisfaction. *Personality and Social Psychology Bulletin, 25*(8), 1049–58.

Streitmatter, R. (2004). *Sex sells: The media's journey from repression to obsession.* Cambridge, MA: Westview Press.

HANDOUT: WRITING A NONSEXIST
TELEVISION ADVERTISEMENT

In "A (Bad) Habit of Thinking" Jane Caputi argued that a "pornographic worldview" suffuses our culture by providing us with images of the objectification and subordination of women. In *Killing Us Softly 4*, Jean Kilbourne showed numerous examples of advertising images that represent women as being valued only for their physical beauty. The following group exercise is designed to help you develop skills in creating images of women and men that are nonsexist and do not rely upon appeals based on physical attractiveness or sexuality. Your group is to assume the role of an advertising agency "pitching" a script to the executives of the company that makes the product you are assigned below.

Television Ad Writing Group Exercise

Your group assignment is to write and perform a 30-second script for a TV commercial selling the product below assigned to your group. *You should avoid using any sexual stereotypes, sexual objectification, or sexual appeal in the characters or the words.*

You should come up with a name for your product, and write a visual script and a sound script. Your visual script should describe the setting and objects the viewer would see, any graphics used, and descriptions of people in the ad and what they are doing. Your sound script should describe alongside the visual script any music the viewer would hear, as well as sound effects used, monologue, dialogue, and announcer's words (if any). You will not need to turn in your script, but you will need to demonstrate your script by performing it for the class, so having a fully developed script is imperative. A 30-second script of this type would typically be about two pages long with appropriate spacing for ease of use.

Products

- Group #1—women's perfume
- Group #2—men's shampoo
- Group #3—women's underarm deodorant
- Group #4—women's body wash
- Group #5—men's cologne

Being a Man: Challenging or Reinforcing Embodied Masculinities in the University Classroom

Jessica J. Eckstein, PhD
(Western Connecticut State University)

Appropriate Course(s) and Level

Any level interpersonal, relational, family, popular culture, or gender communication course.

Appropriate Class Size

10–50 students or more.

Learning Goals

- To become aware of dominant cultural narratives related to diverse masculinities.
- To be able to identify masculinity as operating at macro, societal levels.
- To recognize one's own role in supporting masculinities as interpersonal constructions.

Estimated Time Required

Assigned homework in preparation, and then 30–40 minutes in a single class period.

Required Materials

- Means to affix magazine pictures to front of classroom (tape, pins, etc.).
- Magazines or access to ads via the Internet.

Rationale

In a 2006 issue of *Esquire* magazine devoted to the American man, a professor detailed his concerns surrounding a recent gendered shift in academia:

> I watched as my colleagues expressed an increasing disdain for men in the class-room . . . I went to faculty lunches dealing with disruptive students, only to realize that what we were talking about was primarily male behavior, that men themselves were in some fashion perceived to be the disruption . . . I watched as nearly every significant social problem was laid at the feet of the male student population . . . Everything about them that is male—their physicality, their hunger for stimulation, their propensity to argue—seemed clipped by the academic world I lived in. I was not waiting for the birth of a men's movement so much as I was looking for a little discussion, a chance to engage boys in the same way women engaged girls forty years ago. What did my university do in the face of these problems? It formed a task force on the status of women. (Chiarella, 2006, p. 96)

The above lament represents one perspective concerning the role of males and masculinity as addressed within academia. As Palmer-Mehta (2006) noted, "While traditionally it was femininity that was seen as inherently weak and pathological, today . . . it is masculinity that is regarded as the troubled gender" (p. 182). A contrasting perspective is that 20 years of progress for women has done little to erase hundreds of years of male-dominated academia. Additionally, many believe universities, as social institutions, have a responsibility to nurture a female-oriented perspective in the individuals they turn out into a male-oriented world-at-large. A final dominant rhetoric insists that inequality—whether for men or women—does not exist in *their* academic world.

There exist a myriad of approaches to dealing with gender in the university classroom. In many cases, however, instructors have adopted their own comfort-level-driven approach to discussions about gender. They may be unknowingly reinforcing their own larger cultural stereotypes (simply because it's what they were taught), or many may unconsciously reinforce the biases their students bring into the classroom. Even educated, "forward-thinking" instructors may be subject to their own biases, as both media and social interactions involve gender-persuasion/enforcement that "recycle[s] gender ideology rather than minimizing or challenging gender stereotyping" (Johnson & Young, 2002, p. 477). A failure to scrutinize masculinities (as well as femininities) implies belief structures are "norms" that need no further examination. Indeed, not including activities on masculinities (while conducting them in regard to women and femininity) may indicate to students that masculinity and possible hegemonic norms are the standard by which to view the world—in other words, thinking we only study femininity because *it* is the anomalous societal form. Activities treating masculinities as separate entities—types of gender (just like femininities) that are enacted through various forms—can challenge the perception of masculinity as the norm (for both students and instructors).

Current gender scholars who theorize and measure these two gender constructs tend to find they are more orthogonal (i.e., simultaneously co-occurring) than polarized in nature (Brems & Johnson, 1990). In other words, one individual can embody both masculinity and femininity. Further, masculinity and femininity are each multidimensional constructs, with diverse representations in larger culture and situated in interpersonal relationships (Connell, 1995; Kimmel, 1996). By looking at images as cultural artifacts representing embedded belief structures, this classroom activity addresses the larger nature of gender as socially constructed (and assigned to particularly sexed bodies) in specific cultures. The activity problematizes masculinity on two fronts: as produced by mainstream narratives at a macro level and as idealized by individual students on an individual, micro level.

Preparing for the Activity

1. I recommend first preparing and providing a lecture prior to this activity to introduce (at a minimum) the following ideas:
   - Sex (biological physiology; e.g., male, female) as distinct from gender (bodily, personality, and communication enactment; e.g., masculine, feminine).
   - There is not one masculinity; there are many forms. Most often attributed to Connell (1995), one dominant classification of masculinity types includes hegemonic, complicit/accommodating, subordinate, and protest manifestations.
   - All gender enactments are based not only on historical relationships between the sexes but also on ongoing interpersonal, social relationships between them. Media persuasion, in particular, is viewed by many scholars as a cultural reinforcement of gender identities and subsequent roles enacted (Palmer-Mehta, 2006). However, this is only half the story. Masculinities are tied to both macro- and micro-level relationships across time and cultures. Embracing the perspective of many communication scholars, Johnson and Young (2002) noted that personal traits may be learned in the process of an individual becoming a gendered participant in their culture.
   - All genders are performative—a negotiated outcome, as well as a negotiating tool in personal interactions (Palmer-Mehta, 2006). Personal, and in many cases biological, appearance has been argued as important to the behavioral and identity roles enacted by individuals (Connell, 1995).
   - There are both positive and negative psychological and sociological outcomes of communicating different types of masculinity. Kimmel (1996; 2008) provided both historical and current sociological accounts of these processes in regard to American men.
2. After introducing students to these basic ideas of gender relationships and embodiment, I introduce the following as take-home work:
   - Think about two of your ideal men in popular culture today; ones to whom you are personally attracted or who represent your ideals of what an attractive man "should be." For the instructor: "attractiveness" is a term used because of its vagueness and adaptability; it maximizes students' interpretations of a multifaceted construct.
   - One of these men must be stereotypically masculine and attractive, as agreed upon culturally.
   - One of these men must be someone who most people in your culture would *not* agree is ideally attractive.
   - Bring in a large (preferably color) picture of each of these men.

- Do not label or otherwise identify yourself on the front of these pictures.
- Although all pictures will be viewed in class, picture providers will remain anonymous.

Facilitating the Activity

1. On the day of the activity, as students enter the classroom, instruct them to place their pictures face-down in a pile by the door. Make certain that no student's name is on any of the images to protect student privacy.
2. Once all students have entered, mix/shuffle the pictures to increase the anonymity of the activity.
3. Have students assist in taping or otherwise affixing pictures to the front of the room to maximize visibility. It is important that the pictures not be classified in any particular order.
4. After providing an opportunity to view the images, identify, with class help, any of the men who are not obviously apparent (usually less popular actors/musicians and some sports figures).
5. Then ask each person to silently ask, Which of these men is most attractive "as a man" to me (e.g., "Pick your top 5")? Have them write this list in their notes.
6. I continually remind students that our ideas of masculinities are heavily tied to sexuality (e.g., hegemonic males cannot be homosexual). Thus I reiterate that I have intentionally forced both the men and women in the class to choose their attractive preferences in *men*; this also allows students to begin connecting their own "attractions" to concepts of cultural normativity in a hegemonic context. After we have concluded the debate surrounding the different men posted at the front, I remind the class that individuals learning and maintaining (i.e., enacting) their gender are thought to be influenced by cultural surroundings, whether through positive imagery (possibly in media) or through negative reinforcement (possibly from peers). As a result, it is important for us to continually be aware of the ways in which we are influenced by others.

Discussion Questions

- Which men—from those posted at the front—do you feel are most unattractive?
- Which men are—in your opinion—the obviously not culturally-agreed-upon attractive men?
- How do the culturally-agreed-upon attractive men differ physically (e.g., hair, dress, attitude, physical profession) from your idiosyncratic preferences?
- What about your specific upbringing, subculture (e.g., religious, rural/urban, personal style), and experiences may have shaped what you see as attractive/unattractive in men? Which of the images you chose is similar to or different from the concepts of manhood you experienced as "ideal" when you were growing up?
- How does seeing men in contrast to other men—both culturally ideal and not-ideal—shape the way we saw the men posted at the front?
- How do your ideas of attractive masculinity for pop culture icons differ from your assessments of individual men in your life?

- Identify obvious examples of Connell's (1995) masculinity types. (There typically are a diversity of masculine types/masculinities, but also, we are usually unable to identify a truly "hegemonic" man: attention to fashionable dress, hair style, or hygiene are feminine attributes; careers involving artistry, music, or acting involve high levels of emotional expression; and anything other than normative hetero-sexuality eliminates one from mainstream "values." As argued by Connell (1995) and others (Connell & Messerschmidt, 2005; Kimmel, 1996), the masculinity (i.e., hegemonic) to which academics typically attribute society's "evils" rarely exists in any individual man.)

Typical Results

- I have implemented this activity in both urban and rural settings, at community colleges and universities, with male and female students, in the Midwest and on the East Coast, in courses devoted to gender and more general communication classes. This activity is highly adaptable because the students bring in their own pictures; therefore, the activity remains culturally relevant over time.
- Usually a major outcome of this activity is the class's recognition that the men found to be most culturally attractive are the most "objectively" plain in appear-ance, accomplishments, and profession. In contrast to the idiosyncratic prefer-ences, there is often little that is exceptional about the most "masculinely" attrac-tive man. The attractive-to-me-but-not-to-the-culture men are typically effeminate in some way (e.g., in appearance, behavior, sexuality). This is important to note because whereas everyone brought an image of the latter man to class, the class largely converges on its recognition that their idiosyncratic preferences are not the larger culture's. Depending on the level of traditionalism in students, there may be little overlap between the two.
- The goal here is to illustrate and problematize the taken-for-granted of both hege-monic normativity *and* the socially constructed nature of masculinity (as not neces-sarily tied to biological imperatives). When students begin to see the diversity (or lack thereof) of images chosen by their male and female (inevitably possessed of diverse sexualities) classmates, they begin to see the ways in which their classmates are equally (or perhaps not) influenced by larger, macro-level constructions of mas-culinity, as demonstrated through media representations *and* interpersonal experi-ences. Constructions of "ideal men" (as exhibited in bodily form) may or may not be diverse, but inevitably this discussion reveals that the men were chosen for their "attractiveness" according to very different means. For example, in past iterations of this activity, when asked to explain why they chose particular men (and those specific images/planned representations of them), both men and women began to reference nonphysical aspects of those individuals (e.g., "He's really good at this, so he's cool" or "Just the way he acts" or "He dates so-and-so"). This is another opportunity to raise the issue of embodiment as extending beyond physical, bodily features.
- Inevitably, issues of sexuality will arise in the discussion. This allows the activity also to touch on the ways that physical embodiment (and behaviors *and* communi-cation) shapes our perceptions of masculinity. Students can get extremely specific with the physical analyses at this point.

- Following this activity, in general classes (where masculinity is not the focus of the course), my students consistently express a desire to learn *more* about the specifics of masculinities—in terms of cultural expectations, communication of this gender type by individuals and larger cultural structures, and psycho-social outcomes and antecedents of different masculinities for both men and women who enact and interact with them. This demonstrates the extent to which students (both men and women) respond positively to masculinities as an area of inquiry—when not taught from a masculinity-as-inherently-negative approach.

Limitations and Cautionary Advice

- The nature of this activity is such that it requires an instructor who can effectively manage side-conversations (by bringing them in to the main discussion), who can quickly and appropriately address insensitive (or outright prejudicial) comments, and who is able to rein in students to the main Discussion Questions after the picture analyses have concluded. If these skills are not possessed by the instructor, the activity runs the potential of merely reinforcing students' dominant and hurtful gender attitudes and beliefs.
- On the other hand, instructors should consistently be challenging their own gender prejudices. Too often students are alienated by the belief that anyone teaching a university-level gender activity is already biased against men. Of course, this activity could be adapted to incorporate female images, but students have heard endless stories of the ways "women in the media" are portrayed bodily; a mistake would be to have this activity merely "flip the coin" by putting men in a scopophilic-object light. Instead, this activity challenges us to look closer at the ways embodiment operates, how a "mere image" is associated with expectations and normative behaviors in our lives, and why/how our socially ingrained notions of masculinity are influenced by our own relational experiences and sexual proclivities. We all have biases, and it is important to contemplate these before beginning this activity. Often, I have shared some of my previous preconceptions with the students as a way to show that no one is perfect or ideal in their sex-gender beliefs—that would be largely impossible in our society. Rather, the goal (for instructors and students) should be to continue questioning our assumptions about men, women, and their various genders.

Alternative Uses

- This activity can easily be adapted to address issues of race, power, age, etc.
- The Discussion Questions could be assigned as a take-home, reflective assignment; however, the in-class discussion remains important to examining the diversity of opinions.

REFERENCES

Brems, C., & Johnson, M. E. (1990). Reexamination of the Bem sex-role inventory: The interpersonal BSRI. *Journal of Personality Assessment, 55,* 484–98.

Chiarella, T. (2006 July 11). The problem with boys . . . is actually a problem with men. *Esquire, 146*(1), 94–96. www.esquire.com/features/the-state-of-the-american-man/ESQ0706SOTAM-BOYS_94.

Connell, R. W. (1995). *Masculinities.* Cambridge: Polity Press.

Connell, R. W., & Messerschmidt, J. W. (2005). Hegemonic masculinity: Rethinking the concept. *Gender & Society, 19*, 829–59.

Dickinson, G., & Anderson, K. V. (2004). Fallen: O. J. Simpson, Hillary Rodham Clinton, and the re-centering of White patriarchy. *Communication and Critical/Cultural Studies, 1*(3), 271–96.

Johnson, F. L., & Young, K. (2002). Gendered voices in children's television advertising. *Critical Studies in Media Communication, 19*(4), 461–80.

Kimmel, M. (1996). *Manhood in America.* New York: Free Press.

Kimmel, M. (2008). *Guyland: The perilous world where boys become men.* New York: HarperCollins.

Palmer-Mehta, V. (2006). The wisdom of folly: Disrupting masculinity in *King of the Hill. Text and Performance Quarterly, 26*(2), 181–98.

20

Communicating Gender Expectations:
An Analysis of Boys' and Girls' Toys and Games

Elizabeth Tolman, PhD
(South Dakota State University)

Appropriate Course(s) and Level

Undergraduate gender studies, gender and communication, or women's studies courses.

Appropriate Class Size

20–30 students.

Learning Goals

- To illustrate how gender is socially constructed through boys' and girls' games and toys.
- To have students identify examples of boys' and girls' toys and games that promote communication rules.
- To have students analyze the implications of toys and games on gender construction.

Estimated Time Required

One 60- or 75-minute class period.

Required Materials

- Handout for each student (see Handout B).
- Discount store in close proximity to campus or access to toys.

Rationale

Oftentimes gender and communication courses offer instructors the opportunity to present information about how cultural expectations are communicated to boys and girls. This teaching activity illustrates how gender expectations are communicated to children through the toys and games that are available and marketed to children. Students complete field research and illustrate their understanding of gender construction in the assignment and in-class discussion. The pedagogical outcomes of having students conduct field research outside of class, as a class, are significant. This engaged learning helps students participate in more critical analysis of gender construction.

Ivy (2012) defined sex as "biological designation of being female or male" (p. 25) and gender as "cultural construction that includes biological sex (male or female), psychological characteristics (femininity, masculinity, androgyny), attitudes about the sexes, and sexual orientation" (p. 25). Ivy reviewed prior research about male and female characterization in video games. She argued for the potential impact of video game play and exposure. Nelson (2005) conducted a toy inventory of family homes with children ages 3 to 5 in Sweden. Sweden is a country that encourages gender equality, so Nelson believed the study would reveal fewer gender-typed toys. However, the study identified strong gender-typed toys. Certainly the types of toys and games available to children in the United States are worthy of analysis and discussion.

Preparing for the Activity

1. Explain the assignment in class, prior to meeting at the store. You can present the examples provided in Handout A to give students guidance about what to look for when conducting the field research, but another option is having students conduct the field research without presenting examples for each communication rule. Although students may initially have difficulty seeing the nuances of gendered appeals in toys and games, it will challenge students to look beyond the examples provided.
2. For this activity, you and your students meet at a discount store (Walmart, Kmart, Target, etc.) that sells kids' toys and games. Typically, the class meets at the store during an assigned class period. This works well because you are available to answer questions about the activity, and the students can share some of their initial findings with each other while they complete the activity. (If access to a nearby store is not possible, suggestions are provided in Alternative Uses.) For each student, you should make one copy of Handout B with the eight communication rules.

Facilitating the Activity

1. Once at the store, you should provide copies of the Handout.
2. While the students are completing the field research at the store, you should be available to answer questions and help students develop connections between the communication rules and the toys and games.

3. Once the students are done collecting data, you may choose to process the activity either in the store or in the following class period with the provided Discussion Questions.

Discussion Questions

- What types of toys and games do you consider appropriate for boys? Why?
- What types of toys and games do you consider appropriate for girls? Why?
- What toys and games do you consider gender neutral? Why?
- How, if at all, have the types of toys and games that are available today changed from when you were a child?
- Do the toys and games that you identified in the field research set up expectations for traditional gender roles? Why or why not?
- In your opinion, what types of toys support a masculine culture (cultures where men are expected to be assertive and tough)?
- In your opinion, what types of toys support a feminine culture (cultures in which both men and women are modest and concerned with quality of life)?
- Do the toys and games that you identified in your field research contribute to the process of becoming "gendered"? Why or why not?
- According to Ivy (2012), children learn to "understand themselves as individuals separate from others" and begin to "respond to others as members of a particular sex" (p. 58). Do the toys and games you identified help children differentiate between men and women and help them see themselves as a boy or girl? Explain your answer.
- If you are a parent or plan to be a parent, based on your findings from this research, will you promote gender-neutral toys and games or will you be comfortable having your child/children play with toys and games that illustrate the communication rules for boys and girls? Explain your answer.
- Beyond the toys themselves, how did the store's displays of girls', boys', or gender-neutral toys compare or contrast with one another?
  - Did the store have blue shelves for boys' toys, pink shelves for girls' toys, and neutral-color shelving for infant/ toddler and gender-neutral toys?
  - What are the potential implications of this labeling by the store?

Typical Results

- Students enjoy applying course content outside the traditional classroom.
- In addition, they enjoy sharing their findings with the class in the following class period. Students get excited about sharing the toys and games they found and how they illustrate the communication rules.

Limitations and Cautionary Advice

- Depending on the size of the class, store employees may ask what your students are doing and why they are taking "notes" when they should be shopping. To avoid any issues, the instructor could notify the store manager prior to the class trip to the store.

- Some students may not have transportation to the store. Students are asked to make arrangements to carpool to the store.

Alternative Uses

- Students could complete this assignment individually and not meet as a class at a store, reporting their findings during class on an assigned date.
- The activity could also be adapted to an online course, and students could post their findings in a discussion board. Their initial findings could serve as a starting point for discussions about these course concepts.
- If the instructor is unable to have the class meet during a class period at a discount store due to location and time constraints, students could be assigned to find an example of a toy or game that illustrates one of the communication rules and bring that toy or an image of the toy to class. Or the instructor could use websites from discount and toy stores to illustrate the communication rules.
- Another variation is bringing in examples of the toys and games for small-group discussion. The instructor can borrow these items from friends and family or shop at garage sales to find these items.
- The instructor may choose to have students not only analyze the products but also the presentation of the products. For example, in many stores, the shelving is the color blue for boys' toys, pink for girl's toys, and a neutral brown for games and gender-neutral toys for infants and toddlers. This can lead to discussion about how the store has labeled what toys are appropriate for girls and boys just based on the color of the shelves.

REFERENCES

Ivy, D. K. (2012). *GenderSpeak: Personal effectiveness in gender communication*. Boston: Pearson.

Nelson, A. (2005). Children's toy collections in Sweden—A less gender-typed country? *Sex Roles, 52*(1/2), 93–102. doi: 10.1007/s11199-005-1196-5.

Wood, J. T. (2013). *Gendered lives: Communication, gender, and culture*. Boston: Wadsworth.

HANDOUT A: INSTRUCTOR EXAMPLES HANDOUT

Wood (2013) outlined ways that boys' and girls' toys and games cultivate communication rules.

Gendered Communication Rules for Boys' Toys and Games (Wood, 2013, p. 127)

1. "Use communication to assert your ideas, opinions, and identity."
   Lawn mowers, grills, leaf blowers, and power tools: These toys suggest that outdoor work and manual labor have value. Mowing the lawn, grilling meat, and building things are activities that are appropriate for boys and help to establish their identity.
2. "Use talk to achieve something, such as solving problems or developing strategies."
   Walkie talkies: Boys can use the toy to find each other.
   Strategy-based board games: Boys communicate and strategize during the game. Boys secretly place their ships in squares and work to sink their opponent's ships.
   Wooden blocks and other construction materials: Boys can build objects or buildings. In doing so, they illustrate their ability to achieve a goal.
3. "Use communication to attract and maintain others' attention."
   Swords or other weapons: Boys can role-play with the toy and use it to gain and maintain attention from those around them.
   Noise-making cars and other toys: Boys can use the cars to race and make car noises.
4. "Use communication to compete for the "talk stage." Make yourself stand out; take attention away from others, and get others to pay attention to you."
   Hero Mask: Boys can act like a super hero and gain others' attention through their talk and physical activity. For example, a boy may talk or act like a super hero in order to stand out from those around him.
   Talking Hand Drill: The yellow drill rotates and talks. It says, "It's drilling time. What can we fix next? Wow, you're a pro, Take me for a spin, work and play, having lots of fun today, Nice work partner, A job well done, What can we fix next?" The toy illustrates the "talk stage" because of its numerous sayings, its ability to draw attention to the child, and the child's potential to take attention away from others when playing with the toy.

Gendered Communication Rulesfor Girls' Toys and Games (Wood, 2013, p. 128)

1. "Use communication to create and maintain relationships. The process of communication, not its content, is the heart of relationships."
   Friendship Board Game: The game promotes girls working together to achieve a goal and maintain a friendship. The game does not promote criticism or competition.
2. "Use communication to establish egalitarian relations with others. Don't outdo, criticize, or put down others. If you have to criticize, be gentle."

Text Phones: These oftentimes pink phones can be used by two girls to communicate with a friend. The toy promotes the need to develop and maintain equalitarian relationships with other girls.

3. "Use communication to include others; bring them into the conversation, respond to their idea."

   Tea sets: Girls can pretend that they are having a tea party. While playing with the tea sets, girls may engage in talk, respond to each others' ideas, and work to include each other in the conversation. The communication that occurs while using the tea set illustrates that talk has value and is the essence of relationships.

4. "Use communication to show sensitivity to others and relationships."

   Baby Doll: Girls show sensitivity by caring for their doll. One doll has teeth that the girl can brush. Another doll can be fed and changed. This toy illustrates that caring for others is an important part of being a girl.

   Doll houses: The toys illustrate different types of family members and how they live together in a house. Girls can role-play with the family figurines in the doll house. The toy highlights the fact that relationships have value for girls and can be positive.

HANDOUT B: FIELD RESEARCH HANDOUT

Wood (2013) outlined ways that boys' and girls' toys and games cultivate communication rules (pp. 127–28). For each communication rule, identify and discuss *two* toys and/or games that illustrate that particular communication rule. Provide the name of the toy or game. In addition, include a 2–3 sentence description of how the toy or game illustrates the communication rule.

Gendered Communication Rules for Boys' Toys and Games

1. Use communication to assert your ideas, opinions, and identity.

2. Use talk to achieve something, such as solving problems or developing strategies.

3. Use communication to attract and maintain others' attention.

4. Use communication to compete for the "talk stage." Make yourself stand out; take attention away from others, and get others to pay attention to you.

Gendered Communication Rules for Girls' Toys and Games

1. Use communication to create and maintain relationships. The process of communication, not its content, is the heart of relationships.

2. Use communication to establish egalitarian relations with others. Don't outdo, criticize, or put down others. If you have to criticize, be gentle.

3. Use communication to include others; bring them into the conversation; respond to their ideas.

4. Use communication to show sensitivity to others and relationships.

Engendering Material Culture: The Gendered Packaging of Bath and Beauty Products

Michael J. Murphy, PhD
(University of Illinois Springfield)

Appropriate Course(s) and Level

Introductory to advanced courses in women's/gender studies, media studies, material culture studies, art/design, marketing/advertising courses.

Appropriate Class Size

Up to 35 students, in classrooms with enough space to allow for small-group work.

Learning Goals

- To understand the distinction between biological sex and sociocultural gender by showing how cultural beliefs about gender are materially encoded in mundane consumer products.
- To understand that gendered cultural discourses take material as well as visual and textual form.
- To practice analytical and descriptive skills employing multiple senses: sight, touch, sound, etc.
- To develop and apply a vocabulary of gender adjectives to describe the world around us.

Estimated Time Required

One 75-minute class but could be adapted for shorter classes by dividing lecture and analysis parts of the activity.

Required Materials

- A selection of highly gendered personal bath and beauty product containers.
- Analysis handout (see Handout).
- Reading on the gendering of Clinique product packaging (Kirkham & Weller, 1996).

Rationale

How is it that an object can be perceived as "female" or "male" when it doesn't have a biological sex? This exercise helps students analyze the gender of material culture so they can better understand how ideas about gender can exist independent of biological sex or individual psychology. It also helps them understand how gendered cultural beliefs are conveyed from generation to generation, and why they are so slow to change despite the fast pace of social change—gender is everywhere, all around us, encoded in the material world (Hochschild & Machung, 2012).

Though the two terms are often used interchangeably in popular culture, gender-studies scholars distinguish between *sex* (biology, physiology, morphology, anatomy; maleness and femaleness) and *gender* (the meaning given to sex in a given time and place, including norms, ideals, and expectations for males and females). The internalization of these norms through a process of socialization produces *gender identity*: our sense of ourselves as male or female. How we make this sense of self known to others is called gender performance or gender expression.

The social behavior of males and females (what they do) is often guided by our cultural beliefs about gender norms and ideals (what males and females are supposed to do; what is considered masculine or feminine). A primary vehicle for the communication of gender norms and ideals is cultural practices and artifacts (i.e., language, music, theater, art, literature, fashion/clothing, food, consumer goods; Lorber, 1995; Peoples, 2001; Warnke, 2010). Scholars who study material cultural maintain that we can understand any society's cultural beliefs, including its beliefs about gender, through careful analysis of its cultural artifacts (Prown, 1982; Summers, 1993). However, students can struggle to analyze beliefs about gender as they are encoded in material cultural artifacts.

Because personal bath and beauty products are central to the care, treatment, and stylization of bodies in accordance with a society's gender ideals, their product packaging is often highly gendered, offering a rich vein that can be mined to understand a specific culture's gender ideals. In general, product packaging encourages consumers to associate values and beliefs with a specific product such that the subsequent purchase of that product affirms those beliefs and enables their presentation to the larger society. This is done through the careful and intentional selection of every aspect of a product and its packaging: size, shape, color, texture, words, and pictures. One of the ways manufacturers differentiate products for female and male consumers is through *gendered* product packaging. In actuality, most bath and beauty products differentiated for male and female consumers (i.e., deodorant) have very similar active ingredients; it is the aesthetics of product design and packaging that encourages consumers to view such products as "male" or "female" (Kirkham & Weller, 1996).

Gendered product packaging taps into existing consumer beliefs about gender and encourages us to augment our gender identities by consuming such products and using them to express our gender. As such, the consumption and use of gendered consumer goods is one of the myriad ways that we "do" gender as a social performance (West & Zimmerman, 1987). But because these products shape and style the sexed body in accordance with binary gender norms, they are also one of the ways the cultural fiction of binary sexual difference is produced, maintained, and exaggerated—despite a mountain of evidence that males and females are more alike physically than they are different. This binary—or rather, the *belief* that sex and gender are binary in nature—is a significant source of oppression for everyone, not just those who cannot or do not wish to conform to social norms for sex and gender (Birke, 1992).

For example, Tim's biological *sex* is male, and he holds specific beliefs about the *gendered* behavior and appearance (i.e., the masculinity) of males in his society. AXE body spray is designed, named, packaged, and marketed using aesthetics that appeal to Tim's previously held beliefs about male *sex* and masculine *gender*. (Unilever, the maker of AXE products, knows about these beliefs because it surveyed guys like Tim as part of its product development process.) Because of the successful connection between Tim's beliefs and Unilever's marketing strategies, Tim's use of AXE body spray as part of his overall *gender expression* affirms his sense of *gender identity*. It's one of the ways he "does" masculine gender and becomes culturally intelligible as male in his society. And because hegemonic masculinity is constructed in the contemporary United States as the opposite of femininity, his use of AXE also participates in the ongoing binary social construction of sex and gender in his society.

Preparing for the Activity

1. For the day you will conduct this activity, assign students an article on the gendering of advertising and product packaging of Clinique products (Kirkham & Weller, 1996).

2. Place on the syllabus and remind students to bring a "highly gendered" personal bath or beauty product from home on the day(s) they will conduct this analysis. I instruct students that "highly gendered" means products for which there is little doubt as to whether it is intended for use by females or males. College students' bathrooms typically contain several product types that work well for this assignment: bath gel/body wash, shaving creams, razors, deodorants, hair products, and colognes/perfumes. The activity involves analysis of a single product, but it is good to have several options to choose from, so ask everyone to bring something.

3. It is helpful for this exercise to have first explained the conceptual distinction between *sex* and *gender* to help students understand how gender is a social construction that is perpetuated through cultural discourses, beliefs, and artifacts (Lorber, 1995).

4. Bone up on dichotomous beliefs about gender in Western culture. Broverman et al. (1972) offered a nice summary of the major sociological aspects of gender while Summers (1993) discussed the historical gendering of aesthetic issues like line, color, texture, and form.

Facilitating the Activity

1. If you have not already covered these concepts in your course, and depending on the background of your students, prepare and deliver a brief lecture on the conceptual difference between *sex* and *gender*, and the general concept of gendered product packaging. (In 50-minute class sessions, this can be done on day one with analysis of bath products on day two.)

2. After your brief lecture, divide the class into small working groups. I find groups of no more than 4 students will involve all students but allow the group to move through the questions in the allotted time. Each student should bring their bath product with them to their group.

3. Distribute the Handout, briefly explain the activity, and answer any questions.

4. Allow groups to analyze their products using the questions on the Handout (20–30 min.).

5. Circulate among groups to monitor progress and push students to move beyond the more obviously gendered aspects of their product (e.g., color, shape). An extra-credit question is included to engage the faster students in the class.

6. Ask groups to report findings to the class as a whole. Allow at least 40 minutes total for a class of 30 students. Have each group report answers to all questions on their sheet before moving to the next group.

7. Facilitate a class discussion with the Discussion Questions.

Discussion Questions

- What general principles of gendered cultural beliefs can we derive from this analysis? What characteristics make a product seem "female/male"? Write answers on the board and attempt to derive trends and themes through discussion.
- Are there any contradictory or confused gendered product packaging? Provide an example.
  ° Does this represent a marketing mistake or does it have some other purpose?
- Why do you think manufacturers find it necessary to "gender" bath and beauty product packaging?
- How much do you think these gendered qualities affect consumers' buying decisions?
  ° How would consumers' buying habits of such products be influenced if they weren't so highly gendered?
- How would you describe the relationship between manufacturers and consumers when it comes to gendered bath products?
  ° Are consumers passive/helpless "victims" of gendered bath products or are they complicit in the gendered meaning of bath products? Why or why not?
- Why should we care about gendered product packaging?
- Does the gendering of consumer bath and beauty product packaging relate to larger social issues like equality between the sexes in employment, education, religion, law, and government?

Typical Results

- For many students, this exercise helps them understand how cultural beliefs about gender are present in the most mundane cultural artifacts: personal bath products. They acquire new respect for the pervasiveness of such beliefs and gain a deeper understanding of how gender is larger than individual behavior, psychology, or biology.
- Students also begin to understand how gender ideologies are conveyed through material form, in less than obvious ways, and are therefore "invisible" to most people, and why normative gender beliefs are so slow to change and difficult to resist.

Limitations and Cautionary Advice

- As you monitor student work, be prepared to advise students in their choice of which product to analyze. The more highly gendered the object, the easier the analysis. Ambiguously gendered or minimally designed products are the most difficult, and you should steer students to analyze products appropriate to their ability and background. As noted, it helps to have every student bring a product, then to guide students in the selection of the best one from among the available choices.
- Students having a better grasp of the foundational concepts will produce a deeper level of analysis. Those with little experience in cultural or gender analysis can struggle with this assignment. Also, some students have a difficult time seeing the package design of bath products as a vehicle for gendered cultural beliefs; bath products are so familiar, they can struggle to make them "strange." Commonly, students have a difficult time assigning gendered adjectives to the material aspects of the product (except shape and color). They tend to have more experience with analysis of images and texts and will consequently struggle to address the gendered associations of texture, etc. This is where instructor preparation is crucial (see References and Additional Readings).
- When you are monitoring group analysis, if you have a group that is struggling, try inversion analysis. Ask why the product wouldn't be successfully marketed to males (if it's a product aimed at females and vice versa). What gendered messages does it send that a different group of consumers would find objectionable or repulsive? Sometimes this tactic can "unstick" a stuck group.
- Be prepared for some students to disagree with the gendered associations of a particular aesthetic characteristic (i.e., pink = feminine). Acknowledge that, yes, individual beliefs and behaviors can vary, but this only shows that cultural beliefs about gender are not "natural" or biological. If they were, they wouldn't vary historically, cross-culturally, or individually. It is important to acknowledge students' individual perspectives while encouraging them to think in terms of *widely held* and *enduring* beliefs about gender as encoded in cultural artifacts. An individual may find "softness" to be masculine, but that aesthetic characteristic has been gendered feminine for a very long time in Western religion, culture, and philosophy. This can be a useful entry point into a discussion about the balance between individual beliefs about gender versus the historical weight of long-held beliefs as

encoded in material cultural artifacts, as well as a consumer's ability to resist or contest the gendered messages in these products.

- Be prepared for students to reduce cultural beliefs about gender to "gender stereo-types." Though technically this exercise uncovers gender stereotypes in product packaging, I find the term itself shuts down analysis rather than furthers it since many students have been trained to see stereotypes as false and derogatory ideas about racial, sexual, and ethnic minorities. By contrast, cultural beliefs about gender are not necessarily negative or inaccurate, and they can have real effects on gendered behavior and the sexed body. Cultural beliefs about gender are no more "true" or "false" than the material world is "true" or "false." On the contrary, the materialization of cultural beliefs about gender in bath product packaging both *reflects* and *produces* gender in society. For example, the widely held cultural equa-tion of softness with femininity drives many women to shave their legs, condition their hair, moisturize their skin, and pumice their heels. In this example, the female body becomes a cultural artifact that (literally) incorporates widely held cultural beliefs about gender (how the female body should appear and feel; femininity). The "soft" female body—partially a gendered construct—is then cited as evidence of "essential" female softness, a characteristic used to justify and legitimate social inequality between women and men.

Alternative Uses

- This activity can be applied to analysis of most any form of material cultural ar-tifact—furniture, clothing, automobiles, etc.—though students not familiar with material culture studies methods or foundational women's- and/or gender-studies concepts often have an easier time if you start with smaller, more familiar, and more obviously gendered artifacts.
- The process outlined in the Handout questions could also be applied to historical cultural artifacts and/or ideologies about race, class, nationalism, and politics.
- In advanced classes, less-gendered or ambiguously gendered objects could be analyzed, as well as the concepts of resistance, contestation, and negotiation by subversive or gender nonconforming consumers. Although the large majority of gendered consumer products reflect the wider gender binary social structure, they present numerous openings for creative nonconforming consumers to turn these products to ends other than those intended by the manufacturers.

REFERENCES

Birke, L. (1992). In pursuit of difference: Scientific studies of women and men. In G. Kirkup & L. S. Keller (Eds.), *Inventing women: Science, technology, and gender* (pp. 81–102). London: The Open University.

Broverman, I. K., Vogel, S. R., Broverman, D. M., Carlson, F. E., & Rosenkrantz, P. S. (1972). Sex-role stereotypes: A current appraisal. *Journal of Social Issues, 28*(2), 59–78.

Hochschild, A., & Machung, A. (2012). *The second shift: Working families and the revolution at home*. Revised edition. New York: Penguin.

Kirkham, P., & Weller, A. (1996). Cosmetics: A Clinique case study. In P. Kirkham (Ed.), *The gendered object* (pp. 196–203). Manchester, UK: Manchester University Press.

Lorber, J. (1995). *Paradoxes of gender*. New Haven, CT: Yale University Press.

Peoples, J. G. (2001). The cultural construction of gender and manhood. In T. Cohen (Ed.), *Men and masculinity: A text reader* (pp. 9–18). New York: Wadsworth.

Prown, J. (1982). Mind in matter: An introduction to material culture theory and method. *Winterthur Portfolio, 17*(1), 1–19.

Summers, D. (1993). Form and gender. *New Literary History, 24*(2), 243–71.

Warnke, G. (2010). *Debating sex and gender*. Oxford: Oxford University Press.

West, C., & Zimmerman, D. (1987). Doing gender. *Gender and Society, 1*(2), 125–51.

ADDITIONAL READINGS

Donald, M., & Hurcombe, L. (Eds.). (2000). *Gender and material culture in historical perspective*. New York: Palgrave Macmillan.

Martinez, K., & Ames, K. (Eds.). (1997). *The material culture of gender/The gender of material culture*. Wilmington, DE: Winterthur Museum.

Pink, S. (2004). *Home truths: Gender, domestic objects, and everyday life*. London: Berg.

HANDOUT: GENDER ANALYSIS OF BATH/BEAUTY PRODUCT PACKAGING

1. *Select*. From the products your group brought to class, select *one* that seems very masculine or feminine. Often this is a product that is clearly intended for males or females, but not both. Ask if you need help!

2. *Describe*. Every aspect of a product's packaging was selected by a designer and market-tested with potential consumers—there's nothing "natural" or "accidental" about product packaging! Make a list of single words or short phrases that describe the *physical* and *aesthetic characteristics* of the product's packaging. Consider the size, shape, color, texture, font, words, and images (if any). Be specific.

3. *Meaning*. Every product packaging choice is intended to evoke specific *meanings* or *feelings* in the minds of consumers. For the characteristics you listed above, make a list of their common *meanings* or *feelings* (i.e., black = strong, bold, decisive). When you hold the product in your hand, how does its size, shape, and texture make you feel? What emotions or attitudes do you associate with your product's physical characteristics? Note: a characteristic may have many possible meanings; product designers aim for common/majority meanings in order to reach the greatest number of consumers.

4. *Gendered meanings*. For each meaning/emotion/cultural *association* of your product's design *characteristics*, decide if it is typically considered *masculine* or *feminine* (i.e., black = strong = masculine). How *strongly* gendered are these characteristics and their associated meanings? Are there any "mixed messages" in the gendering of your product's packaging? Explain.

5. *Gendered persuasion*. Consider how these gendered meanings/emotions/associations might influence the consumer to view the actual product (not the packaging; its contents). In other words, what do the gendered aspects of the product packaging promise the product will "do" for the consumer's gender? Do you find these gendered messages convincing? Why or why not?

6. *Outside the box*. Imagine you are a product designer and you need to market this same product to a different sex (different than the one you believe it is intended for). What different decisions would you make about the product's physical attributes and their gendered meanings? Why would you make these choices? Are all products able to be "re-gendered" by redesigning product packaging, or are their limits to what a package can do for the "gender" of a product? Why or why not?

VI

BODY

Voicing Gender: Critically Examining Expectations about Gender and Vocalics

Lisa K. Hanasono, PhD
(Bowling Green State University)

Appropriate Course(s) and Level

Gender, interpersonal communication, nonverbal communication, performance studies, impression management, communicating identities, and introduction to human communication.

Appropriate Class Size

This activity was originally designed for smaller classes of less than 40, but it can be adapted to larger classes (up to 150 students).

Learning Goals

- To examine how the human voice is a gendered performance.
- To help students understand a person's gendered vocal performance does not always accurately indicate his or her biological sex.
- To identify and critically evaluate gender stereotypes affiliated with the human voice.
- To challenge students to explain how they use their own voice's pitch, tone, volume, and rate to perform gender.

Estimated Time Required

20 to 30 minutes.

Required Materials

- Standard classroom audiovisual equipment that can play music videos found on the Internet.
- Selection of audio clips (see Preparing for the Activity).

Rationale

From pop music to everyday conversations, vocalics can play an important role in social perception processes. Vocalics are the nonverbal characteristics of a person's voice, such as its volume, pitch, tone, articulation, and rate (Beebe & Beebe, 2008; McCornack, 2010). Instead of focusing on *what* a person says (i.e., the verbal content), vocalics describe *how* a person orally communicates. *Volume* refers to the loudness of an articulated message. *Pitch* indicates how high or low a person's voice sounds. Changes in pitch are called vocal inflections; individuals who do not vary the pitch of their voices are typically described as *monotone*. *Tone* refers to a voice's clarity or timbre. For example, an individual with a raspy or hoarse voice would have a harsher tone than an individual with a breathier voice (Verderber, 2000). *Rate* refers to the speed at which a person speaks; most native English speakers articulate 165 to 180 words per minute (Rubin, 1994).

Individuals often use vocal tone, pitch, volume, and inflection to infer other people's gender, biological sex, sexual orientation, attractiveness, and personality (Mack & Munson, in press; Weirich, 2008). For example, Harms (1961) reported that most participants could correctly identify another person's gender, ethnicity, and social class by simply listening to a recording of the individual's voice for 10 to 15 seconds. Amir et al. (2011) found untrained listeners correctly identified the gender of children's recorded voices 81.8 percent of the time. There are perceived gender differences in a variety of vocal characteristics. Specifically, people tend to perceive voices that are higher in pitch (Andrews & Schmidt, 1996), breathier in tone (Borsel, Janssens, & De Bodt, 2008), and smoother to be more feminine in quality than masculine.

Although researchers have documented perceived gender differences in vocalics, the speech perception process is often unquestioned and can result in the application of problematic stereotypes (Strand, 1999). Simply listening to the quality of a person's voice can lead to erroneous assumptions about a person's gender. Just because a person sounds "feminine" or "masculine" does not necessarily mean he or she self-identifies with a particular gender. For example, an actor who performs a soprano solo may sound feminine, but he may self-identify as a masculine person. By completing this activity, students will gain a greater understanding and appreciation of the complex relationship between vocalics and gender.

In addition, students frequently conflate the concepts of gender and biological sex. Some students use the terms interchangeably, while others talk about gender when they are actually referring to a person's biological sex (or vice versa). The study of vocalics can help students explore and understand the differences between socially constructed gender and biological sex.

Preparing for the Activity

1. You will need to find two songs that feature singers whose voices challenge traditional gender performances. A plethora of free examples can be found on YouTube. One recommended clip features the talented voice of Moises Castillo, an acclaimed male soprano. In this clip, Castillo performs an operatic song from "Poema en Forma de Canciones" (Tapia, 2002). As a male soprano, Castillo is able

to hit high notes that are traditionally associated with female/women's voices. Another recommended clip features the vocal talents of Thai singer Bell Nuntita (2011). Nuntita is able to sing in a lower register that is traditionally considered masculine; her vocalics are masculine even though she presents as a woman. It is the disjunction between biological sex and gendered vocalics that makes these two examples useful for the study of gender and vocalics. Ultimately, the activity should feature one song by a person who demonstrates more "masculine" vocalics and another song that features a voice with more "feminine" vocalics.

2. Before the class period starts, you should preset the selected songs, using the classroom's audiovisual equipment.

Facilitating the Activity

1. At the beginning of the class period, introduce the concept of vocalics (e.g., Duck & McMahan, 2011) to the students. After briefly discussing the fundamentals of pitch, tone, volume, and inflection, explain how people can perform gender through vocalics. Then explain that people make inferences about others' identities by simply listening to their voices.

2. Next give students the Vocalics Worksheet (see Handout).

3. Play an audio clip of the first song; during this time, students should quickly write down their perceptions of the singer's vocalics, demographic attributes (e.g., gender, age, race, biological sex, sexual orientation) and personality traits on the Vocalics Worksheet.

4. Then play an audio clip of the second song and ask students to describe the second singer on the same sheet of paper. It is important to note that students should *only hear* the audio tracks of the songs. They should not be exposed to the music videos' visual cues yet. If you only have video versions of the songs, you can simply turn off the projector in your classroom, so students won't get a sneak peek at the singers' physical appearances.

5. Once the audio recordings have played, ask students to share their written descriptions with the rest of the class. Students should share their perceptions about each singer's physical appearance *and* personality traits. If possible, students should form a consensus about the identities of the mystery singers.

6. Finally, reveal the identities of the singers by showing *video* recordings of the songs. Usually students will be surprised by the discrepancies between the way the singers were portrayed in their written descriptions and the way they were actually portrayed in the music videos.

7. Once both music videos have been screened, debrief the activity using the Discussion Questions.

Discussion Questions

- What are some common gender stereotypes affiliated with the human voice?
  - How do people learn about these stereotypes?
  - Why are these generalizations problematic?

- What aspects of each singer's voice in the audio track led you to believe he or she would appear in a particular way?
- How did the singers' actual physical appearances compare to your initial perceptions?
- How do you use your voice's pitch, tone, volume, and rate to perform gender?
  - How conscious are you of the use of vocalics in regard to your own gender performance?

Typical Results

- Students typically love this activity! Because the relationship between people's vocal gender expression and their biological sex is often taken for granted, many students find this activity to be novel, interesting, and educational.
- This activity teaches students to reflect on their own beliefs, biases, and expectations about the human voice and gender. It also helps students realize how their own voices perform gender in everyday interactions.

Limitations and Cautionary Advice

- You should pick your music videos wisely *before* your class meeting. The video clips should feature relatively unknown singers so students will not guess the performers' actual identities. In other words, it would *not* be a good idea to play music videos by popular recording artists because most of the students are familiar with these singers.
- The videos should also feature voices that challenge stereotypes about gendered voices.
- It is important to *not* show the music videos to the students until the *end* of the activity. Sometimes instructors will accidentally show the video clips (instead of playing the audio tracks). The element of surprise plays a key role in this activity's success.

Alternative Uses

- You are welcome to use the recommended songs, or you can select your own. As an alternative to music videos on YouTube, you could purchase or rent music videos of professional singers (university libraries often have eclectic music collections).
- This activity can be adapted to a written assignment. Instead of posing the discussion questions to students in class, you can simply play the clips and ask students to respond to some of the discussion questions in a 1–2 page reaction paper. This approach encourages each student to reflect carefully on his or her perceptions about gender, biological sex, and the human voice. In addition, this short writing assignment will allow you to provide personalized feedback to your students.
- This activity highlights how human voices express gendered identities. However, gender is only one identity marker affiliated with vocalized performances. This

same activity could be used to teach students how people attribute other identity markers (e.g., race, ethnicity, age) to human voices.

• In addition, this activity highlights how audio *and* visual cues shape social perceptions. Instructors who specialize in media studies might use this activity to teach students how the medium (e.g., radio broadcastings versus televised music videos) can shape people's impressions of the artist.

REFERENCES

Amir, O., Engel, M., Shabtai, E., & Amir, N. (2011). Identification of children's gender and age by listeners. *Journal of Voice, 26*, 313–21.

Andrews, M. L., & Schmidt, C. P. (1996). Gender presentation: Perceptual and acoustical analyses of voice. *Journal of Voice, 11*, 307–13.

Beebe, S. A., & Beebe, S. J. (2008). *Public speaking: An audience-centered approach* (7th ed.). Boston: Pearson.

Borsel, J. V., Janssens, J., & De Bodt, M. (2008). Breathiness as feminine voice characteristic: A perceptual approach. *Journal of Voice, 23*, 291–94.

Duck, S., & McMahan, D. T. (2011). *The basics of communication: A relational perspective* (2nd ed.). Los Angeles: Sage Publications.

Harms, L. S. (1961). Listener judgments of status cues in speech. *Quarterly Journal of Speech, 47*, 164–68.

Mack, S., & Munson, B. (in press). The influence of /s/ quality on ratings of men's sexual orientation: Explicit and implicit measures of the 'gay lisp' stereotype. *Journal of Phonetics*.

McCornack, S. (2010). *Reflect and relate: An introduction to interpersonal communication.* Boston: Bedford/St. Martin's.

Nuntita, B. (2011). Bell sings Mak Kwa Rak and Kwam Lub. www.nuntitabell.com/latest-video-clips.

Rubin, J. (1994). A review of second language listening comprehension research. *Modern Language Journal, 78*, 199–221.

Strand, E. A. (1999). Uncovering the role of gender stereotypes in speech perception. *Journal of Language and Social Psychology, 18*, 86–99.

Tapia, J. C. (2002). Cantares from "Poema en forma de canciones." www.youtube.com/watch?v=hOoTuhboF7Y.

Verderber, R. F. (2000). *The challenge of effective speaking* (11th ed.). Belmont, CA: Wadsworth.

Weirich, M. (2008). Vocal stereotypes. Proceedings from the 2nd ISCA Workshop on Experimental Linguistics, Athens, Greece.

HANDOUT: VOCALICS WORKSHEET

Please use this worksheet to record your perceptions of Singer #1 and Singer #2.

Singer #1
Vocalics: Please describe the singer's vocalics.
Perceptions: Based on your knowledge of the singer's vocalics, please describe the person's
Singer #2
Vocalics: Please describe the singer's vocalics.
Perceptions: Based on your knowledge of the singer's vocalics, please describe the person's

23

Performing and Analyzing
Gendered Nonverbal Communication

Deborah Cunningham Breede, PhD
(Coastal Carolina University)

Appropriate Course(s) and Course Levels

A variety of communication classes—including gender, interpersonal, and nonverbal—yet also meets a variety of objectives within sociology, psychology, women's and gender studies, and world languages and cultures. Suitable for introductory as well as upper-level courses.

Appropriate Class Size

12–30 students.

Learning Goals

- To articulate and exemplify differences in nonverbal forms of communication often attributed to sex, gender, gendered performance, age, geography, ethnicity, and other standpoints common in modern American culture.
- To identify and critique some of the many cultural, political, and historical explanations for such differences in gendered nonverbal communication.
- To adapt and regulate individual communication styles to conform to a variety of gendered styles and norms of nonverbal communication.

Estimated Time Required

One 75-minute or longer time block; plan for a two-day process in classes that are shorter. Part(s) of the activity are easily adaptable for homework assignments as well (see Alternative Uses).

Required Materials

- Pencil or pen.
- Traditional or electronic notebook.
- Copies of the Handout (see below).

Rationale

Social constructionists/symbolic interactionists (Blumer, 1969; Mead, 1934) theorize that through language, human beings are able to create meaning and symbolically construct their realities, including their social worlds. Researchers in nonverbal communication have extended this line of thought to suggest social norms governing nonverbal communication teach, sustain, and reify cultural gender norms (Burgoon & Le Poire, 1999; Hall, Halberstadt, & O'Brien, 1997). Simply defined here as information transmitted without using words, types of nonverbal communication include body language, paralanguage, spatial usage, and self-presentation (Verderber & Verderber, 2013). Body language (eye contact and motion, facial expressions, gestures, posture, and touch); paralanguage (vocal pitch, volume, rate, quality, intonation, and use of vocal markers); our use of space (including personal space, acoustic space, and territory); and our self-presentation (physical appearance, artifacts, and use of scent) all involve distinct and culturally bound gender performances. In addition, according to Hybels and Weaver (2007), nonverbal communication is often subconscious. Like most of us, students don't often relate their everyday behaviors to their perceptions and performances of culturally appropriate gendered nonverbal behaviors. Moreover, many students unquestioningly accept these culturally imposed demands, roles, and expectations as "natural," "easy," and/or "normal," sometimes leading to troubling stereotypes, ethnocentrisms, and sexisms (Hall, E. T., 1959; Ivy, 2012; Wood, 2013). Therefore, this activity is designed to introduce students to the gendered "performance of everyday self" (Goffman, 1959) that occurs through nonverbal social communication.

Preparing for the Activity

1. There is little preparation required for this activity.
2. You may choose to make copies of the optional Handout (see below).

Facilitating the Activity

1. Ask students to define and/or exemplify nonverbal communication. What is it? What are some examples of it? Make sure all examples of nonverbal communication listed on the Handout are discussed.
2. Distribute Handout. Referencing the Handout, ask students to brainstorm by themselves a list of differences in the ways in which men and women generally use nonverbal communication within American culture. Ask students to share their lists. Ensure, again, that all of the examples listed on the Handout are discussed. Some students will usually observe that other students are displaying artifacts different from the traditional norm (female students in sports attire, for example).

3. Briefly discuss the differences between sex and gender. Note that these terms are often used interchangeably, but that sex generally refers to biology and/or anatomy; gender generally refers to the ways in which cultures distinguish differently between the sexes through assignment and performance of culturally approved roles. This is a good time to introduce differences in nonverbal gendered norms existing in other cultures, if they have not already been discussed. It is also important to talk about variations in gendered nonverbal performances that occur within our own culture: differences that often emerge in this discussion are different norms of dress in various parts of the country or different uses of artifacts among various genders.

4. Team each student with a partner. It is useful to try to make these pairings mixed sex if possible. Give students the following instructions:

> Go somewhere right now where you know students are gathered. This may be the quad, an athletic field, or another outside venue (weather permitting); a library, computer lab, bookstore, or other academically related space; or a coffee shop, dining hall, sandwich shop, or other food-service space. Sit down somewhere, and for 10 minutes write down examples of the various nonverbal communication behaviors you observe, and how they differ among men and women. Note any gender differences or other differences in traditional behaviors. Then sit with your partner for 10 minutes, compare notes, and compile results to share with us. All students should return within 30 minutes.

5. When students return, facilitate a brief discussion about the various nonverbal communications they observed and how that varied among sexes and genders they observed. As students are listing, discussing, and comparing their observations, the instructor should note some of the behaviors that were observed, especially those "counter" performances that could be exemplified in the classroom in the next step.

6. For the final section of the activity, I modify one of Bodey's (2009) introductory activities designed for use with Wood (2013). However, you could also use some of the students' observations you noted previously that emphasize gendered norms of nonverbal "tasks." For example, you could ask students to
   - Stand up. Pick up your pen or pencil. Drop it on the floor. You must now pick it up, bending only your knees, not your back. Your rear cannot stick up or out, and you must hold down the back of your shirt while you do so. Do not fall.
   - Sit down. Draw your body in so that your elbows are at your side. Press your knees together. Hold this pose for at least 30 seconds.
   - Stand up again. Pull in your stomach, clasp your hands together in front of you, and say in a soft, high-pitched voice, "Good Afternoon/Good Evening Professor. Thank you for this eye-opening activity."
   - Sit down. Relax. Spread out. Spread your legs and arms out as far as you can. Use space. Hold this position for at least 30 seconds.
   - Stand up again. Drop your pen or pencil. This time, in order to pick it up, you must drop into a crouch or bend at the waist. Do not fall.
   - Now, hold your chin up, throw your shoulders back, and say in a deep strong voice, "Good Afternoon/Good Evening Professor. Thank you for this eye-opening activity."

This activity exemplifies the discomfort most of us have when asked to nonverbally communicate in ways different from the ways in which we have been socialized. Generally speaking, you will find that most men are uncomfortable and/or unable to perform the first three tasks on this list, while women are uncomfortable and/or unable to perform the last three.

7. Briefly discuss the students' discomforts in attempting/performing the tasks. This is a good time to link these performances and discomforts to observations about other nonverbal gendered norms; for example, the ways in which men's clothing generally allows greater freedom of movement than does women's. Process with the Discussion Questions.

Discussion Questions

- Why do men and women use eye contact differently? What are some of the miscommunications that sometimes result because of misinterpretations of eye movement and eye contact?

- Why do men and women use space differently? How do modern American architectural norms, home and office decorative norms, and spatial layout and design norms contribute to gendered use of space?

- What are some of the ways in which artifacts are gendered? How do gendered artifacts affect the ways in which we use nonverbal communication? Does the gendering of artifacts remain consistent over time? Why or why not?

- How did some of your observations of gender performances in these contexts (athletic fields, libraries, restaurants) differ from each other? How do we "choose" our gendered performances and adapt them to different contexts?

- How do race, age, ethnicity, nationality, religion, geography, and other standpoints affect the gendered performance of these nonverbal behaviors?

- How do the norms of nonverbal communication within modern American culture contribute to stereotypes, ethnocentrisms, sexisms, and other discriminatory language and practices?

Typical Results

- This activity displays for students the social construction of gender performance in our culture and paves the way for more demanding and complex performances and activities throughout the rest of the semester. While sometimes apprehensive at first, students are typically able to generate multiple examples, ask provocative questions, and understand and restate the gendered differences in norms, expectations, and performances in nonverbal communication.

- Be prepared for students to ask many follow-up questions the day after this activity; it tends to invite students to observe and question a variety of gendered nonverbal communications once they have left class.

Limitations and Cautionary Advice

- One of the strengths of this activity is that it presents students with an opportunity to generate examples and apply concepts to their own performances of nonverbal communication. This is also one of the activity's challenges. Timing is everything in this activity, and it is often difficult to move from one segment of the activity to the next because of students' interest in the topic.

- The distinction between generalizing typical gendered nonverbal communication and stereotyping is a fine one. Therefore, I find frequently distinguishing between generalizations and stereotypes, sex and gender, and self and society to be necessary.

- This activity is modifiable for students with particular disabilities; for example, be sure to partner a student who is vision impaired with a student who is not. The student who is vision impaired can easily listen for paralanguage differences while the student who is visually oriented can then observe behaviors. Or, perhaps, in the event of wheelchair-bound students, be sure to assign that team a location more easily proximate than other locations may be.

Alternative Uses

- This activity can be extended into a complete unit that includes more detailed discussions of gender and sex, gender performance and sex performance, and verbal communication differences as well as nonverbal communication differences, among others.

- The activity can be adapted to more in-depth and lengthy research projects for students as well as individual homework assignments to allow students to reflect on, apply, criticize, and synthesize these concepts in a variety of contexts.

- The activity is modifiable for online courses. For example, students can brainstorm types of nonverbal communication on the course's online discussion board, complete individual observations in accessible locales, and then share results via a discussion board, homework assignment, or Skype. If the online forum requires a Skype connection, even the alternate nonverbal gender performances can be facilitated, or students can complete those individually and journal about their discomforts with the activity.

REFERENCES

Blumer, H. (1969). *Symbolic interactionism*. Englewood Cliffs, NJ: Prentice-Hall.

Bodey, K. R. (2009). *Instructor's resource manual*. Boston: Wadsworth Cengage Learning.

Burgoon, J. K., & Le Poire, B. (1999). Nonverbal cues and interpersonal judgments: Participant and observer perceptions of intimacy, dominance, and composure. *Communication Monographs, 66*, 105–124.

Goffman, E. (1959). *The presentation of self in everyday life*. Garden City, NY: Doubleday Anchor.

Hall, E. T. (1959). *The silent language*. New York: Anchor Books.

Hall, J. A., Halberstadt, A. G., & O'Brien, C. I. (1997). "Subordination" and nonverbal sensitivity: A study and synthesis of findings based on trait measures. *Sex Roles, 37*, 295–317.

Hybels, S., & Weaver, R. L., III. (2007). *Communicating effectively* (8th ed.). New York: McGraw-Hill.

Ivy, D. K. (2012). *GenderSpeak*. Saddle River, NJ: Pearson Education.

Mead, G. H. (1934). *Mind, self and society*. Chicago: University of Chicago Press.

Verderber, K. S., & Verderber, R. F. (2013). Inter-act: Interpersonal communication (13th ed.). New York: Oxford University Press.

Wood, J. T. (2013). *Gendered lives* (10th ed.). Boston: Cengage Learning.

ADDITIONAL READINGS

Arliss, L. P., & Borisoff, D. J. (Eds.). (2001). *Women and men communicating: Challenges and changes* (2nd ed.). Long Grove, IL: Waveland Press.

Borisoff, D., & Merrill, L. (1998). *The power to communicate* (3rd ed.). Prospect Heights, IL: Waveland Press.

Findlen, B. (Ed.). (2001). *Listen up: Voices from the next feminist generation*. New York: Seal Press.

Foss, S. K., Domenico, M. E., & Foss, K. A. (Eds). (2013). *Gender stories: Negotiating identity in a binary world.* Long Grove, IL: Waveland Press.

Lorber, J., & Moore, L. J. (2007). *Gendered bodies: Feminist perspectives*. Los Angeles: Roxbury Publishing.

Tannen, D. (2001). *You just don't understand*. New York: Quill.

HANDOUT: TYPES OF
GENDERED NONVERBAL COMMUNICATION

(Note: Handout can be adapted to serve as an observation sheet)

- Artifacts: Personal objects such as clothing, jewelry, and furnishings that represent our identities, self concepts, and group affiliations.
- Proxemics: Use of space, including personal space, distance, and territory.
- Haptics: Use of touch, including personal touch and the use of physical force.
- Kinesics: Use of body language, including facial motion (eye contact and eye movement) and body motion (gestures, posture, and movement).
- Paralanguage: Vocal cues, including pitch, volume, rate, quality, intonation, and the use of fillers such as "um" and "uh."
- Physical appearance/Self-Presentation: Bodily appearance, including weight, shape, size, physical features, and use of scent.

Gender-Norm Violation and Analysis

Tamara Berg, PhD
(Winona State University)

Appropriate Course(s) and Level

Introductory to intermediate courses in women's/gender studies, cultural studies, communication studies, and psychology.

Appropriate Class Size

Up to 40 students in classrooms with enough space to allow for small-group work.

Learning Goals

- To identify common culturally constructed gender norms.
- To critically analyze the power of gender norms, the social pressures to conform to them, and the challenges encountered when one transgresses a gender norm.
- To reflect upon the process of violating masculine and feminine gender norms and the impact these norms have on larger cultural issues.

Estimated Time Required

One 75-minute class is appropriate, but the activity could be adapted for shorter classes by completing the planning and acting out of a violation portion of the exercise during one class and carrying out the analysis and discussion in the following class.

Required Materials

- Varies according to the planned violations. Students should decide what materials they need to carry out this activity, drawing from their personal items as needed.

Props also may be supplied by the instructor. Some examples of "violations" and needed props that have been carried out in the past include:
° A woman spitting in public.
° A man with pastel-painted nails asking passersby what they think about his manicure and offering to paint other men's nails.
° A man carrying a purse.
° A woman carrying a heavy box or other large item while walking with an empty-handed man by her side.
° A man wearing a skirt.
° A woman offering to open a door for a man to walk through.
° A man walking to and from a dorm shower with a towel wrapped at armpit level and/or wrapped on his head.

Rationale

Risman (2004) argued we need to understand gender as a social structure in order to analyze the ways in which gender influences us as individuals and to examine how it controls the institutional dimensions of our society. This exercise gives students the opportunity to understand how strong socially constructed norms are, how those norms limit the actions of men and women, and how challenging it is to transgress gender norms. Lorber (1995) argued gender differences are socially constructed to justify sexual stratification and gender inequality. "The continuing purpose of gender as a modern social institution is to construct women as a group to be subordinate to men as a group" (p. 33). Kimmel (2008) focused on the detrimental effects socially constructed norms of masculinity have had on men.

The social construction of gender is undoubtedly a complex concept, but it is common for students to view gender as a simple case of "either/or"—if you are a man you act a certain way; if you are a woman you act a certain way, and these gendered behaviors are inherent. This exercise facilitates an understanding that gender is "performed" through a combination of countless signals using clothing, cosmetics, hairstyles, the way we talk, body language, and much more. As students plan and carry out a gender-norm violation in a public space, they will experience what it feels like to violate a cultural norm related to gender and/or sexuality. Cultural constructions of masculinity and femininity influence all aspects of life, including personal identity, and therefore the act of transgressing an identified norm results in a number of repercussions, both for the transgressor (the student) and those witnessing the transgression (the public). By analyzing their personal reactions to the act of transgressing as well as the public's response to their actions, students come to understand via their experience how strong gender norms are in our culture.

Preparing for the Activity

1. For the day you will conduct this activity, assign students one or more readings on the social construction of gender (see Kimmel, 1999; Lorber, 1995) or prepare a brief lecture on this material.

2. Note on the syllabus that students will participate in an exercise that will take them outside of the classroom.
3. Bring any needed/desired props.

Facilitating the Activity

1. Introduce the activity by explaining the concept of a gender-norm violation. Give examples of what constitutes a gender-norm violation (see examples in Required Materials).
2. Divide students into teams to brainstorm their gender-norm violations (team size may vary depending on class size, but 3 to 5 in a group works well). Stress that violations must not break any laws. Discuss options for conducting the violation, which will vary based on the planned transgression: 1) One student performs the violation while the others observe as bystanders (students could switch roles if feasible), or 2) All group members participate in the violation. Encourage students to discuss possible props that may be used. Focus on facilitating a discussion of how to carry out the violation and what possible issues could arise—either with the proposed scenario or with possible repercussions resulting from the violation. Have students focus on keeping the situation safe and legal no matter what the violation.
3. Once their violations have been approved by you, allow students to move to a public space to perform their gender-norm violations. Ask them to think about where potential audiences will be (a cafeteria, commons, bookstore, coffee shop, etc.). Ask them to let you know where they are going. Circulate among groups to monitor progress. Allow at least 20 minutes for the groups to enact the transgressions and record their findings.
4. Return to the classroom and allow 25 minutes to discuss the outcome of the violations. Encourage students to reflect on their experiences, focusing on their personal reactions while enacting the violations as well as the public reaction.

Discussion Questions

- What happened before, during, and after the gender-norm violation?
- How did you feel as you were transgressing a gender norm?
- If you were observing, how did you feel while watching the transgression?
- If you felt nervous or embarrassed or scared during any part of the exercise, where might those feelings be coming from?
- If you felt excited or empowered during any part of the exercise, where might those feelings be coming from?
- What was the public response to the transgression?
- If the public response was negative, what do you think was behind the response?
- If the public response was positive, what do you think was behind the response?
- How, if at all, were you surprised by your feelings or the reactions of others?
- Drawing from your experience, how do cultural constructions of masculinity and femininity influence our actions and choices?

- Drawing from your experience, how do cultural constructions of masculinity and femininity influence society in general?
- Where do gender norm expectations come from? How powerful is their influence on behavior?

Typical Results

- This activity has been a popular and effective assignment that exposes students to the reality of socially constructed gender norms and reinforces the idea that society dictates norms of masculinity, femininity, and sexuality.
- Students generally remark on either how difficult or how exciting it was to transgress gender norms in a public space, and they often express a respect for those who violate gender norms as well as a deeper understanding of how powerful the cultural forces are that keep us compliant with even seemingly "minor" gender norms (i.e., men should open doors for women, not the other way around).

Limitations and Cautionary Advice

- For this activity to be successful, it is necessary to address the fact that many people live their lives transgressing gender norms. It is important that students approach this exercise without exploiting stereotypes (i.e., cross-dressing may be an effective gender-norm violation, but it needs to be done in a way that does not turn the violation into a caricature).
- It is also necessary to provide adequate debriefing time for the students—they will want to share what happened during their violation, and facilitating an analysis of their experiences as well as the public reaction to their violation is an important part of this exercise. Note that the facilitation should not just be about students' experience but also about how it relates to course material.

Alternative Uses

- This exercise can be extended to violations of other culturally constructed norms: race, class, age, ability, etc.
- This exercise also affords a powerful blogging or journaling opportunity if the assignment is structured to allow students to blog about their experiences either on a course website or other Internet forum.
- This exercise is also a good tool to begin a discussion about transgender issues. Students learn that society often reacts to gender transgression by trying to discourage the behavior, in some way silencing or punishing the individual. Some people, simply because their gender expression differs from the norm, are subjected to emotional trauma or physical harm. The experience of publicly transgressing a gender norm can be a powerful point of entry into thinking about why gender norms are so powerful, what and whom they control, and which social norms they enforce.
- This activity also could be used as a take-home assignment, but there is the risk that the students won't actually perform the violation. A detailed written analysis of their experience could help to mitigate this risk.

REFERENCES

Kimmel, M. (1999, October/November). What are little boys made of? *Ms*, pp. 88–91.

Kimmel, M. (2008). *Guyland: The perilous world where boys become men.* New York: HarperCollins.

Lorber, J. (1995). *Paradoxes of gender*. New Haven, CT: Yale University Press.

Risman, B. J. (2004). Gender as a social structure: Theory wrestling with activism. *Gender and Society, 18*(4), 429–50.

VII

WORK

25

Gender at Work: Revealing and Reconciling the Influence of Gender Norms on Perceived Occupational Roles

Jessica Furgerson, MA
(Ohio University)

Appropriate Course(s) and Levels

Lower-level courses in women's and gender studies, sociology, communication, or psychology.

Appropriate Class Size

10–35 students, but can be adapted to very large classes (see Alternative Uses).

Learning Goals

- To explore the normative assumptions surrounding gender and occupation.
- To encourage student reflection on the factors that have contributed to the formation of their own gender stereotypes.
- To examine the link between gender stereotypes and occupational segregation.

Estimated Time Required

10 minutes of preparation and approximately 30 minutes of class time.

Required Materials

- Name the Profession worksheet (see Handout).

Rationale

Despite the passage in 1963 of the federal Equal Pay Act, which formally outlawed discriminatory compensation practices, informal sex discrimination is still prevalent in the United States. As Gabriel and Schmitz (2007) explained, "Occupational differences between men and women are a persistent presence in the U.S. labor market. Traditional blue-collar occupations such as operatives and craft continue to be male dominated, while women remain concentrated in service and clerical occupations" (p. 1). For example, in 2007, 79 percent of clerical and support jobs were filled by women while 91 percent of production and craft/trade based jobs were filled by men (Gabriel & Schmitz, 2007). These differences, known as occupational sex segregation, continue to exist. Cartwright, Edwards, and Wang (2011) noted, "Service-providing industries, as a whole, have about twice the percentage of female employees as do goods-producing industries (54.5 percent and 27.3 percent, respectively)" (p. 39).

Although educational level and other socioeconomic factors contribute to occupational sex segregation, cultural stereotypes and assumptions surrounding work and gender are also a major factor. In her book *Delusions of Gender* (2010), Fine argued,

> When we categorize someone, as we inevitably do, gender associations are automatically activated and we perceive them through the filter of culture beliefs and norms. This is sexism gone underground—unconscious and unintended—and social psychologists and lawyers are becoming very interested in how this new, covert, and unintended form of sexism disadvantages women . . . in the workplace. (p. 66)

Despite our desire to remain unbiased or gender neutral, social and cultural norms cause us to unconsciously form associations between gender and occupational roles. Kmec, McDonald, and Trimble (2010) contended, "Widely shared gender status expectations about masculinity and femininity shape societal beliefs about men's and women's work-related capabilities" (p. 215). These expectations are transmitted from childhood through toys and media representations, which socialize us from a young age to associate certain skills, career goals, and occupations with either men or women. Fine (2010) also stated, "The implicit associations of the mind can be thought of as a tangled but highly organized network of connections," which, for instance, often results in the pairing of agentic words (i.e., competitive) with males and communal words (i.e., supportive) with females (pp. 4–5). "These status expectations are stereotypes that define 'appropriate' work for women and men, thereby making gender a prominent basis for matching workers to jobs" (Kmec, McDonald, & Trimble, 2010, p. 215). Given the significance, and often-unacknowledged prevalence, of these stereotypes, this activity seeks to help students see and analyze their own stereotypical associations between gender and work.

This activity pushes students to discover and reflect on the influence of gender-based assumptions and stereotypes within these contexts. By engaging students in an activity that doesn't simply tell them about gender norms but exposes their own gender biases, this activity provides students with experiential knowledge, allowing them to understand the influence of gender stereotypes on their own cognitive associations. The coupling of this activity with the debriefing Discussion Questions provides students with the opportunity to reflect on the ways they formed their own gender-based assumptions and stereotypes as well as the implications of gender stereotypes within not only the occupational context but society overall.

Preparing for the Activity

1. Conducting the exercise *prior* to any lecture on gendered profiles of specific occupations and sex-segregation helps prevent students from providing answers based on what they believe is the correct answer based on the course or the instructor. Students should engage in the activity prior to discussing the material for the day, ensuring that their responses are not biased and that the intent of the activity is not discovered prior to its completion.
2. Prior to the start of class, photocopy one worksheet (see Handout) for each student.

Facilitating the Activity

1. Begin by handing out a worksheet to each student. Instruct students to write their name on the back of their worksheet so that the responses can be tallied without being matched to any students.
2. Instruct students to read all of the instructions prior to beginning, and answer any questions that students may have. Encourage students not to think too much about the worksheet, and to simply put down the first name that comes to mind.
3. Collect the worksheets from the students.
4. Tally the responses to each of the occupations, determining how many students provided a man's name or a woman's name. Do not share this information until you begin debriefing the activity.
5. Pass the worksheets back to the students.

Discussion Questions

- What kind of names did you write down for Doctor? What about CEO?
- What kind of names did you write down for Nurse? What about Secretary?
- Which professions did you write down a man's name for?
- Which professions did you write down a woman's name for?

At this point, reveal the numbers you tallied earlier for each answer. Revealing these numbers allows students to see the prevalent preponderance of gender stereotypes by highlighting the number of students who associated a given profession with either a man's or a woman's name.

- Are any of these professions exclusive to one gender or the other?
- Are any of these professions more suited to one gender than the other? For example, do some jobs require more physical strength than a woman may possess?
- What aspects of the profession make it more suited to one sex/gender or another? Are these dependent on one's sex (male/female) or merely associated with one's sex?
- What jobs did you typically consider "men's" jobs? What characteristics of these jobs make them masculine?

- What jobs did you typically consider "women's" jobs? What characteristics of these jobs make them feminine?
- What kinds of information, experiences, and knowledge influenced your selection of names for each occupation? Did the wording of the position title affect your answer? If the profession had been Policeman, Waitress, or Senator, would that have changed your response?
- How, if at all, can we avoid gendering of certain professions?
- Should we recognize the sex of the person that holds the position by saying "female athlete" or "male nurse"? Why or why not?
- Does changing how we refer to these occupations affect the existence of these gender associations? Why or why not?
- How could we create a more gender-neutral society to help break down assumptions about which jobs are appropriate? (For example, if more young girls were encouraged to play with fire trucks and more young boys to play "house," would it be possible to lessen the existing occupational segregation within the labor force?)

Typical Results

- This activity has continually encouraged and facilitated high-level critical thinking about the role of gender associations and stereotypes. Although the objective of the activity may seem obvious to educators, students rarely catch on. Students, especially those who consider themselves sensitive to issues of gender disparity and socialization, often are shocked to learn they too employ these very stereotypes regularly.
- By conducting the activity prior to a lecture on the role of gender in the workplace, the responses given by students are honest, and the discussion much more revealing and insightful.
- The response to this activity has been overwhelmingly favorable, as students have commonly used this activity as a springboard for self-reflection and critical inquiry about the prevalence of gender associations within their own mind and society as a whole.

Limitations and Cautionary Advice

- Although this activity typically goes well, students who have not thought about these issues before may be reluctant to disclose the factors that influenced their choices. To help students feel more at ease discussing the sometimes sensitive issue of gender stereotypes, students should be selected on a volunteer basis, and instructors should also be willing to share any experiences that contributed to the formation of their own stereotypes about gender and work. Conducting the discussion in such a way encourages students to feel comfortable answering honestly.
- Instructors should be prepared to modify the Discussion Questions based on the feedback they receive to promote critical and productive discussion of gender norms.

• Finally, it is important to have a conversation about the importance of gender diversity in the workplace in addition to a discussion of the influence of gender norms.

Alternative Uses

• The basic objective of this activity can easily be adapted to fit the needs of other content areas. For example, instead of asking students to provide a first name for each occupation, ask students to write down a race for each position; doing so can help students learn about racial norms and the complex relationship of race and class.
• Rather than tallying in class, the instructor can ask for a hand-count.

REFERENCES

Cartwright, B., Edwards, P. R., & Wang, Q. (2011). Job and industry gender segregation: NA-ICS categories and EEO-1 job groups. *Monthly Labor Review Online, 134*(11).

Fine, C. (2010). *Delusions of gender: How our minds, society, and neurosexism create difference* (1st ed.). New York: W. W. Norton & Company.

Gabriel, P. E., & Schmitz, S. (2007). Gender differences in occupational distributions among workers. *Monthly Labor Review Online, 130*(6).

Kmec, J. A., McDonald, S., & Trimble, L. B. (2010). Making gender fit and "correcting" gender misfits. *Gender & Society, 24*(2), 213–36.

Taylor, C. J. (2010). Occupational sex composition and the gendered availability of workplace support. *Gender & Society, 24*(2), 189–212.

ADDITIONAL WEBSITES FOR INSTRUCTOR PREPARATION

• Bureau of Labor Statistics—Current Employment Statistics. www.bls.gov/ces/.
• Center for Women Policy Studies. www.centerwomenpolicy.org/programs/poverty/default.asp.
• United States Department of Labor—Equal Employment Opportunity. www.dol.gov/dol/topic/discrimination/ethnicdisc.htm.

HANDOUT: NAME THE PROFESSION

Instructions: Next to each profession, please write a first name that would suit a person who holds this position. You do not need to write the name of someone you know with this occupation. If possible, do not duplicate names.

Doctor
Librarian
Lawyer
Teacher
Veterinarian
Stockbroker
Secretary
CEO
Dental Hygienist
Scientist
Plumber
Retail Salesclerk
College Professor
Nurse
Police Officer
Politician
Real Estate Agent
Professional Athlete
Nutritionist
Restaurant Server
Lobbyist
Journalist

Analyzing Media Representations of Powerful Women in the Workplace

Sarah Stone Watt, PhD
(Pepperdine University)

Appropriate Course(s) and Level

Introductory and advanced courses in women's/gender studies, media studies, gender and communication, organizational communication, business communication, and public relations.

Appropriate Class Size

15 or more students where classroom space allows for small-group work.

Learning Goals

- To critique perceptions of what makes a "powerful woman" in the workplace across industries.
- To reflect upon the ways in which men and women in the workplace may be portrayed differently.
- To understand the ways media framing contributes to wider cultural perceptions of sex and gender in the workplace.

Estimated Time Required

30–40 minutes.

Required Materials

- Magazine list of powerful women, such as the *Forbes* list "The World's 100 Most Powerful Women."
- Sheryl Sandberg's (2010) TED talk "Why We Have Too Few Women Leaders" (optional).

Rationale

In a 2010 TED talk, Facebook chief operations officer Sheryl Sandberg made the bold claim that "women are not making it to the top of any profession anywhere in the world." Although there are *some* women at the top, they are few and far between. Sandberg (2010) quantified the problem by highlighting the small percentages of women as heads of state (4 percent), members of parliament (13 percent), and top-level corporate executives (15–16 percent) around the world, explaining that the numbers "have not moved since 2002 and are going in the wrong direction."

These numbers may be hard for American college students to grasp in light of the feminist movement's gains, the high percentages of women entering and graduating from college, recent high-profile political campaigns, and the cultural myth that women today can be anything they want to be. Young women who see these achievements are ready to embrace the choices they have and the empowerment they perceive as a result of feminism. They often are hesitant to believe that feminism is still needed to accomplish true equality in a variety of areas, particularly employment. Feminist scholars recognize this phenomenon as post-feminism—taking into account feminist gains to create a sort of "*faux*-feminism," in which, McRobbie (2009) explained, "the young woman is offered a notional form of equality, concretized in education and employment, and through participation in consumer culture and civil society, in place of what a reinvented feminist politics might have to offer" (p. 2). This depoliticization of equality for women comes through the promotion, within popular culture, of those areas of life in which women can *perform* equality without necessarily achieving it, such as sexuality and consumption.

Across the media landscape in particular, women are offered role models who depict the playing field as level. A long line of television shows portraying female empowerment in the workplace such as *Murphy Brown*, *Ally McBeal*, *Friends*, and *Sex in the City* have painted a persuasive picture of empowered women who love their jobs but struggle for fulfillment in their personal lives (Rockler, 2006). These shows, along with news reports highlighting how miserable women are at work (Buckingham, 2009) offer evidence that women are integrated into the workforce, but they would rather be at home. News reports complicate the picture further by highlighting those women who are striving to have it all, creating an "alpha mom" who has kids and a helpful spouse and, as a result, is happier than other working women (Olsen, 2011).

Recognizing that women are better represented in the lower echelons of the workforce, that women may face unique challenges in balancing work and personal life, and that media representations influence our perception of workplace equality, college students should have the opportunity to explore media messages regarding powerful working women. Each year *Forbes* magazine publishes its list "The World's 100 Most Powerful Women," which I offer to students as an illustration not only of women who hold great power but also of how the media depicts them. Using the list, I invite students to consider the powerful positions women hold, the skills that appear to be valued by business-minded audiences, and the language this publication uses to frame women in power.

Preparing for the Activity

1. Locate a recent list of powerful women that offers some description of the women and their accomplishments. The *Forbes* list is ideal because it offers brief biographical information, highlights of major accomplishments, and pictures of the women on the list. This gives students a brief but detailed image of each woman to work with. Similar lists, such as the *Fortune* "50 Most Powerful Women in Business" will also work. You may choose to print copies of the list or invite students to use their laptops to access it during class.

2. Determine which categories within the list are most relevant to your class. Although *Forbes* offers an overall ranking of the top 100, they also categorize the women by type of industry, such as business, politics, nonprofit, sports, and celebrity/lifestyle. Students will work in groups to analyze the women in one category and then come together to make comparisons across categories.

3. Once you know which areas you would like students to focus on, create a worksheet (see Handout) for each area that contains the primary issues/questions you would like the group to consider. For example, you might want them to take note of the number of women in their assigned category, the countries represented, and the information offered regarding their job and their personal life, along with any other issues you have discussed concerning women in the workplace. In my course I cover prominent stereotypes of women in the workplace such as the sex object, mother, child, and iron maiden (Wood, 2011), and I ask students to look for signs of those stereotypes in the descriptions of the women.

4. Prior to dividing the class into groups for this activity, it can be helpful to deliver a lecture or lead a class discussion regarding sex and gender in the workplace. You may find it useful to cover the historical development of gender in the workplace, the types of jobs women and men have held in previous time periods, changing assumptions about gender roles at work and home, and stereotypes for women and men in the workplace. You might also discuss the disparities in representation of women and men in different types of work and highlight the lack of women in powerful positions (Sandberg's talk is helpful for addressing this issue). Finally, take time to discuss media representations of women and men in the workplace and invite students to identify existing images that inform the current cultural understanding of gender and work.

Facilitating the Activity

1. Divide the class into small groups of 3–5 students.
2. Make sure each group has a copy of the *Forbes* list "The World's 100 Most Powerful Women" and a worksheet to focus their discussion.
3. Allow students enough time to work together to answer the questions on the worksheet. Aim for at least 15 minutes of small-group discussion and analysis.
4. When the groups have answered the questions, have each report their findings to the class as a whole and process the information and experience with the Discussion Questions.

Discussion Questions

- What similarities and differences did you perceive across categories?
- What countries appear on the list most often?
  - How, if at all, does this surprise you?
  - Why do you think these countries appear most often?
- What stereotypes appear most often?
  - What words or pictures signal the presence of those stereotypes?
- Based on your interactions with the list, what is your perception of women in the workplace?
- How, if at all, do you think a list of the most powerful men might be different from the list you analyzed today?
- How, if at all, do you think these media representations of women in the workplace will influence your future careers?

Typical Results

- This activity centers on women, yet in the debriefing students tend to talk about a variety of issues related to sex, gender, and work. The preceding lecture, Sandberg talk, and group activity appear to get them thinking about multiple related concepts. After completing the activity students tend to want to discuss how *Forbes* frames the women on the list, the students' perceptions of appropriate roles for women and men, and students' anxieties about work and personal life after college.
- During the discussion it is important to highlight the limited amount of space that *Forbes* writers have to represent each woman. The lack of space and the writing style imply that the magazine offers only the facts in their most condensed form and leaves out what the writers and editors perceive to be trivial details. Students may observe that the entries often focus on particular accomplishments and challenges the women have overcome. In doing so, the magazine highlights the assertiveness of women in high-power positions. This is an important observation because it contradicts repeated reports that women are behind in the workplace because they "don't ask" or are less assertive than men (Babcock & Laschever, 2007; McFarland, 2011). For many entries, the magazine will list information about the woman under the heading "Fast Facts." The bulleted points offer space for a few additional details, usually including at least one personal element such as family activities, favorite foods, and hobbies.
- In discussions regarding the workplace students tend to share their perception of gender roles and work in their own families. Some are passionate in their appreciation or disdain for the way their parents managed work and family and will make active comparisons to the way the women in the list appear to negotiate those boundaries.
- Students often share their own anxieties about entering the workforce. This issue becomes more salient as students perceive mounting pressure to find a job in an uncertain economy. When this discussion occurs, female students tend to be the most concerned. They do not express great concern about making less money,

encountering discrimination, or experiencing sexual harassment. Rather, they focus on their fears about failing to achieve an appropriate work-life balance. Perhaps this highlights the fact that the post-feminist narrative is well engrained among today's young women who believe they can have it all but worry about what they might lose in the process. It is important to discuss the students' concerns and point to the personal and political approaches they might take to reduce the problem. It is also important to gauge the extent to which males in the class share these concerns. In these discussions, men are often surprised that women fear work-life imbalance or that women are concerned about this balance at a point in their lives when they do not yet have a career or a family. The most productive part of this discussion tends to be when both groups consider why the other feels the way they do. This discussion highlights the ways that our culture socializes men and women to think about work and family, and it prompts conversations about how to bring about cultural change in this area.

Limitations and Cautionary Advice

- The most obvious limitation to this exercise is that it focuses heavily on the representation of *women* in the workplace. Men may feel left out of the picture or, if you're not careful, vilified as the gatekeepers in a discriminatory system. There are at least two ways to address this. First, talk about stereotypes of men in the workplace along with the stereotypes of women, and discuss the implications of each of the stereotypes in terms of power. Men tend to recognize that their stereotypes, such as the sturdy oak and the breadwinner, do limit them in real ways but also tend to more readily place them in positions of power. They also realize that women's stereotypes, such as the sex object and the child, tend to be more disempowering. Second, I sometimes assign a reading that highlights the changing nature of men's roles within the family, especially the pressures they feel as a result of increased family responsibilities alongside unchanging workplace responsibilities (see Additional Readings).
- Another limitation is that the heavy focus on traditional understandings of work can give the impression that full-time parenting is not a legitimate occupation. It is important to mention the hard work it takes to maintain a home and family and to confer legitimacy on that option. You may choose to use the term "paid employment" in place of "work." At the same time, remember to highlight the fact that, for most families, having one adult at home full-time is not financially possible.

Alternative Uses

- If you are interested in highlighting the differences between the framing of men and women and the disproportionate number of men in power, you might choose to use the *Forbes* list "The World's Most Powerful People" instead. This list contains women but is dominated by men. Many of the same questions can be asked, but this list offers the opportunity to make direct comparisons between representations of women and men.

- If you are interested in the changing nature of representations, you could compare "The World's 100 Most Powerful Women" lists over time. For example, interesting observations might be made in comparing Sarah Palin's representation on the list on 2010, when she was ranked sixteenth and her industry was listed as politics, versus 2011, when she was ranked 34th and her industry was listed as celebrity/lifestyle.
- This activity can also be adapted to classes focused on different topics such as entertainment, history, politics, and international studies. To do so, simply choose a list that is more relevant to your topic. Some possibilities include
  - "Time 100: The World's Most Influential People," *Time*
  - "Women in Entertainment: The Power 100," *Hollywood Reporter*
  - "Washington's 100 Most Powerful Women," *Washingtonian*
  - "Power Night: 100 Most Powerful Arab Women," Arabianbusiness.com
  - "The 25 Most Powerful Women of the Past Century," *Time*

REFERENCES

Babcock, L., & Laschever, S. (2007). *Women don't ask: The high cost of avoiding negotiation—And positive strategies for change.* New York: Bantam.

Buckingham, R. (2009 September 17). What's happening to women's happiness? Huffington Post. www.huffingtonpost.com/marcus-buckingham/whats-happening-to-womens_b_289511.html.

Forbes. (2010 October 25). The 100 most powerful women (p. 66).

McFarland, S. (2011 October 14). Study: Women ask for raises but aren't heard. CNN. http://business.blogs.cnn.com/2011/10/14/study-women-ask-for-raises-but-arent-heard/.

McRobbie, A. (2009). *The aftermath of feminism: Gender, culture, and social change.* Thousand Oaks, CA: Sage Publications.

Olsen, L. (2011 October 6). Are women less happy in the workplace? U.S. News: Money. http://money.usnews.com/money/blogs/outside-voices-careers/2011/10/06/are-women-less-happy-in-the-workplace.

Rockler, N. (2006). "Be your own windkeeper": Friends, feminism, and rhetorical strategies of depoliticization. *Women's Studies in Communication, 29*(2), 244–64.

Sandberg, S. (2010 December 21). Sheryl Sandberg: Why we have too few women leaders [Video]. www.ted.com/talks/lang/eng/sheryl_sandberg_why_we_have_too_few_women_leaders.html.

Wood, J. T. (2011). *Gendered lives: Communication, gender, and culture* (9th ed.). Boston: Wadsworth, Cengage Learning.

ADDITIONAL READINGS

Curry-Johnson, S. D. (2001). Weaving an identity tapestry. In B. Findlen (Ed.), *Listen up: Voices from the next feminist generation* (pp. 51–58). Emeryville, CA: Seal Press.

Ehrenreich, B. (2002). *Nickel and dimed: On (not) getting by in America.* New York: Holt.

Neuborne, E. (2001). Imagine my surprise. In M. Crawford & R. Kessler Unger (Eds.), *In our own words: Writings from women's lives* (p. 273). Boston: McGraw-Hill.

Scott, P. (2010 July). The new American dad. *Parents* (pp. 84–91).

HANDOUT: ANALYZING MEDIA REPRESENTATIONS OF POWERFUL WOMEN IN THE WORKPLACE

Your group will focus on the women in the *Forbes* list "The World's 100 Most Powerful Women." The questions on this worksheet will help you locate information that you will later compare with other groups who are looking at women listed in other industries such as sports, politics, finance, music, and food. Please use the biography, photograph, "Fast Facts," and any other resources available about the women in your category to answer the following questions:

1. How many women appear in your category?
2. What age group appears to be most/least represented in your category?
3. What country are most of the women in your category from?
4. What commonalities do you notice among the women (include commonalities in content and representation)?
5. Are there any unique details that appear to distinguish some women from others?
6. Which of the stereotypes discussed in class (sex object, mother, child, iron maiden) do you see represented in the descriptions of the women in your category?
   a. What types of evidence are presented for those stereotypes?
   b. Do you see any other stereotypes or generalizations being made regarding the women in your category? Explain.
7. Describe the group of women represented in your category in three sentences or less (no run-ons).

Let's Go to Work: Discovering the Prevalence and Place of Gender and Sexuality Expectations in Organizations

Jeanette Valenti, PhD
(Metropolitan State College of Denver)

Appropriate Course(s) and Level

Introductory to advanced students in organizational/business communication and women's/gender studies.

Appropriate Class Size

Up to 40 students. In classes over 40, it can become difficult to manage the discussion.

Learning Goals

- To discover how organizations present information about gender and sexuality in the workplace or organization within its written policies or handbooks in workplaces.
- To learn to recognize the overt and covert messages about gender and sexuality within a workplace's formal practices and policies.
- To analyze and discuss how the overt and covert messages presented in formal policies may affect sexuality and gender expectations and behavior within the organization.

Estimated Time Required

One 85–100 minute class session so there is enough time for students to read their workplace policies, talk about and analyze them in small groups, and then bring conversation into a class-wide discussion.

Required Materials

- A selection of employee handbooks or some form of written company guidelines and policies (see Preparing for the Activity).
- The worksheet of instructions and question prompts (see Handout).

Rationale

Although most students may be able to think of obvious examples of how gender and sexuality are present in the workplace (i.e., certain types of establishments that feature scantily clad women serving wings), they may be unaware of the prevalence of more subtle and oftentimes gendered messages about expected and accepted behavior in the workplace. Such messages often are found in the employee handbook, or the formal written policies and procedures created by an organization. Example of these messages may include information about how a company handles relationships in the workplace, maternity/paternity leave policies, sick leave and family leave, and guidelines for attire.

In the past, men have been the prevalent occupiers of business and institutional life, and both formal and informal policies and procedures reflected masculine norms (Ashcroft & Mumby, 2004; Wood, 2010). Today, although 1 in 2 workers are women and most women work outside of the home (Allen, 2004; Wood, 2010), formal workplace policies and procedures still often reveal gendered practices. Formal written practices (such as scheduling, leave, dress codes, etc.) articulate the ways an organization/workplace views gender and gender roles. Many companies have official written policies that underscore gender differences or inequities (such as maternity but not paternity leave or dress-code discrepancies), while other companies seem to be gender neutral. Many policies and procedures present in organizations perpetuate unfair treatment and promote subtle discrimination against both men and women; thus, this activity challenges students to examine both overt and covert gendered expectations within organizations.

Through first selecting an employee handbook, then reading and analyzing it, followed by discussing it, students are actively learning about sexuality and gendered messages in their own world (Tileson, 2007). Through this type of engagement, students are more likely to understand and retain information (Bonwell & Eison, 1991).

Preparing for the Activity

1. This activity does require some advanced preparation because of the necessity of gathering workplace/organization employee handbooks. Ideally, every student should bring a handbook to class. This activity is most effective if the employee handbooks are from places where the students have worked, are working, or want to work. Students will typically be more interested in the activity if the manual/handbook is from a workplace to which they have some sort of tie or in which they have an interest.

2. On the syllabus and/or course calendar, remind students to bring a handbook or printout of a workplace's current written policies and procedures. If they do not have a handbook for their current place of employment, policies and procedures for different organizations are easily found through Internet search engines (use

search terms such as "employee manual" and "employee handbook"). Some handbooks can be quite extensive, and it is ideal for students to read through their handbook before class, but students may not follow through, so giving time in class to read the handbooks is helpful.

3. Although each student should bring his or her own handbook, it is a good idea to bring a few backups.

Facilitating the Activity

1. At the beginning of the activity, give students time to read their handbook and complete the worksheet (20–30 min.).

2. After most (if not all) students have completed the worksheet individually, divide the class into small discussion groups (3–5 individuals). Within the groups, students should take turns sharing their thoughts and answers from their chosen organization (as described on the worksheet). Be sure to wander around the class to ensure questions are answered and students stay on task (20–30 min.). Encourage the students to think about how they feel about the different organizations' policies, and which policies they believe are best.

3. Reconvene the class as a whole and discuss the standout findings and reactions from the small-group discussions and facilitate with the discussion questions provided below (20–60 min.).

Discussion Questions

- From the information you found (or didn't find!) in the handbook, what surprised you about the policies and procedures in regard to gender and sexuality?
  - What did you like or what didn't you like? Why?
- Why do you think it is necessary for companies to stipulate overt or formal policies that encompass gender and sexuality?
- From the written policies and procedures, what conclusions can you draw about the place of gender and sexuality in company culture?
- In addition to written policies and procedures found in a handbook, a workplace has "unwritten" rules about how things work. What are some examples, from your own experiences, of subtle or "unwritten" covert gendered policies?
  - From your own experiences, how are these unwritten rules shared?
  - From your own experiences (including media stories and exposure), do you think that formal written policies and procedures always match unwritten ones? Give examples of how this may or may not be the case.
- What can be the effects (both positive and negative) of company policy in reference to gender and sexuality?

Typical Results

- This activity first and foremost helps the individual student learn about at least one "real-life" organization's formal policies and procedures where gender and sexuality is concerned. By thoughtfully completing the worksheet questions, each student has individually engaged in analyzing and learning about overt and covert gender and sexuality messages. Through discussion with classmates, the learning continues as the information is further analyzed, and the student's ability to recognize communication gender and sexuality in formal policies is increased.

- In class, once the factual questions have been answered and students begin conversing about their answers to the discussion questions, they begin to have fun talking about sexuality and gender in the workplace.
- Although some (usually young) students do not have real work experience, other students have already experienced decades in the workplace. These varying perspectives, combined with other diversifying factors such as socioeconomics, race, age, gender, and family background lead to strong discussion.
- Vigorous debating is usually common in at least one or two parts of the discussion, and it is important that you are prepared to keep the conversation on track.

Limitations and Cautionary Advice

- I have found that this entire activity works better when students are required (and know they are required) to turn in their completed worksheet at the end of class, which keeps most students focused, on task, and more thoughtful and complete in their answers. Completing the worksheet is crucial since student engagement is key in the learning process for this activity.
- This activity isn't a discussion of legislation, quotas/affirmative action, or the Family and Medical Leave Act; rather, it is *how* companies enact, enforce, and implement these, in addition to making their own policies. Some students have the tendency to want to argue about affirmative action, etc. Depending on what majors there are in your class (business, communication, economics, etc.), the dynamic of the discussion (even within groups) can be very different.
- Beware of the tendency to go over time! You might consider allowing an extra "cushion" in the next class period to continue conversations. Some classes are very talkative, others are not.
- Some students may not bring handbooks that have much relevant information. For example, a handbook might only discuss the proper way to make a pizza and not include any human-resource type of information about leave, relationships, dress code, etc. Be sure to have a few backup handbooks as part of your preparation so students without appropriate material can have something to use.

Alternative Uses

- This exercise works well if students are assigned to read their handbooks and complete the worksheets before class so they can simply get into groups, share their findings, and then broaden into the class discussion. This is an easy way to shorten the length of time devoted in class to the activity or to allow for more time to focus on discussion.

- This activity could be adapted and used in classes that are shorter in length by reading and doing small-group discussions one class period and a class-wide discussion the next.
- This activity has a natural extension or follow-up activity: What are (or can be) the results of policies and procedures about gender/sexuality in the workplace? Cases about sexual discrimination, hiring biases, lawsuits, etc. (e.g., the Ruby Tuesday lawsuit, Texas Roadhouse, Mavis Tire, etc.). The Equal Employment Opportunity Commission (www1.eeoc.gov/index.cfm) is a fantastic resource for examples of "real-life" cultural cases concerning workplaces and policies about gender/sexuality.
- An interesting addition to this activity would include a comparison of a company's current policies with its policies in the past—examining what has changed and what has not.
- This exercise can also be effective when it is primarily a small-group activity when students in a small group read and answer the questions together about the same policy.
- This exercise can be turned into an analysis paper in the area of gender/sexuality and/or business/organizational communication. For this analysis, students could select a written workplace policy, describe how the policy relates to gender and/or sexuality, and discuss this using the theories and concepts discussed in class.

REFERENCES

Allen, B. (2004). *Difference matters: Communicating social identity.* Long Grove, IL: Waveland Press.

Ashcroft, K., & Mumby, D. (2004). *Reworking gender: A feminist communicology of organization.* Thousand Oaks, CA: Sage Publications.

Bonwell, C., & Eison, J. (1991). Active learning: Creating excitement in the classroom. *AEHE-ERIC Higher Education Report, 1.* Washington, DC: Jossey-Bass.

Tileson, D. W. (2007*). Teaching strategies for active learning: Five essentials for your teaching plan.* Thousand Oaks, CA: Sage Publications.

Wood, J. T. (2010). *Gendered lives, communication, gender, and culture* (9th ed.). Boston, MA: Wadsworth Publishing.

ADDITIONAL READINGS

Craig, L., & Mullan, K. (2010), Parenthood, gender and work-family time in the United States, Australia, Italy, France, and Denmark. *Journal of Marriage and Family, 72*, 1344–61. doi: 10.1111/j.1741-3737.2010.00769.x.

Gottfried, H., & Reese, L. (2004). *Equity in the workplace: Gendering workplace policy analysis.* New York: Lexington Books.

Ray, R., Gornick J. C., & Schmitt, J. (2010) Who cares? Assessing generosity and gender equality in parental leave policy designs in 21 countries. *Journal of European Social Policy, 20*, 196–216.

HANDOUT: ORGANIZATIONAL POLICIES

In your organization's handbook, find and record (feel free to use the back of this paper) information about

1. Maternity and Paternity Leave (Who gets it, for how long, is it paid, etc.? What message does this communicate about gender roles and responsibilities in this organization? Are there details about whether same-sex couples can receive maternity/paternity leave, and if so, what are they?)

2. Family Leave (What are the specifications for family leave? Is it gender specific or gender neutral? For example, does it mention mothers, or fathers, or both? What message does this express about different genders in this organization?)

3. Dress Code (Are there separate descriptions of appropriate attire for men and women? How specific are the guidelines? What is acceptable for men? What is acceptable for women? Is one section more detailed than another? What—if any—rationale is given for the dress code? Based on this information, what can you conclude about the organization's stance on sexuality, as communicated through attire? Also, based on this information, what gender differences are reflected?)

4. Workplace Relationships (Are romantic/sexual relationships allowed between employees in this organization? Can any employee date any other employee, or are there restrictions between bosses and subordinates? Are there stipulations or guidelines given if dating relationships do exist? Is there any mention of moral clauses—i.e., certain activities such as extramarital affairs that might be considered unethical? Based on this information, what can you conclude about the organization's stance on the sexuality of its employees?)

5. Misc. (Did you find any other mention of gender, relationships, or sexuality in your handbook? If so, describe it here.)

What's the Policy? Exploring Sexual-Harassment Policies in Organizations

Joy L. Daggs, PhD
(Northwest Missouri State University)

Appropriate Course(s) and Level

Organizational communication, business law, organizational psychology, family studies courses, gender and communication. Sophomore level and above.

Appropriate Class Size

Up to 30 students.

Learning Goals

- To understand the definition of sexual harassment across various organizations.
- To explore the similarities and differences across different types of organizations regarding sexual-harassment policies.
- To think critically about the influence sexual-harassment policies have on workplace culture and interactions.

Estimated Time Required

45–60 minutes of actual class time.

Required Materials

- A copy of your state's policies related to sexual harassment (the law that describes what the state minimum standards are for a sexual-harassment policy for organizations) and/or similar information retrieved from the federal level, such as the Equal Employment Opportunity Commission (EEOC).
- A copy of your college or university's sexual-harassment policy for faculty or students or both.

- Copies of sexual-harassment policies from employers to share with the class (it helps if students bring in policies from their own employers).

Rationale

According to the Equal Employment Opportunity Commission (2011), there were 12,000–16,000 complaints of sexual harassment annually from 1997 to 2011. Herman Cain even halted his 2012 presidential campaign after allegations of sexual harassment surfaced. Dougherty (2001) asked women why they do not report sexual harassment. The participants stated that they feared no one would believe them. A cultural backlash against feminism tends to blame the victim or dismiss the victim as making up the charges in search of financial gain, despite research supporting the significant emotional and physical toll sexual harassment can have on a victim. Paradoxically, the study participants themselves did not believe anyone who reported sexual harassment.

With these challenges facing victims of sexual harassment, education is important to understand what sexual harassment is and how organizations define sexual harassment and procedures for investigating and punishing sexual harassment. Despite the existence of these policies, Dougherty and Smythe (2004) showed a clear disconnect between an organization's policies for sexual harassment and how organizational culture tolerates sexual harassment. The present activity can help students facilitate discussion regarding such issues.

Preparing for the Activity

1. Place on the syllabus, and remind students beforehand, to gather sexual-harassment policies from their employers or other sources to be used on the day of the activity. These organizations can include internships the students may be completing or, if a student is not employed, the policy from a parent or guardian's workplace or, if possible, the policy of an organization for which the student wishes to work. Allow students at least 1–2 weeks' time to locate these policies. Policies should be listed in employee handbooks or possibly posted at the workplace. Students can also ask the organization's director of human resources for a copy of the policy. If the organization is simply one the student would like to work for, students should be able to contact the organization's Human Resources Office if the policy is not available through the company's website. Encourage the students to start early.

2. Contact your state's Division of Labor Office either directly or through the organization's website to obtain a copy of the state minimum standards for sexual-harassment policies. Although most organizations go beyond state laws in their own policies, it is important to have your state's policies to share what the absolute minimum is organizations must have for a sexual-harassment policy. Then go to your institution's faculty and staff handbook(s) to find the policy for sexual harassment. Finally, go to the student handbook to find out the policy for sexual harassment.

3. In the class period prior to the activity, do a general lecture about sexual harassment. A great supplement to the lecture is the *PBS Now* special "Is Your Daughter

Safe at Work?" (www.pbs.org/now/shows/508/index.html). This news program spotlights the prevalence of sexual harassment of teens at work. It has a run-time of approximately 25 minutes. You should familiarize yourself with EEOC statistics on sexual-harassment cases to give your students a background.

Facilitating the Activity

1. Start the class by sharing your state's policies and definitions for sexual harassment (either through paper copies or projection). By doing this, you establish a baseline of expectations for sexual-harassment policies in your state so the students can see the absolute minimum required by law for organizations as defined by their state.
2. Move on to your institution's policy for sexual harassment. If you have different policies in the student handbook and the faculty handbook, discuss this as a class (see Discussion Questions). This will allow students to see a comparison between their institution as a workplace for faculty and staff and as an institution of higher education with policies for relationships between students, faculty, and staff.
3. After your institution's policies have been reviewed, have each student come to the front of the classroom and give a description of their workplace's policy. These should be no more than 2 minutes each.
4. Process the information found in the policies using the Discussion Questions.

Discussion Questions

- How clear is your organization's definition of what behaviors or messages constitute sexual harassment? What, if anything, is missing from this definition?
- What procedures are in place for filing a sexual-harassment complaint?
  - How effective do you believe these procedures are?
  - How do these procedures influence the number of individuals willing to report sexual harassment?
- What actions are to be taken by your organization to investigate a sexual-harassment complaint?
- What consequences should happen if a claim is substantiated?
  - Do you believe these consequences are harsh enough? Why or why not?
- What was the most surprising thing you found out about sexual-harassment policies doing this exercise?
- What major similarities did you see among the various policies?
- What major differences did you see among the various policies?
- How did the policies compare to the state minimum policies?
  - Were they more extensive or just the bare minimum?
  - Why do you think this was?
- How do your college/university policies compare to those of other work organizations?
- What are your perceptions of organizations that have more-developed policies for exploring sexual harassment versus organizations that have the state minimum policy?

- In light of this analysis, how easy do you feel it would be to file a sexual-harassment complaint? How do you think this affects the number of complaints that are filed?
- What, if anything, would you change about your state's sexual-harassment policies? Your organization's?

Typical Results

- In doing this activity, I have found some organizations have one sentence that says, "We do not tolerate sexual harassment," while others have clearly defined actions and messages that are defined as sexual harassment. Many policies outline consequences for substantiated cases of sexual harassment. Some may simply define sexual harassment without outlining any kinds of consequences.
- The activity can result in some interesting discussions about the definitions of sexual harassment and how to be aware of behavior that could be construed as sexual harassment.
- The activity can also help to make students think about some of the issues they may face in the workplace after graduation. Students typically do not have clear expectations about what they will encounter in the workplace.

Limitations and Cautionary Advice

- If students are working for a small restaurant or business, they may not have access to a written policy. In that case, encourage the students to sit down with the owner of the business to interview them about the reasons behind not having a clear policy or what they see their policy to be. Or you might suggest that students find a policy from a company they would perhaps like to work for in the future.
- Despite the social recognition of sexual harassment as a problem, there will still be some resistant students who feel that sexual harassment is something that a person "makes up" for financial gain or that it is not really a problem. They may also mention a *Saturday Night Live* sketch that featured Tom Brady stating that the best way to avoid a sexual-harassment lawsuit is to be attractive and desirable. Remind the students that *Saturday Night Live* is simply a television program that exists for humor and does not reflect the proper ways to address major social concerns.
- Another issue that students may bring up is the "proof" of sexual harassment. How do you "prove" someone said something that was inappropriate? Explore this idea to show that message intent is not what constitutes sexual harassment; it is message perception. This can lead to an interesting discussion about utilizing an organization's director of human resources. At this point, you might simply suggest that if there is suspicion that something is inappropriate, the best thing to do is to report the action. Then, if there are other employees with similar experiences, the director of human resources has documentation. This discussion can also handle the idea of "making up" allegations of sexual harassment. If the director of human resources sees a pattern, then it is less likely that several people are "making up" sexual harassment.

Alternative Uses

- Rather than having each student individually present his or her policy, it could be useful to have the students work in small groups and present their findings regarding similarities and differences among the small group's policies. It may be helpful to create a handout for the small groups to use to guide their interactions based upon the Discussion Questions.
- This activity could be adapted for family leave policies or other workplace policies regarding fairness and equity. This could include same-sex partnership recognition, or other policies that relate to fairness and inclusion in the workplace.

REFERENCES

Dougherty, D. S. (1999). Dialogue through standpoint: Understanding men's and women's standpoints of sexual harassment. *Management Communication Quarterly, 12*, 436–68. doi: 10.1177/0893318999123003.

Dougherty, D. S. (2001). Women's discursive construction of a sexual harassment paradox. *Qualitative Communication Reports, 2*, 6–13.

Dougherty, D. S. (2006). Gendered constructions of power during discourse about sexual harassment: Negotiating competing meanings. *Sex Roles, 54*, 495–507. doi: 10.1007/s11199-006-9012-4.

Dougherty, D. S., & Smythe, M. J. (2004). Sensemaking, organizational culture, and sexual harassment. *Journal of Applied Communication Research, 32*, 293–317. doi: 10.1080/0090988042000275998.

Equal Employment Opportunity Commission. (2011). *Sexual harassment charges EEOC & FEPAs Combined: FY 1997–FY 2011*. www.eeoc.gov/eeoc/statistics/enforcement/sexual_harassment.cfm.

VIII

GLOBAL/INTERSECTIONAL ISSUES

29

Crash: Seeing the Power of Intersectional Analyses

Sal Renshaw, PhD
(Nipissing University, Canada)

Appropriate Course(s) and Level

Introductory to advanced courses in gender, women's and sexuality studies, sociology, cultural studies, and media studies.

Appropriate Class Size

Appropriate for a range of class sizes, including large lecture classes. Ideally the space would permit students to break into small groups.

Learning Goals

- To demonstrate how intersectionality works in a situated example.
- To develop critical literacy in understanding the complexity of equality analyses by providing a concrete conceptual toolkit which can be effectively applied to "real-world" examples.
- To develop a sense of the significance of context/situation in understanding oppression.
- To develop a greater awareness of the way gender analyses are both more rigorous and more powerful with an intersectional approach.

Estimated Time Required

30 minutes minimum, and 45 minutes to allow for more complex connections.

Required Materials

- DVD of the film *Crash* (Haggis, 2004).
- Reading: Bell (1997).
- *Crash* Analysis Handout to focus small-group discussion (see Handout).

Rationale

This exercise pairs a theoretical reading with the screening of an 8-minute excerpt from the film *Crash* (2004). The reading introduces students to the key terms and categories that form the core of an intersectional theoretical approach to thinking about social justice and oppression. Bell (1997) enumerated six features of oppression, and these features become the conceptual toolkit for this classroom exercise. They include the following ideas: that oppression is pervasive, hierarchical, complex, multiple, and cross-cutting of relationships; that oppression is often internalized, and that the various "-isms," like sexism, racism, and classism, have both shared and distinctive characteristics. The reading further elucidates the "-ism's," and it introduces concepts such as hegemony and ideology, and agency and resistance, as well as the importance of thinking about individual as well as group identities. It is implicit that Bell (1997) took an intersectional approach to thinking about oppression, and this is most evident in the section on the cross-cutting nature of the "-ism's." But it may be worth highlighting the central tenets of this term.

Typically, the term "intersectionality" is associated with the work of feminist critical race theorist and legal scholar Kimberlé Williams Crenshaw, who used it to refer to the inseparable nature of the categories of sex, gender, nation, and class. Crenshaw challenged the seemingly universal nature/use of the category of woman by highlighting that for some women, namely African American women, their experience of their identities as women was inseparable from their race. In other words, the category "woman" couldn't meaningfully describe these particular women's experience, at least to the extent that attempts to do so extracted sex from race. Sex couldn't be parsed out as if it was somehow lived in a way that was separable from the wholeness of the person, a wholeness that includes race and class and myriad other particularities of identity. Although we can intellectually conceptualize them as discrete, the categories are not actually lived this way; they are lived as intersecting and inseparable, as simultaneously emergent and dynamic. Intersectional analyses not only reveal the inadequacy of universalizing models of identity, they also show us that identity categories meaningfully shift and change in relation to context, and in order to attend well to questions of justice and equality, we must attend to those contexts. At the heart of an intersectional analysis is the recognition that all our identities come to meaning in relation to others and in relation to particular situations. Although we may experience privilege in one context, we may experience oppression and exclusion in another, and although our individual experiences are unique to us, they are also inseparable from the systemic matrices of power into which each of us are born and over which we have little control as individuals.

The following is a brief outline of the details of the *Crash* segment used for this activity, as well as a brief account of some of the reasons why it is so relevant to an intersectional analysis. The more familiar the instructor is with the clip, the more that can be done with it. It is richly complex despite its brevity. The clip opens with a working-class white man in his 40s, LAPD Officer John Ryan (Matt Dillon) speaking on a public phone to an African American woman Shaniqua Johnson (Loretta Devine) who works at his father's HMO. Ryan is frustrated with what he thinks is the HMO's refusal to provide adequate care for his ailing father. The call ends with Ryan asking Shaniqua her name to which he responds, "Shaniqua? . . . Yeah, big fuckin' surprise that is." The racist and classist undercurrents are evident in his contemptuous tone despite the fact that he makes no explicitly racist or classist statements. The seeming subtlety of Ryan's racism and bigotry is an important point to draw to the attention of students. Shaniqua's response to Ryan is to hang up on him. The scene then transitions to Ryan and his rookie partner, Tom Hanson (Ryan Phillippe) beginning their evening patrol. Clearly, Ryan is still seething over the phone call. Despite discrepancies in its driver's sex, age, and appearance, not to mention the car's actual license plate, they pull over a Lincoln Navigator vaguely similar to one that had been carjacked earlier that evening. They instruct the obviously affluent African American couple, television director Cameron Thayer (Terrence Howard) and his wife Christine (Thandie Newton) out of the car. Although Ryan knows the couple is not responsible for the carjacking, when he sees Christine in the passenger seat sitting up and wiping her lips, Ryan believes "they were up to something," and the context of sexuality is set here. Cameron is cooperative, but Christine quickly becomes indignant and resistant. During the course of the confrontation, Ryan's resentment and anger is increasingly taken out on Christine whose gender he takes issue with—telling her she has "quite a mouth on her"—before ending up blatantly sexually assaulting her on the pretense of administering a weapon search. Through much of the interaction with Christine, Ryan is actually staring tauntingly at her powerless husband, who can do little but watch. Cameron's awareness of his own vulnerability as a black man in the face of the law is uncomfortable to witness. It undeniably evokes the history of slavery and domination when in the end, Cameron's options are so few he has to submit to Ryan's ultimatum that he either apologize or face the alternative of being taken into custody.

When Ryan finishes assaulting Christine and intimidating Cameron, the couple is released, and in the following brief scene at the Thayer's house, the reality of the history of race relations in America is painfully in evidence as Christine's rage takes the form of mimicking her husband's passivity and compliance in the face of Ryan as if he were a slave conceding to his master. Christine is wildly angry that, in her view, Cameron inexcusably did nothing while she was violated, and in her rage, she also verbally retaliates by denigrating his masculinity and challenging his racial status. Cameron is no saint either; he responds in kind, maligning Christine's sexuality, suggesting she had once taken on a whole equestrian team, and implying that he was the actual victim in what had just happened and that what he did was all he could do in the circumstances. The underlying gender discourses about what constitutes a "real man" and a "real woman" are also evident in this scene as the categories of sex, gender, race, and class become the weapons of choice in a very painful and seemingly very personal interaction between them. Again, we see that none of us, even in our most personal moments, can escape our classed, racialized, and gendered cultures or their histories.

This brief segment from *Crash* offers students a rich opportunity to see what they consider to be a "real-world' example of how the categories of sex, gender, class, and race intersect in complex ways in specific contexts, and the film is also a powerful mnemonic strategy. When used early in a course, the exercise can and often does remain a touchstone for later classes.

Preparing for the Activity

1. It is important that you be familiar with the film as a whole in order to establish the context for the excerpt shown.
2. Setting up the time codes ahead of time will ensure that the tech demons are kind. The timings for the relevant sequences are
   - 15:32 . . . we see two Asian men in a diner for a brief second while the voice-over kicks in. The voice-over is Officer Ryan, and he is seen talking on the phone to his HMO about his father. This is an important frame for the subsequent scene. The HMO scene rolls into the following scene with an affluent African American couple being pulled over by police as they drive home from an evening out. Let this scene play all the way through and cut it at 22:34.
   - Move forward to 23:17 to pick up the scene between the couple, Christine and Cameron, when they get home. End the clip at 25:07. This scene is especially important in providing more material on internalized oppression and the intersections of race and gender.

Facilitating the Activity

1. Prepare a brief presentation on the major terms and concepts related to intersectionality from the Bell (1997) reading.
2. Distribute the Handout, and go over it briefly with the class before the screening. Students need to have the questions in mind as they watch because their task is to identify in the clips examples reflecting the concepts from the reading.
3. Screen the clips from *Crash*.
4. After the screening, break into small groups of 6–8 depending on the class size, and instruct the small groups to discuss the connections to the readings and complete their worksheets.
5. Allow students to work in groups for about 15–20 minutes.
6. At the end of group-work time, ask each group to designate a representative to report their findings to the entire class.

Discussion Questions

- What is the class of each of the characters? Explain how you know.
- How do you believe class influenced the characters' interactions?
- What kind of attitude do Christine and Cameron have toward the police when they are initially pulled over? Are they intimidated? Are they stressed? Why or why not?
- What happens to trigger the change in the way the police relate to Christine and Cameron? What is the connection to race and gender in this situation?
  - How, if at all, does the white working-class cop exploit the masculine institution of law in a way that challenges the masculinity of an African American man?
  - How, if at all, is the woman considered to be property?
  - How, if at all, are historical issues of property and privilege displayed in this scene?

- Identify the way class, race, and gender are all part of the accusations Christine and Cameron hurl at each other when they get home.
- What specifically overrides the sense of class entitlement that Christine and Cameron seem to have when they are first pulled over?
- How, if at all, is Officer Ryan an unrelenting figure of masculine power and domination?
  - At what points do you see his power and privilege become ineffective?
- How does age function to mediate power between the male characters?
  - How do you believe Officer Tom Hanson felt watching the interaction between Officer Ryan and the couple?
  - Why do you think Office Tom Hanson acted this way?

Typical Results

- Students have a significant increase in critical literacy with respect to equality analyses that can then be more readily applied in other "real-world" circumstances.
- Students express a heightened awareness of the way context meaningfully alters the experience of oppression and privilege.
- Students demonstrate an awareness of the way gender analyses are both more rigorous and more powerful with the use of an intersectional approach.

Limitations and Cautionary Advice

- As with any explicit depiction of sexual assault, there is a real need to be alert to the way it can be provocative for some members of the class.
- This is equally true of the effect of parsing out just how subtle and complex the systemic effects of racism can be. There can be a real resistance on the part of white students who are first encountering what it means to think deeply about anti-racist work, and it can often trigger students of color into silence.
- Before the exercise begins, consider giving students a heads up about these possible effects and encourage them to set limits for themselves as they need to. This might mean leaving the room during the screening. As much as possible, I reassure them the context of the classroom will be as safe as we can make it for conceptually exploring issues that are actually lived very personally. It is also worth being very cognizant going into the exercise that it will be experienced very differently by different demographics. Being sensitive to these differences will help you prepare the students.

Alternative Uses

- Although this exercise was designed to introduce intersectionality in the university classroom, it would also be a powerful tool in any anti-racist training. Its attention to complexity works to undermine stereotypical and reflexive responses to thinking about gender and race, and its attention to the way class operates so powerfully to modify privilege and oppression adds a significant element that does not always receive sufficient attention in discussions of oppression.

REFERENCES

Bell, L. A. (1997) Theoretical foundations for social justice education. In M. Adams, L. A. Bell, & P. Griffin (Eds.), *Teaching for diversity and social justice: A sourcebook* (pp. 3–15). New York: Routledge.

Crenshaw, K. W. (1994). Mapping the margins: Intersectionality, identity politics and violence against women of color. In M. A. Fineman & R. Mykitiuk (Eds.), *The public nature of private violence* (pp. 93–118). New York: Routledge.

Haggis, P. (Director). (2004). *Crash* [Motion Picture]. Lions Gate Films.

HANDOUT: *CRASH* INTERSECTIONAL
ANALYSIS, CLASS EXERCISE[1]

Directions: Using your knowledge of intersectionality and the movie, complete the worksheet providing clear examples of each of the listed categories. Be sure to explain how the example supports the category.

Pervasive:
Restrictive:
Hierarchical:
Complex, Multiple, Cross-Cutting Relationships:
Internalized:
Racism:
Classism:
Sexism:
Individual and Group Identity:
Privilege:

NOTE

1. Adapted from Bell, L. A. (1997). Theoretical foundations for social justice education. In M. Adams, L. A. Bell, & P. Griffin (Eds.), *Teaching for diversity and social justice: A sourcebook* (pp. 3–15). New York: Routledge.

Us and Them: Teaching Students to Critically Analyze Gender in a Global Context

Amy Eisen Cislo, PhD
(Washington University in St. Louis)

Appropriate Course(s) and Level

Introductory to advanced courses in women's/gender studies, media studies, history, marketing/advertising courses, anthropology, political science, and sociology courses.

Appropriate Class Size

10–30 students.

Learning Goals

- To learn that U.S. cultural beliefs about gender are not universal.
- To explore how non-white women are used globally as symbols of disadvantage, weakness, and sympathy.
- To critically examine how some U.S. media group all women in poorer countries into one unified idea of what Mohanty (2003) has called "the third world woman."
- To recognize the needs of women are unique to their home country and outsiders may misread customs within another country that may seem like gender oppression.
- To apply gender-analysis skills to media analysis.

Estimated Time Required

If you are showing the media in class, a 75–90 minute class would be ideal; but if you assign the viewing/reading as homework, you could complete this activity in one hour.

Required Materials

- Speeches, advertisements, or nonfiction books that encourage English speakers to think about the plight of people in countries outside of Canada, Europe, and the United States. Often these advertisements and books focus on women to emphasize the need to send aid or money. But they can also be short news segments that appeal to Western expectations about women's rights. Possible sources include
  - Any of the ads sponsored by Nike called "The Girl Effect" on YouTube.
  - Mortensen, G. (2006). *Three cups of tea.* New York: Viking.
  - Kristof, N., & WuDunn, S. (2009). *Half the sky.* New York: Alfred A. Knopf. (A chapter or two will suffice. The chapters are very short.)
  - A "news" segment on women outside of Western countries.
  - An organization's webpage like womenforwomen.org.

Rationale

Feminist scholars have come to recognize the ways in which they have ignored their own privilege and have focused too much on their own oppression. The writings of black feminist scholars asked white women to rethink their ideas about their own oppression and to recognize the ways in which they exert a kind of privilege over non-white women (e.g., Collins, 2000; Hooks, 1984; Walker, 2004). This recognition of privilege had a twofold effect on scholarship. Within the United States, it became clear to scholars that when studying gender, they must recognize the significance of intersectionality (a person's race, class, sexuality). This recognition of privilege led to the realization that it was no longer acceptable to speak of women's issues as if all women in the United States shared the same background and had the same needs. Scholarship and activism recognized the importance of studying the ways intersecting oppressions led to different experiences when it came to core U.S. women's issues such as access to health care, reproductive rights, domestic violence, and pay equity.

This activity encourages students to deconstruct the idea of "us and them." In other words, students should begin to recognize that U.S. ideas about gender are not universal, and we must rethink the colonial discourse of privileging white-skinned people over brown/dark-skinned people. Furthermore, we must overcome the idea that all brown-skinned women and men are the same. Much like the early feminist scholarship that assumed that the needs of white, middle-class, heterosexual women were the concerns of all U.S. women, early scholarship on women around the world assumed the concerns of U.S. women were shared by all women globally.

Abu-Lughod (2002) and Mohanty (2003) explained the risks of making assumptions about universal womanhood. Abu-Lughod emphasized the way many Western people misunderstood veiling and assumed that to be veiled was to be oppressed. Their assumption of veiling includes a misunderstanding of the culture and posits men who are married to veiled women as domineering oppressors. Abu-Lughod pointed out Muslim women do not need to be rescued from their veils because many women choose to wear them and understand the veil as a symbol of privilege. Going further to explore scholarship on non-Western women, Mohanty (2003) criticized the thinking behind the phrase "third world woman." She emphasized that using "woman," instead of the plural "women," reveals how the concerns of brown-skinned women are lumped into one. Usually North American scholars assume women in Africa or the Middle East are victims of male violence. Furthermore, Western scholarship perpetuates the idea of women as universal dependents. This exercise uses a similar lens to Mohanty's to analyze visual or textual representations of non-white women who are depicted as helpless victims in countries outside the United States, Canada, and Europe. Students should begin to recognize how ideas about power and gender intersect to depict brown-skinned men as violent and domineering to their women who are helpless victims in need of Western aid.

Preparing for the Activity

1. Read a selection from Mohanty (2003) or Abu-Lughod (2002) to make sure you understand the theoretical background of the idea of "third world woman."
2. A selection from Mohanty, Abu-Lughod, and/or McIntosh (1988) could be assigned to your students in advance. These readings articulate the fundamental theoretical underpinnings of exploring white/Western privilege.
3. Make sure that students look up the following words and are able to explain them: colonialism, imperialism, privilege, oppression.
4. Be prepared to give a brief historical overview of colonialism.
5. Identify a selection of images and texts to be analyzed in class. Either assign them in advance, or use class time to work together on the material.

Facilitating the Activity

1. Take time to talk about what we in the United States/Canada consider to be appropriate gender roles. Ask students to think about whether or not the following are masculine or feminine activities: caring for children, making financial decisions, driving a car, voting, teaching, giving money, spending money, mowing the lawn, leading a country, cleaning. If students answer that all of the activities could be either masculine or feminine, then you can point out they assume that we live in an egalitarian society. If students come up with different answers for the above questions, then you can point out how some activities are gendered masculine or feminine, and thus, we assume that some things are women's responsibility and some are men's responsibility.
2. Ask students how they learned which activities are masculine or feminine, which are men's work and which are women's work. If students are unable to recognize gender roles, the following questions should help them: Who do you usually see mowing a lawn? Who do you usually see caring for children? If a man and a woman are going somewhere together in a car, who would you expect to drive?
3. Take time to point out how gender roles are confirmed in U.S. society through things like etiquette and media representations. Here you may use a recent commercial for dish detergent or some other home product to point out that home activities are usually marked feminine. It might also be beneficial to point out that although we have gender-typical ideas about private life (i.e., the home), we tend to think of public life as egalitarian. In other words, we think women and men should have the same basic rights like voting or working rights.

4. Now ask students if gender roles and gender expectations are the same in other countries. In other words, is gender universal or particular? Global or local? If students have lived abroad and are able to articulate cultural differences, then point out how some activities are deemed masculine in one culture and feminine in another. If your students have no international experience, move on to the next part of the activity and allow the question about cultural differences to remain unanswered until later. To keep the question at the forefront, you may want to write it on the board: Are the activities we consider masculine or feminine the same in other parts of the world?

5. Next brainstorm with the class activities that are limited by gender. What can men do in the United States/Canada that women cannot? This preparation will allow you to point out what is considered normal for men and women in the United States so that you can move on to thinking about whether or not these gender expectations are superimposed on men and women outside the United States/Canada.

6. At this point, you can show your chosen media or begin discussion of the reading you assigned and process with the Discussion Questions.

Discussion Questions

- Does the medium make clear which country is the focus?
- How does the medium attempt to make clear what the gender expectations are in the part of the world that the medium addresses?
- How are the women in this medium described? List adjectives.
- How, if at all, does the medium suggest that the women depicted should be doing the same things as U.S./Canadian women?
- In what ways does the medium convey the idea that that the women are oppressed?
- In what ways does the medium demonstrate that help is needed?
- Do the reasons listed for help correspond to the list we made about expected gender roles for men and women in North America? How?
- Do we get any sense of specific laws or cultural values of the woman's home country? Why or why not?
- What does the medium imply about men?
- List adjectives used in the medium that describe men.
- What does the medium imply about the relationships between men and women? When the medium posits women as victims in a given country, what does that say about men? What does it say about the stability and power of the country described?
- In what ways does the image/video (if you are using images) make clear that you, the viewer, can help? What is the angle of the camera lens? How are you, the viewer, positioned?
- How is the appeal for aid linked to U.S./Canadian gender-role expectations?
- Are there any white people in the medium? If so, what are they doing? If not, why not?
- What does this medium say about privilege? Who has privilege? Who is oppressed?

• In what ways could we change the medium content to avoid the idea of a privileged "us" and a helpless "them"? Is there a way to change the content so we do not impose our culturally specific gender expectations on a person living outside our culture?

Typical Results

• Students should begin to recognize the way U.S./Canadian gender expectations are attributed to women outside of these countries without regard for the culture in the media. Furthermore, students should begin to recognize how brown-skinned women are often associated with helplessness and portrayed as victims of uncompassionate men in their home countries.
• Ultimately, students should come to recognize that gender roles are learned from living within a culture and that U.S./Canadian gender roles should not be used as a global norm. Creating a kind of civilized "us" assumes we have gender roles worked out, that we respect women, and that our men are powerful, perpetuating a colonial idea of the brown-skinned other, or "them." Students should come away from this activity as global (non-colonial) citizens.

Limitations and Cautionary Advice

• I have intentionally avoided the use of the term "Western" because the goal of the activity is to avoid overgeneralization. To make clear to students that gender roles are culturally specific, it is best to be specific about the countries of comparison. Even among English-speaking countries, there is variation in gender expectations.
• Because racial and ethnic stereotypes are deeply imbedded in U.S. culture, it is possible students will be challenged for the first time to think about the ways in which privilege is associated with whiteness. Instructors can acknowledge this uneasiness, but it is certainly more difficult for a non-white instructor to facilitate a discussion with white students about white privilege.
• The widespread assumption that life is better for women in the United States/ Canada than in most other parts of the world makes it difficult for students to acknowledge that the cultural practices of others may be appreciated by women in the other culture.
• Be prepared for questions to arise. A student once asked me if it was a bad thing that a nonprofit organization lumped all brown-skinned women into a monolithic whole if in the end the organization was able to raise money to help these women. This ethical question could be used as a homework assignment in which students must take a position for, or against, sending contributions to organizations that employ colonizing tendencies.

Alternative Uses

• Assign either Mohanty (2003) or Abu-Lughod (2002) and also a medium of your choice. Have students evaluate the medium as if they were the author (Mohanty or

Abu-Lughod). Would the author approve of the way women are depicted in this medium? Why or why not?

- Turn the activity inward to explore the representation of non-white women in U.S./Canadian/European media. How are the representations similar to the way U.S./Canadian/European media depict non-white women in other parts of the world?

REFERENCES

Abu-Lughod, L. (2002). Do Muslim women really need saving? Anthropological reflections on cultural relativism and its others. *American Anthropologist, 10*(3), 783–90.

Collins, P. H. (2000). *Black feminist thought: Knowledge, consciousness, and the politics of empowerment* (2nd ed.). New York: Routledge.

hooks, b. (1984). Black women shaping feminist theory. In Kum-Kum Bhavnani (Ed.), *Feminism and "race"* (pp. 33–39). Oxford: Oxford University Press.

McIntosh, P. (1988). White privilege: Unpacking the invisible knapsack. In V. Taylor, N. Whittier, & L. Rupp (Eds.), *Feminist frontiers* (9th ed.) (pp. 12–18). Boston: McGraw-Hill.

Mohanty, C. (2003). *Feminisms without borders: Decolonizing theory, practicing solidarity.* Durham, NC: Duke University Press.

Walker, R. (2004). Foreword: We are using this power to resist. In V. Labaton & D. Martin (Eds.), *The fire this time: Young activists and the new feminism.* New York: Anchor.

Claiming Your Baggage: Gender, Sexuality, and Nation in American Popular Culture

Christina Holmes, PhD
(DePauw University)

Appropriate Course(s) and Level

Introductory courses in women's/gender studies, mid- or upper-level courses in transnational feminisms, media studies, comparative or area studies, and religious studies.

Appropriate Class Size

35 students or less, but the lesson can be adapted for online learning environments of varying class sizes.

Learning Goals

- To develop media literacy and an ability to critically analyze representations of gender, race, sexuality, religion, and nation in the popular-culture resources of Americans.
- To recognize the ways mediated images have shaped our understandings of "otherness" while facilitating our own gendered, raced, religious, and sexualized identities as American women and men.
- To better open our minds to hear the stories of women from another national and/or religious context.
- To gain familiarity with transnational feminist concepts such as "othering," "ethnocentrism," "Orientalism," and "world-traveling."

Estimated Time Required

45–90 minutes, depending on the nature of the class discussion.

Required Materials

- A select popular-culture blog post, magazine article, advertisement, or music video that represents women from non-Western cultures as "othered" or implicitly depicted in contrast to American women or American values. I have used several issues of *Marie Claire*, a magazine that has a long-standing tradition of introducing readers to women in the non-Western world (along with issues such as genital cutting, sex trafficking, high fashion for veiled Muslim women, etc.). I use this magazine because *Marie Claire* presents itself as one of the more feminist-oriented popular women's publications that attends to transnational issues. As such, it is an especially rich site for analysis.
- Cultural Artifact Analysis worksheet (see Handout).
- Readings that contextualize American students' engagement with *The Complete Persepolis* (Satrapi, 2007; or your selected text) or transnational feminisms more generally (optional).

Rationale

Students both enjoy and can learn much from in-class activities that make use of popular cultural artifacts such as music videos, magazines, advertisements, and blogs. Although American popular culture may not seem like an obvious entry point into conversations about transnational feminisms or women in a global perspective, Western cultural artifacts can be a great way to incite discussions about the interlocking concepts of gender, sexuality, and nation. Starting with an artifact, such as a music video that showcases the people of another, "othered," nation, prompts students to make the familiar (popular culture) strange while learning how these representations construct their beliefs about other cultures, regions, or religions. "Othering" is an imperialist act of representing another from a different culture (through text or image) in contrast to the values we hold—this may mean representing the "othered" woman as primitive or traditional, hypersexual, passive, or fanatically religious in contrast to the images of the modern, sexually and politically liberated woman found in much American popular culture. Thus the aim of this classroom activity is to utilize an artifact that depicts non-Western women differently than typical representations of Western or American women; this facilitates self-reflection among students so they may develop a perspective that questions popular representations of non-Western women and begin to focus on how difference itself is constructed.

Edward Said's book *Orientalism* (1979) usefully presents students with an understanding of how texts and images construct our understandings of people and places, empowering some and disempowering others through popular culture, academic institutions and scholarship, and other institutions that create social consciousness. Although that work remains relevant today, and Orientalist discourses still bear on our students' understandings of the Middle East, it is important to update our pedagogical toolbox with scholarship that more accurately reflects the narratives of "otherness" now available to students. Botshon and Plastas (2009) argued after the terrorist attacks on the United States on September 11, 2001, that representations of Middle Eastern and Muslim women are especially important sites for analysis as distortions of the women's passivity and their potential for violence alongside their male counterparts have come to dominate in American media. Following their assessment of the usefulness of discussing Western hegemonic constructions of "the veiled woman" and of Islam more generally, I argue students are less likely to read a text such as *The Complete Persepolis* (Satrapi, 2007)—a frequently assigned (and justifiably so) book for transnational feminist courses or course units—from an ethnocentric viewpoint after they have had an opportunity to "unpack" their own "cultural baggage."

There is a wealth of feminist and other critical pedagogy that suggests the most effective teaching starts from where the students are—keeping one eye there and one eye on where they could be (Freire, 1996; Horton, 1997). When introducing a class to the topic of transnational feminisms and non-Western women for the first time, I find it helpful to situate my pedagogical choices in the landscape of Lugones's (1987) notion of "world traveling" and Mohanty's (2002) model of a comparative solidarity framework in education. Both scholars work in the field of cross-cultural feminist studies, emphasizing the importance of recognizing your own standpoint before endeavoring to better understand another's, especially across important differences such as culture, race, ethnicity, and religion.

Lugones (1987) offered a model for moving beyond arrogant perception that silences, erases, or stereotypes those who are different from our conception of ourselves. Instead, she advocated the development of "loving perception"—a view that more fully recognizes another's sense of self and worldview by trying to see "others" through their own eyes and yet learning to look at ourselves, too, as they might see us. The move from arrogant to loving perception relies on "world traveling." As a "world" traveler, students learn to see the belief systems and worldview that shapes their own understanding of social reality, learn to recognize how that mediates their view of other "worlds," and, finally, learn to listen to others carefully as they describe the worlds that shape them. Lugones argued that those who exist outside of dominant cultures and lack privilege often develop this skill as a survival strategy, but it is a skill all of us must urgently develop.

Similarly, Mohanty (2002) described three pedagogical models for cross-cultural knowledge acquisition in the feminist classroom. First, she presented the feminist-as-tourist model that typically addresses women from other cultures as victims and oppressed by their culture, and looks at cultures as entirely separate entities. This model does not turn the gaze back upon the viewer nor does it consider current and historical relations between East and West. This model is potentially the most dangerous approach because it does not challenge students to think about the role of ethnocentrism in cross-cultural analysis—the other culture is judged uncritically against the norms and expectations one has internalized as relevant for one's own culture.

The second is the feminist-as-explorer model that employs an area-studies approach to learning about women in other cultures—it may, for example, focus on women in the Middle East, but the syllabus would not contextualize such approaches in a broader picture of how Middle Eastern studies have been deeply complicit in the project of U.S. imperialism with historical ties to the Cold War era (Mohanty, 2002). Moreover, although these approaches may not tend toward ethnocentrism as much as the first model, Mohanty noted that "unless these discrete spaces are taught in relation to one another, the story told is usually a cultural relativist one, meaning that differences between cultures are discrete and relative with no real connection or common basis for evaluation" (p. 521).

Finally, Mohanty (2002) advocated for a third model, the feminist solidarity model. This pedagogical approach is a comparative one wherein "what is emphasized are relations of mutuality, coresponsibility, and common interests, anchoring the idea of feminist solidarity" (p. 521). This model brings issues of power to the foreground and looks at how global and local processes shape women's lives both here (in the American classroom) and abroad within frameworks that address cultural and historical specificity.

What do these pedagogical frameworks mean for the use of American magazines, music videos, or other artifacts in the classroom? As students confront their own socialization and internalization of images of non-Western women, popular culture acts as a bridge to open discussion for a range of understandings about the intersection of gender and sexuality with race, nation, and religion. Moreover, it does so while emphasizing the ways in which capitalism and Western media mediate available narratives and subjectivities for feminists in the American classroom. For example, many news and magazine articles that depict women dressed in hijab continue to represent the women as "traditional," oppressed, or voiceless despite their increasingly visible participation in heavily televised events such as the Arab Spring protests in Egypt and other regions across the Middle East beginning in late 2010.

The activity detailed here develops media literacy skills that highlight American confusion over the role of veiling in the lives of Muslim women and the ambivalent responses Western feminists have taken on the topic. It raises the question of the "otherness" of Islam and Iran in American media post 9/11 as American media and politics sought out a nationalist counter-image of progressive Christianity and liberal democracy. The activity I describe here is just one example of how magazine articles, blog posts, music videos, and advertisements can jump-start conversations about difference in the classroom.

Preparing for the Activity

1. Although this activity is widely adaptable, I suggest using it as an introduction to discussions of veiling and comparisons of American to Islamic or non-Western feminisms. It is helpful to begin conversations about women in another national and cultural context by deconstructing our own assumptions about "us" and "them" and discovering how deeply entrenched these ideas are through students' consumption of popular media.

2. In order to conduct the activity, copy relevant sections of the magazine or advertisement or make the ad, music video, or other cultural artifact available to all students by projecting it from a classroom computer. This artifact must present an "othered" or "us vs. them" perspective.

3. This activity can be used on its own, without supplemental reading, to gather information about where students are at in their understanding of media literacy and representations of non-Western women. It can also be used alongside readings covering key ideas such as "ethnocentrism" and "othering" (see References and Additional Readings).

4. For courses that do not have a focus on media studies, you may also want to give students a brief background lecture on media literacy and the politics of representation that asks them to think about the creator, medium, and message of a text. You may find the discussion questions on media literacy included on the Handout sufficient to prod students to think critically about the artifact; nonetheless, a list of short, accessible, readings that introduce media literacy is provided (see Additional Readings).

Facilitating the Activity

1. At the beginning of class, explain that the goal is to analyze the representations of Muslim or non-Western women that circulate in Western media and to note that these representations are not neutral reflections of reality but are carefully constructed images that carry important messages about how we think of ourselves as well as how we think of women from a different cultural and/or religious context. These representations will be interpreted for what they mean to American readers within the current cultural and historical moment.
2. Once you have finished explaining the reasoning behind the activity, distribute the chosen artifact and the Cultural Artifact Analysis worksheet (see Handout) to students and divide the class into groups of 3–4 students.
3. Instruct the students to work through the worksheet with their small group. While the students talk in their groups, be sure to walk among the groups and check in with students to ensure that they are moving through the questions in a timely manner.
4. Allow approximately 20–30 minutes for students to read through their articles or to watch an advertisement carefully several times and discuss the Handout in their groups.
5. After that time has passed, bring the class back together to facilitate a large discussion. Have each group share their answers to the questions and allow students to respond to each other when opinions differ to draw out as many different perspectives as possible.
6. Use the Discussion Questions to process the activity and artifact as a class.

Discussion Questions

- What messages are Western readers supposed to take away from this artifact? Which major narratives or discourses does the creator seem to be drawing from in constructing this advertisement, music video, or magazine spread?
- How, if at all, does this artifact challenge any stereotypes or common representations of Muslim, Middle Eastern, and/or American women?
- What purpose do you think this artifact serves for the creator and audience?
- How will today's activity affect your reading of an autobiographical or fictional transnational feminist text? Do you think you will be better able to recognize and resist your own tendencies to impose ethnocentric frames or discourses on the reading?
- What specific reading strategies and tools for critical analysis can you borrow from the artifact exercise as you read transnational feminist texts? What sorts of questions will you want to keep in mind as you read?

Typical Results

- Students often embrace this assignment enthusiastically and have varied opinions regarding how to read the women presented in different popular-culture artifacts, which makes for a good and lively class discussion. This activity benefits from employing the full class period to allow students to explore their ideas about media, socialization, "otherness," and the ways their own gender and sexuality are linked to representations of non-Western "others." Typically students are very interested in learning to read magazines and other media they often read for pleasure against the grain, and they have much to say as they learn to develop a new lens for looking.
- I have found that providing the conceptual framework of comparison found in Lugones (1987) and Mohanty (2002) alongside an emphasis on media literacy before students begin their analysis of the images or texts impacts the quality of their contributions. Clearly explaining the activity objectives and providing key definitions of such terms as "ethnocentrism" or "Orientalism" before students look at the artifact can help focus the discussion better. Emphasize that the Discussion Questions will guide their thinking, but the questions are open-ended and may not have a single correct answer.

Limitations and Cautionary Advice

- Students may get caught up in the idea that these representations offer "authentic" examples of Muslim womanhood or American feminism, for example, and they may need to be reminded that these are images and texts that are entirely constructed and created by a specific producer for a specific audience. The artifacts say a lot more about the writers, photographers, editors, producers, readers and/or viewers of the artifact than it does about the women or culture depicted therein.

Alternative Uses

- Although the directions provided above guide students in a classroom setting through the exercise, this activity is also ideal for online course delivery where discussion forums can be set up and students can be linked to the artifact through the class website.

REFERENCES

Botshon, L., & Plastas, M. (2009). Homeland in/security: A discussion and workshop on teaching Marjane Satrapi's *Persepolis*. *Feminist Teacher, 20*(1), 1–14.

Freire, P. (1996). *Pedagogy of the oppressed* (2nd ed.). New York: Penguin.

Horton, M. (1997). *The long haul: An autobiography*. New York: Teachers College Press.

Lugones, M. (1987). Playfulness, "world"-travelling, and loving perception. *Hypatia, 2*(2), 3–19.

Mohanty, C. T. (2002). "Under Western eyes" revisited: Feminist solidarity through anticapitalist struggles. *Signs: Journal of Women in Culture and Society, 28*(2), 499–535.

Said, E. (1979). *Orientalism*. New York: Vintage Books.

Satrapi, M. (2007). *The complete Persepolis*. New York: Pantheon.

ADDITIONAL READINGS

Jhally, S. (1994). Image-based culture: Advertising and popular culture. In G. Dines & J. Humez (Eds.), *Gender, race and class in the media*. Thousand Oaks, CA: Sage Publications.

Shohat, E., & Stam, R. (Eds.). (2003). *Multiculturalism, postcoloniality, and transnational media*. New Brunswick, NJ: Rutgers University Press.

HANDOUT: CULTURAL ARTIFACT ANALYSIS

Cultural artifacts (advertisement, music video, etc.) require both a creator (either an individual or a team) and a medium (voice, pen, paper, or computer). Representations are never neutral or apolitical. Although texts or artifacts can be read against the grain and may have more than one obvious interpretation, they are created by someone for an explicit purpose. We need to look at the creator, the importance of the medium, and patterns of reception among audiences when understanding how to read popular-culture texts.

Part 1: Media Literacy

- Who is the intended audience for this artifact?
- Who created this artifact?
- What medium did they choose for this artifact and how does that affect how the audience understands the message or discourses embedded in the artifact?

Part 2: Reading Middle Eastern Women

- How are the women characterized? What are their stories or personalities? How much do we get to learn about them? Give examples.
- How do the images and text construct the sexuality of the women?
- What relationships can be seen between the women and the West?

Part 3: East-West Relations

- How are the "West" and "East" being depicted here? What differences between "Western women" and "non-Western women" are presented or implied? What evidence do you have? Point to specific aspects of the artifact to support your explanation.
- What claims about religion, secularism, and modernity are being made? For example, is there a contrast between religion in the "East" and religion in the "West"? Are value judgments implied in this representation? How so?

Part 4: Additional "World-Traveling" Examples (If Time Allows)

- Where else do we find representations of Muslim or non-Western men and women in our popular culture? Provide specific examples.
- How are the stories of these men and women told? What kinds of visual representations of men and women do you see? What are they wearing? What are their facial expressions? What can you assume about their class, sexuality, gender, or religion based on the images? Do they tell their own stories or speak in the advertisement, music video, article, etc.?

About the Contributors

Tamara Berg, director of the Women's & Gender Studies Program at Winona State University in Minnesota, has been teaching about gender and sexuality for more than twenty years.

Mara Berkland is an associate professor of speech communication at North Central College. Her research interests include intercultural communication, communication and social justice within cultures, and the construction of femininity within law and language. The courses she teaches include intercultural communication, communication theory, public speaking, interpersonal communication, human sexuality, and gender studies.

David Bobbitt is an associate professor of communication at Wesleyan College in Macon, Georgia. He is the author of *The Rhetoric of Redemption: Kenneth Burke's Redemption Drama and Martin Luther King, Jr.'s "I Have a Dream" Speech* (2004). He has published articles in the *Journal of Communication and Religion*, the *Florida Communication Journal*, and in the online journals *Enculturation* and *Media Fields Journal*.

Deborah Cunningham Breede is an associate professor of communication at Coastal Carolina University (CCU). A founding member of the Women's Resource Center at CCU, she is a four-time recipient of the College of Humanities and Fine Arts' Outstanding Teaching Award. She earned a bachelor's degree in education from Old Dominion University, and a master's and doctorate in communication from Florida Atlantic University and the University of South Florida, respectively.

Amy Eisen Cislo, PhD, is a lecturer in women, gender, and sexuality studies at Washington University in St. Louis and author of *Paracelsus's Theory of Embodiment: Conception and Gestation in Early Modern Europe* (2010). She has twelve years of teaching experience in women, gender, and sexuality studies and has an equal amount of experience teaching German language, literature, and culture at the high-school and college levels.

Elizabeth Currans is an assistant professor of women's and gender studies at Eastern Michigan University. She is working on a book, provisionally titled '*Protests are the Activists' Prom': Gender, Sexuality, and Counterpublic World-Making in Women's Public Demonstrations*. The book explores how participants in public protests in the contemporary United States coordinated and attended primarily by women claim and remake public spaces, and the ways that gender, sexuality, and race influence our understanding of public space. Her article, "Claiming Deviance and Honoring Community: Creating Resistant Spaces in U.S. Dyke Marches," appeared in *Feminist Formations*. Her research and teaching interests include public protest; grassroots activism; cultural geography and explorations of public space; feminist, queer, and critical race theory; and the intersections of gender, sexuality, and race in cultural life.

Joy L. Daggs is an assistant professor of communication and media studies at Northwest Missouri State University in Maryville, Missouri. She teaches courses in speech communication and public relations. She holds a doctorate in communication from the University of Missouri, Columbia.

Jessica J. Eckstein, PhD, is an assistant professor in the Communication Department at Western Connecticut State University. She has been incorporating popular-culture gender-analytic activities in her classrooms for the past decade and continues to research alternative ideas of gender relations. She is interested in the interpersonal practices of diverse masculinities—of both men and women—and in the communicative identity practices of male victims of domestic violence.

Jessica Furgerson is a doctoral candidate in communication studies at Ohio University where she is also completing her graduate certificate in women and gender studies. Her research areas include gender communication, feminist rhetoric, critical theory, communicative practices of women's movements, and feminist historiography. After completing her doctorate, Jessica plans to continue researching and teaching about communication and women and gender studies issues.

Lisa Hanasono is an assistant professor in the Department of Communication at Bowling Green State University in Ohio. Passionate about teaching communication principles, theories, and skills, Lisa has taught a variety of college courses in interpersonal communication, interviewing, technical communication, persuasion, culture and communication, presentational speaking, introductory Asian American studies, and health communication. As an interpersonal and intercultural communication scholar, her research interests focus on the intersections of gender, race, ethnicity, and communication.

David Hennessee teaches British literature, LGBT literature and media, and composition at California Polytechnic State University, San Luis Obispo. His work has been published in *Dickens Studies Annual*; *Nineteenth-Century Contexts*; and *Nineteenth-Century Gender Studies*.

Edward A. Hinck is a professor and director of forensics in the Department of Communication and Dramatic Arts at Central Michigan University. He teaches courses in argumentation, rhetorical criticism, and communication theory.

Shelly Schaefer Hinck is an associate dean in the College of Communication and Fine Arts at Central Michigan University. She has taught courses in gender communication, interpersonal communication (graduate and undergraduate level), and conflict resolution. She holds a doctorate from the University of Kansas.

Christina Holmes is an assistant professor of women's studies at DePauw University. Prior to arriving at DePauw, she taught courses in women, gender, and sexuality studies, transnational feminisms, feminist approaches to environmentalism, and Chicana literature at Ohio State University.

Navita Cummings James, PhD, is an associate professor in the Department of Communication at the University of South Florida. Her pedagogical activities have included authoring articles, leading teaching workshops, and teaching graduate and undergraduate classes addressing communicating and listening across gender, racial, sexuality, and religious differences. She is a former president of the Southern States Communication Association, former member of the executive board of the National Communication Association, and a current deputy to the General Convention of the Episcopal Church (which is one of the U.S. churches struggling over issues of human sexuality).

Amie Kincaid is an assistant professor of communication at the University of Illinois Springfield. She earned her PhD from the University of New Mexico, and her research and teaching interests focus on issues of race, class, culture, ethnicity, and gender and how they may contribute to power inequities in our interpersonal interactions—specifically in instructional settings.

Christin L. Munsch is a PhD student in sociology at Cornell University with interests in gender, sexuality, social psychology, and violence. She has worked in domestic violence shelters and rape crisis centers and as a women's advocate. Christin is currently completing her dissertation on threatened masculinity and compensatory behaviors.

Michael J. Murphy is an assistant professor of women and gender studies at the University of Illinois Springfield. He teaches courses in critical men's/masculinity studies, LGBTQ/sexuality studies, and visual and material culture studies. He holds a master's degree and doctorate in the history of American art and visual culture, with a graduate certificate in women and gender studies, from Washington University in St. Louis.

Jessica A. Nodulman is a lecturer in the Department of Communication and Journalism at the University of New Mexico. Dr. Nodulman's research focuses on sexual health communication. She is also a post-doctorate research associate at the Center on Alcoholism, Substance Abuse, and Addictions at the University of New Mexico. Her current line of research investigates sex-positive sexuality education.

Robyn Ochs has been invited to hundreds of colleges and universities. She is the editor of the forty-two country anthology *Getting Bi: Voices of Bisexuals around the World*, and her writings have been published in numerous bi, women studies, multicultural, and LGBT anthologies. Robyn has taught courses on LGBT history and politics in the United States. Robyn is an advocate for the rights of people of all orientations and genders to live safely, openly, and with full legal equality, and her work focuses on increasing awareness and understanding of complex identities, as well as on mobilizing people to be powerful allies to one another within and across identities and social movements.

Kerry Poynter has over fifteen years of experience working with LGBTQA students in higher education at a number of institutions including Columbia University, Duke University, New York University, and Western Michigan University. Among his experiences, he has managed a 2,500 sq. ft. LGBTQ location; coordinated four LGBTQ Safe Space Ally Programs; written and was awarded a number of grants; conducted numerous trainings on LGBTQ and allied issues with faculty, staff, and students; assessed campus climates and services for LGBTQ people in fraternity/sorority life, residence life, health services, and human resources; empowered students through peer education; and led advocacy efforts for more inclusive policies for transgender students. His work with Lavender Graduation ceremonies was cited by *Instinct* magazine as the best of LGBTQ offerings on college campuses. Since 2010, he has served as the director of the LGBTQA Resource Office at the University of Illinois, Springfield.

Sal Renshaw is an associate professor at Nipissing University, Canada, and is chair of the Department of Gender Equality and Social Justice, cross-appointed in the Department of Religions and Cultures. She is the author of *The Subject of Love: Hélène Cixous and the Feminine Divine* (2009), and her research interests range from philosophies of love to representations of sexuality and ethics in contemporary media. She has most recently published on representations of queer sexuality in the HBO series, *The L Word*, and she is currently working on a collection of feminist essays, "Screening the Canon," a critical reading through film of key theological concepts such as grace, redemption, and sacrifice.

Elizabeth N. Ribarsky has a doctorate from the University of Nebraska-Lincoln, and she is an assistant professor in the Communication Department at the University of Illinois, Springfield, where she teaches both undergraduate and graduate courses in interpersonal communication. Dr. Ribarsky's research focuses on the construction of individual and relational identities. Specifically, much of her research is devoted to understanding the gendered communication surrounding dating and sexual communication. Her research has been published in various academic journals and books, including *Communication Quarterly*; *Teaching Ideas for the Basic Communication Course*; and *Fix Me Up*, a book examining the reality of reality television.

Hazel J. Rozema is an associate professor in the Communication Department at the University of Illinois Springfield. She has a bachelor's from Calvin College, master's from Michigan State University, and a PhD in communication from the University of Kansas. She teaches courses in family, gender, and interracial communication. She has previously taught at Western Michigan University, the University of Arkansas at Little Rock, Millikin University, and Minnesota State University, Mankato.

Sherianne Shuler is an associate professor of communication studies at Creighton University in Nebraska. She teaches courses related to gender, autoethnography, and organizational communication. Her current research projects include autoethnographic explorations of emotional labor in a health care context, and mothers and daughters negotiating the princess culture. Her PhD is from the University of Kansas.

Susan E. Stiritz is a senior lecturer in the Women, Gender, and Sexuality Studies Program at Washington University in St. Louis, Missouri. She teaches courses in sexuality studies, service learning, sexuality education, law and sexuality, contemporary sexualities, hooking up, and the social construction of sexuality. She holds a doctorate in English and American literature and a master's in social work from Washington University in St. Louis, and a master's in business administration from the University of Missouri in St. Louis. She is a graduate of the St. Louis Psychoanalytic Institute.

Allison R. Thorson is an assistant professor in the Communication Studies Department at the University of San Francisco. She teaches courses in communication and aging, the family, interpersonal, communication, and the dark side of communication. She holds a doctorate in communication studies from the University of Nebraska-Lincoln.

Elizabeth Tolman is an associate professor of communication studies and theater at South Dakota State University.

Shawn Trivette is an assistant professor of sociology in the Department of Social Sciences at Louisiana Tech University. He earned his PhD in 2012 in the Department of Sociology at the University of Massachusetts, Amherst. His teaching and research interests include sexualities, queer studies, intersections of race/class/gender/sexuality, environmental sociology, food and agriculture, qualitative methods, and social network analysis.

Stacy Tye-Williams is an assistant professor of communication studies at Iowa State University. She teaches courses in gender, organizational communication, and theory. She holds a doctorate from the University of Nebraska-Lincoln.

Jeanette Valenti received her PhD in human communication studies from the University of Denver in 2008. She is married with two children and currently living in San Diego where she teaches communication courses online through the Metropolitan State College of Denver and Brigham Young University, Idaho.

Sarah Stone Watt is an assistant professor and director of forensics in the Communication Division at Pepperdine University. She earned her PhD at Pennsylvania State University where she studied rhetoric and women's studies. Her research focuses on the rhetorical development of American feminism, particularly third-wave and post-feminism; media representations of gender and sexuality; and rhetorical constructions of women's health.

Evangeline Weiss has been working with people on concerns of identity, privilege, and power for over twenty-five years. With a master's degree in educational policy studies from the University of Wisconsin, Madison, Evangeline has worked with nonprofits in the United States such as Gay Men's Health Crisis and Hospital Audiences, as well as various universities and public-sector health and human services departments. In addition to LGBT advocacy efforts, Evangeline has conducted affirmative action audits for universities, designed leadership retreats for boards and steering committees, and worked on reproductive rights advocacy for Ipas and International Planned Parenthood in South East and Central Asia. Since 2010, she has served as the leadership programs director at the National Gay and Lesbian Task Force in Washington, DC.

Made in the USA
Middletown, DE
19 March 2019